Praise for *Robbie*

NEW

D1471320

90800100064515

Also by Sean Smith

Kate
Cheryl
Victoria
Kylie: The Biography
Justin: The Biography
Britney: The Biography
J. K. Rowling: A Biography
Jennifer: The Unauthorized Biography
Royal Racing
The Union Game
Sophie's Kiss (with Garth Gibbs)
Stone Me! (with Dale Lawrence)

Robbie

SEAN SMITH

**SIMON &
SCHUSTER**

London · New York · Sydney · Toronto

A CBS COMPANY

First published in Great Britain by Simon & Schuster UK Ltd, 2003
This edition published by Simon & Schuster UK Ltd, 2011
A CBS COMPANY

1 3 5 7 9 10 8 6 4 2

Simon & Schuster UK Ltd
1st Floor
222 Gray's Inn Road
London
WC1X 8HB

www.simonandschuster.co.uk

Simon & Schuster Australia
Sydney

A CIP catalogue for this book is
available from the British Library.

ISBN: 978-1-84983-100-0

Typeset by M Rules
Printed by CPI Cox & Wyman, Reading, Berkshire RG1 8EX

For David and Barbara – always good company

Contents

Introduction: Nan's Song   ix

PART ONE: **ROB**

1	**Two Peas in a Pod**	3
2	**Dodger**	17
3	**The Lads**	28
4	**The Sporting Life**	40
5	**Gary's Gang**	46
6	**The Man in the Mustard Suit**	56
7	**No Girls Allowed**	70
8	**Drugs, Rock 'n' Roll and Sex**	84
9	**Melon**	95

PART TWO: **THE MAKING OF ROBBIE WILLIAMS**

10	**The University of Nights Out**	103
11	**Finding Team Robbie**	111
12	**Angels**	124
13	**Never Ever**	132
14	**Give Back Sum**	143
15	**The Occasional Shag**	153
16	**Me and My Shadow**	164

PART THREE: **ESCAPE TO LA**

17	**Mulholland Drive**	181
18	**Beyond My Wildest Dreams**	195
19	**Tin Tin and the Radio Adventure**	203

20	**Acting Gay**	211
21	**Rude Awakening**	217
22	**Just One Night With Robbie**	228
23	**Field of Dreams**	236
24	**The Return of Robbie Williams**	246
25	**Union and Reunion**	256
	Last Story	269
	Life and Times	271
	Acknowledgements	281
	Select Bibliography and Picture Credits	283
	Index	285

Introduction

Nan's Song

Robert Williams loved his nan, Betty. Most nights after school he would ride his BMX bike over to her little terraced house in Newfield Street for his tea. She was always trying to fatten him up, which might have been the reason he was podgy as a boy. His mother, Jan, who brought him up as a single parent when his father left home, was stuck running her florist's shop, so she relied on her mother-in-law. She says simply that even after her marriage broke up Betty remained her best friend: 'She was special. She was just beautiful: a lovely, caring lady who played an important part in Robert's life.'

Even when he became Robbie Williams and joined Take That, he would still go round his nan's to listen to her stories and borrow two quid so he could go to the gym and try to get fit for all the dancing he had to do. Betty never quite got what it was all about and would make sure he had plenty of biscuits to take with him. She was immensely proud when fame came knocking at her grandson's door, although she had to change her phone number because of all the calls from desperate fans. She even travelled up to Manchester to see him perform with Take That, although the loud screams of the young female fans made her temporarily deaf. When Rob, as his friends have always called him, received his first, slim wage as a pop star, he went straight round to his nan's and paid her electricity bill.

Rob continued to include his nan in his life after he became famous. He took his first celebrity girlfriend, Jacqui Hamilton-Smith, to meet her. They drank Coke and chatted easily in her living room. Betty thought Jacqui was very polite and pretty, and told her, 'Any girl who gets Rob is very lucky.' He later brought his girlfriend Nicole Appleton, of All Saints, round to the house at a time when they were the most talked about couple in music. Betty always wanted to hear all his news. On other occasions, his best mate, Jonathan Wilkes, would join him because he loved talking to Rob's nan. When the local newspaper carried a story about Jonathan's career for the first time, Betty rang up his mother, Eileen, and said, 'Oh, I am so proud of him. Send him my love.'

Rob was distraught when his nan died in 1998. He wrote a song for her, the beautiful 'Nan's Song', as a tribute. It features on the number one album *Escapology*, and is the first song that bears the name 'Robbie Williams' as the sole writing credit. In the lyrics, he describes how his nan used to teach him the kings and queens while she stroked his hair, and how she is always with him and he misses her every day. Rob's father, the comedian Pete Conway, was thrilled to be there when Rob recorded the song in Los Angeles. He said, 'I've been proud of everything he has done but I am really proud of this one. The song for his nan, my mum, is a real tear-jerker.'

On stage in front of 125,000 people at Knebworth in August 2003, Rob said, 'This is for my grandma Betty who passed away five years ago. I love her very much and I know she is probably with me on stage right now – which is a bit scary. This is for all you grandmas.'

He then performed 'Nan's Song'.

PART ONE

ROB

1

Two Peas in a Pod

Rob just wasn't himself. His pal Zoë Hammond could hear it in his voice. This was Rob's first big role, playing the Artful Dodger in *Oliver!* at the Queen's Theatre, Burslem. It was opening night and Zoë had helped him get ready, brushing off his blue tail-coat and making sure his hair was just right. Rob was fourteen and born to play Dodger but Zoë knew he could be prone to nerves. Everything had started normally. She had stood in the wings with him, waiting for his first cue, and whispered, 'Go get 'em' in his ear so he would get an adrenalin buzz as he swept on stage. Zoë saw he was OK and went back to the dressing room to finish preparing for her small role as Beth. She could hear Rob over the Tannoy launch into 'Consider Yourself'.

'It was, like, "that's not him" and I knew something was wrong.' She turned to other children in the cast and remarked, 'What's up with him?'

After fifteen minutes Rob came off the stage. Zoë could see he was upset and put her arms around him, and said, 'I knew the moment you sang your first line. What's up?'

Rob started crying and told her, 'I just said my first spiel and I looked down into the pit, like, and, bugger me, but I've looked up and there is my fucking old man in the front row.' Rob had no idea his dad was coming to see him: 'How I remembered that song and how I remembered any of the words, I don't know. I've got to get a grip before I go back on.'

Zoë recalls, 'He was all tearful. You know lads: they want to be big and bolshie with it but he didn't. Not many lads would open up like that, would they?'

Zoë gave him a little squeeze and a pep talk: '"Right, come on, he's there; he's come to see you, so give him something to be proud of." And he said, "Yeah!", and he went back on. He's put his dad on a pedestal, you see. But when he went back out he was brilliant. It made me cry because I loved him so much at that time.'

Robert Peter Williams was three years old when his father, Pete Conway, had abandoned him, his mother, Jan, and his half-sister, Sally. He said to Jan that he was just popping out for a pint. Rob idolized his father, who was, as he himself said, the most famous comedian ever to come out of Stoke-on-Trent. Pete told jokes, sang Sinatra and had been on the telly.

Amateur psychologists might enjoy analysing young Rob, forever trying to emulate his dad and win his approval. Eric Tams, who knew both father and son well, used to play darts with Pete in a pub in Hanley, and observes: 'Within five minutes of walking into any room, Pete was your friend. It's just the same with Rob. He was the most lovable child. I think it must be inbred. They were like two peas in a pod.'

Peter Williams – his real name – was a Tunstall boy, just as his son would be. These were his streets, full of neat and uniform terraced houses built as homes for the pottery workers. Tunstall is the most northerly of the six towns incorporated into the new borough of Stoke-on-Trent in 1910. Tunstall is very much a small working-class town where families have lived for generations, and you are always likely to bump into someone you were at school with while buying your morning paper or pack of cigarettes. The more ambitious residents aspire to live a few miles away in smarter Newcastle under Lyme. Rob was the same: when he was a teenager he pointed out a modest house as he drove through Newcastle and declared that it was the one he would buy his mum when he became famous. He would eventually buy her a much grander home.

Rob's father was brought up in a terraced house in Newfield Street, just north of the old marketplace where the Sneyd Arms, an old coaching inn, dominates the square. Pete can still be found there from time to time enjoying a drink in the bar. Despite spending much of his working life 'on the road', Pete has always drifted back to where his roots are and describes his years in Newfield Street as 'very happy times'. Rob, too, has Tunstall blood in his veins and has never forgotten the strong sense of community he enjoyed while he was there.

Pete's father, Phil, was a bricklayer and his mother, Betty, worked in a pottery factory. Young Pete was all set for a career in the police force and joined the cadets when he left school at sixteen. He stayed in the uniform for seven years but found that life as a bobby on the beat in late sixties Stoke-on-Trent did not fire his imagination in the same way as the applause of an appreciative audience.

Pete had the knack of making people laugh. If you met him, you remembered him. Eileen Wilkes, the mother of Rob's best friend Jonathan Wilkes, recalls, as a teenager, standing in a long, damp queue to get into a dance when a young man started entertaining everyone: 'He had us all laughing and had such a sense of fun. When the doors opened, no one wanted to go in. We wanted to stay listening to him. It was Pete.' Pete Conway had a charisma that he would pass on to his son.

Despite winning a commendation for tailing a gang of post office robbers while he was off duty, Pete dreamt of being a professional entertainer. At the time, Stoke-on-Trent was a thriving centre on the club circuit. He became a well-known face in Potteries pubs and clubs and was soon successful enough to pack in his job with the police. He still needed a part-time job, however, and found work at a local firm that supplied electrical components.

He chose the stage name Conway by looking at a list of all his fellow employees and putting Pete next to them to see which was the catchiest. In those early days he used to pretend to be a Scouser because 'every comic came from Liverpool. I used to talk down my nose and say how great it was to be here from Anfield even though I hadn't been there in my life!'

The possibility of a long-term career became a reality when he won *New Faces*, a seventies equivalent of *Britain's Got Talent*, in which the hopefuls would sing their songs or tell their jokes before either being congratulated by a panel of 'experts' or, much more entertainingly, being 'hatcheted' by Tony Hatch, writer of the *Neighbours* theme tune and the Simon Cowell of his day. Pete came third in the all-winners' grand final, just behind another up and coming comedian, Les Dennis, who actually *was* from Liverpool.

Eric Tams observes: 'Pete did the rounds, got the feel of the thing, the love for it and then went to *New Faces* when he thought he was good enough. He had a great natural ability to be funny. You would say something and he would always come back with something comical. He would never belittle you though or make a joke at your expense. He would just be amusing.'

Pete's son, Robert Peter Williams, was born in the maternity wing of the North Staffordshire Hospital in Newcastle Road on 13 February 1974. Jan and Pete had been married for nearly four years; it was a second marriage for both of them. Jan already had a ten-year-old daughter, Sally, from her first marriage. Pete had started going out with flame-haired Jan when Sally was just eighteen months old. One of the popular myths about the life of Robbie Williams is that he was born in a pub, the Red Lion at Burslem. He did not help matters when he announced in a television documentary, 'This is where I was born. I was born in a pub on Oliver Reed's birthday.' Only the Oliver Reed part of that was true.

For the first couple of years of his life, home was a dark, gothic-looking house in Victoria Park Road, on the west side of Tunstall Park. From the bedroom window at the front, the view took in a lake packed with swans and Canada geese and a bandstand where brass bands would strike up at weekends. The three-bedroom Edwardian semi had an atmosphere that subsequent owner Sam Evans attributes to 'ghostly happenings', although she is not sure if there were any poltergeists to disturb young Master Robert Williams. In the early seventies, in this part of town, you were more likely to encounter doctors and solicitors and young couples on their way up in life. Pete and Jan Williams wanted to be in the latter category.

Perhaps surprisingly, just twelve months after winning *New Faces*, Pete made the decision to put the family first and became the licensee of the Red Lion, an unprepossessing pub near the Port Vale football ground, which was handy as he was a keen supporter. Rob was two years old at the time. Pete explained, 'I phoned around all the agents and managers and said I couldn't do any more bookings because I had become a licensee. I didn't stop doing cabaret but only performed in Stoke because the pub was now the first concern.'

Pete soon realized he had made a big mistake: 'I became unhappy. It just wasn't me. I missed the goings on and the atmosphere of the entertainment business even though I was still doing a bit.' Pub life was not enough and Jan's dream of a settled family life was about to be shattered. Ironically, she had urged her husband to become a landlord because she was concerned that all the travelling involved in being a professional comic would mean a great deal of time spent away from home.

She could not have guessed that it would make Pete so miserable. Nor could she have predicted that within a year he would walk out on his wife and family and Rob would spend his childhood in a broken home. Before he left so abruptly, Pete introduced Rob to performing. Rob would give impromptu performances of whatever came into his head. Pete proudly recalls that his young son would do superb impressions of Brian Clough and Margaret Thatcher. He got him out of bed one night to perform on the bar of the pub. Jan was not impressed, telling her husband firmly that 'he's not a performing monkey!'

Pete did not see his son for several months after the break-up but says that when he first saw Rob again he was watching *Batman*. 'Hiya, Dad,' he said without taking his eyes off the telly. At the time Pete was sleeping on a pal's floor and is adamant that no one else was involved in his spilt from Jan. He was always a ladies' man, however, and soon took up with a young barmaid from Hanley; they became a popular couple in the local pubs.

One can only speculate on the lasting effect his parents' split had on the life of Robbie Williams. Rob's flippant dismissal that his dad was some bloke who came round every so often, took him to Woolworth's and bought him a toy car can assuredly be taken with a very large pinch of salt.

In 1977, Jan took Rob on holiday to Torremolinos. One afternoon at the Pontinental he seemed to have disappeared, which threw her into a panic until someone said he was downstairs because there was a talent competition taking place. She rushed down to the ballroom, which was in complete darkness: 'All of a sudden there was this spotlight that shone on the stage and this little figure slipped through the curtain. It was Robert. I thought, "What is he doing!" Then the John Travolta song "Summer Nights" came on over the speakers and he was doing all the movements to it and singing away. He won the competition.' Young Rob loved John Travolta and some of the swagger the star had as Danny in *Grease*, and earlier as Tony in *Saturday Night Fever*, seemed to infuse themselves into the character that would become Robbie Williams.

While Pete Conway was striving to live his dream, it was left to Rob's mother, Jan, to play the thankless role of single parent. She was more fortunate than some in that Pete's parents were kind-hearted folk only too pleased to help out while she endeavoured to make a success first of a boutique, followed by a coffee shop and then a florist's. She always appreciated the value of a pound and was quite shrewd about business. When she decided to sell the coffee shop, she waited until she had secured a licence to sell alcohol so that she could increase its attraction for potential buyers. Eileen Wilkes, who has been a friend for more than twenty-five years, says that Jan still has some of the furniture she had when she was first married, despite the grand homes she has since enjoyed thanks to her son's wealth.

Jan moved her young family in to a smart post-war semi in Greenbank Road, Tunstall, opposite the Ancient Briton pub, or the Mill Hill Tavern as it was previously called, which in years to come would be a dream location for the teenage Rob. Behind the pub, a sprawling council estate ran down towards Burslem and Hanley but on the Williams' side of the street the houses were privately owned. Their house was kept tidy but friends remarked that it was a bit higgledy-piggledy with things here, there and everywhere. Rob had the boxroom at the front of the house, with a view across the road to the pub.

It was very much a family home, where everyone would sit round watching a television that was kept in a dark wood cabinet in the lounge. The three-piece suite was green and in the front room there was an upright piano for Christmas singsongs and the creation of one-finger classics. The effect was very homely.

Rob even kept a couple of parakeets. One morning he went into school and told his mates that one of his birds had died the previous evening. They never told him that when they had been round his house the day before, they had been persecuting the poor bird by poking it with a pencil.

The house in Greenbank Road was a happy one. Jan recalls, 'The growing-up part was lovely because we were right by the park and it was easy for Robert to go out and play.' Several of Jan's family lived near and were always popping in, including her father, Jack Farrell, a well-known character in Tunstall who was in the building trade. Jack and Rob were the best of friends.

Jack had married Jan's mother, Janetta, in the Church of the Sacred Heart, just a mile from the house. Jan came from a strong Irish Catholic working-class family. Her great-grand parents had left the poverty of Kilkenny in the south-east of Ireland to try to find a better life in this corner of Staffordshire. It would be stretching credibility to suggest Rob had a Catholic upbringing but Jan did try to instil in her son the value of good manners and common decency.

Jan's father was a man's man and she acknowledges that he played a big part in Rob's life when he was a very young boy. Sadly, he died when Rob was five but not before he had taught his grandson to treat his elders with respect. Rob has never forgotten him and, when he became famous, would check into hotels using the alias Jack Farrell Jnr. He also has Jack tattooed on his right wrist and Farrell on his left.

Growing up, Rob liked nothing better than when his family came round and everyone would pile over to the park for a picnic. Rob would whizz around on his beloved BMX bike until it was time for sandwiches and Coke. He loved his big sister, Sally, who was a rock of dependability for him. Being that much older, she had to get on with her own life while supporting him as much as she could. Rob would always refer to her as 'my Sally' or 'my Sal' and none of his mates realized that she was his half-sister. She was his sister as far as he was concerned. She was very popular with his school friends, who always fancied her but knew she would be forever unattainable. 'Sally was nice,' says his best mate at school, Lee Hancock, simply. Zoë Hammond, who met her when she used to come and watch

Rob perform, agrees, 'She was all right' – a good compliment in those parts.

Jan always tried to involve herself in her son's life, mindful that he did not have an ever-present father to join him. She indulged his love of Showaddywaddy, a fifties throwback group, whose cheery renditions of American rock 'n' roll standards were all over the charts during the first eight years of Rob's life. He wanted to be Dave Bartram, the cool lead singer, and was overjoyed when his mother took him to see their concert at the Queen's Theatre in Burslem. He was seven and it was his first ever concert. He thought it was fantastic and was very disappointed when Jan said he could not have a Teddy boy outfit for his birthday because he would soon grow too big for it.

Jan took up golf when Rob became interested, playing with him at Burslem Golf Club. She was a left-hander and, according to Tim Peers, who used to play golf with Rob, she 'wasn't bad at all'. She also joined the amateur dramatics society to keep Rob company. She was not a great actress – she was usually consigned to the chorus – and preferred the more relaxed, good humour of the local amateur Olde Time Music Hall.

She involved Rob in one of her own passions – horse racing. Jan went out for a couple of years with a man who was a racehorse owner and knew the England and Manchester United captain Bryan Robson – definitely something to grab the attention of a young lad. Rob was much more interested in football than racing, although, when he was old enough, he routinely spent the afternoon in a bookie's in Burslem with his mates.

While she did not exactly spoil him, Jan did her best to make sure Rob was happy and indulged. Jan was popular with the majority of Rob's friends. Tim Peers says she was 'very down to earth'. He observes, 'She was very realistic about things but very supportive at the same time.' Kelly Oakes, whom Rob had a crush on at school, was struck by 'how chilled' Jan always seemed: 'Nothing fazed her.'

Jan was certainly good fun: on the occasions when she was

merry she would launch into her inimitable version of the Doris Day classic 'Sentimental Journey', which Rob and his sister Sally good-humouredly renamed 'My Very Mental Journey'. One day she was singing away in the kitchen when Rob came in. After a minute he said, 'Mum, pretend you are on the radio.' Jan was flattered by her son's suggestion and proceeded to give it her all. 'Now, pretend I have turned you off,' said Rob.

Lee Hancock says, 'He didn't chat about his dad – it was always his mum. She was lovely, a very generous person. There were no rules in the house but she was definitely not one of the lads. She was very much a mum. She would have been an attractive woman in her day.'

She was certainly attractive enough to have a number of boyfriends over the years, not all of whom met with the approval of her son. As well as having to raise two children by herself, Jan faced the dilemma of trying to have a life as well. Inevitably this led to some conflicts and heartbreak for her son, although Rob has always remained 100 per cent loyal to his mother. 'You've only got one mum', he used to say to Zoë Hammond. But not everyone shared his high opinion of his mother.

Pantomime organizer Carole Banks, who met Jan when Rob was in *Chitty Chitty Bang Bang*, recalls, 'I think Jan thought she was the bee's knees when Robert was young.' She remembers he 'kicked off' as a twelve year old when it was suggested the family go to stay with one boyfriend from Nottingham: 'He didn't want to go and I heard him say, "I'm fed up with your boyfriends."' She also recalls Rob being dropped off at his grandmother's house after rehearsals and his nan saying to her, 'Oh, you picked him up again.'

David and Val Ogden, who were also involved in the show, often saw Rob waiting at the bus stop on his own and they would give him a lift back home because his mum was unable to make it. David recalls, 'His mum did leave him to come on his own. She did pick him up sometimes but often she would be late and one of the things I best remember was when I had a conversation with him one time about getting home: "Robert, is your mum picking you up tonight?" "Yeah." "Well, where is she?" "Oh, she's out with her new fella."'

Zoë Hammond recalls his mother turning up to the Queen's Theatre in Burslem: 'She was wearing a fur coat and she's standing there with more lip gloss on than Boots the chemist have and there's this bloke with her looking as smarmy as you like and there was Rob – he just had that look of "here we go again".'

Zoë was present at a heartbreaking scene at the after-show party for *Oliver!* when Rob was fourteen: 'His mum turned up with a brown paper bag and she said, "Here you are Rob", and tossed it to him. And he just looked and I knew by his face he was upset. He walked down the stairs from where we had the party and sat on the steps outside. I followed him down and said, "What's up?" He was really upset and he said, "It's really difficult for me because I love my mum to bits but I don't always agree with her choice. You know what's in the bag? My pyjamas – I'll have to sort out something for tonight." My heart went out to him. I think his mum was trying to find a bit of happiness, looking for Mister Right, but he didn't always agree with who she picked, if you know what I mean. He protected her like you'd never know and it took a lot that night for him just to tell me he was upset. You know how some lads are but he was never like that. He was just down in the mouth about it but never nasty.

'I always felt dead sorry for him because he loved his mum but he felt in the way, sometimes, of what she was doing at the time and yet, despite all of the feelings and all of the confusion he was going through on a personal level, he never went funny with his mum. I found that really weird because I used to say to him, "If it was my mum, I couldn't be doing with it. I don't know how you can just stand by her like you do." He just got on with his life, even though inside it hurt. That was the way it always was. No matter what feelings she gave him as a kid, he never retaliated.' Quite simply, Rob's love for his mother was unconditional. He once told a journalist that his mother did not nag him as a child. 'She just worries about me.'

When Zoë told her own mum, who was at the party, about the incident with the pyjamas, she asked her why she had not asked Rob to go home with them. 'I didn't like to because he was that het up about it,' she replied. 'I just said to him, "What are you going to do?" and he said, "Oh, I'll be all right." Reading between the lines, I was sure he would go round to his nan's.'

While Jan struggled at home to get her son to help with the garden, or do some household chores, which Rob was always hopeless at, or just keep his room tidy, Pete was able to be the hero *in absentia*. Inevitably, the young Rob would see the glamorous side of his father's life and brag a bit about it to his friends back in Tunstall, especially if he had shared the spotlight as well. He wanted to be part of that life and he wanted his dad to be proud of him. When Pete was in a summer show – for instance, he did four seasons at Perran Sands, a Cornish holiday camp – Rob would visit in the school holidays for as long as six weeks. He would always watch the acts and make a mental note of what the audience liked. Pete's friend, Pat Brogan, recalls, 'He would watch his dad work and you can't buy that sort of experience. Pete was a great pro and I am sure a lot of it has rubbed off on Rob.'

Pete's work took him to the great seaside resorts of Britain. Rob, who loved the lifestyle, would be there in Scarborough, Great Yarmouth or Carmarthen Bay. It was not always as glamorous as Pete hoped. On one occasion in Cornwall he returned to his caravan to find the future pop star standing underneath a hole in the ceiling catching the rain in a bucket. During one of those traditional rainy seaside days in Scarborough, Pete taught his son backgammon, a game he still loves to play.

One of Pete's best memories is when one of the camp enter-
tainers, Bill Wayne, in a leotard without his trousers on – as was
often the case to get some laughs on stage – spotted Rob watching from the wings and beckoned for him to follow him on and
copy what he was doing. The act was that he would pretend to
be doing keep fit. Rob went on stage, bold as brass, and did
exactly what Bill did, copying him precisely and expertly. 'The
place was in uproar,' said Pete proudly.

These were happy times for father and son. Rob first got
drunk watching his father perform at a camp in Scarborough,
when he persuaded the barman to slip him bottles of
Newcastle Brown, despite not enjoying the taste. A mutual love
of beer enabled them to become best pals during Rob's
teenage years. His domestic skills, however, did not improve
when he was staying with his father. Pete recalls, 'I would do
the cooking and he would do the washing up and then he
would go out and I would do the washing up again.'

Only Pete can say for sure if he achieved his dream. If all he
wanted was to be a professional entertainer, as he himself has
stated, then he has lived up to those aspirations. The reality is
that he became a 'nearly man' of British entertainment, doing
the rounds of Butlins and Pontin's, or hosting the nightly
entertainment in a variety of large resort hotels, where a few
gags and a spot of crooning would keep the punters happy. He
was once the warm-up man for Norman Vaughan, a Liverpool
comedian, on the television classic *The Golden Shot* but the big
time remained tantalizingly out of reach. When he was the res-
ident MC at the Holme Lacy House Hotel near Hereford, he
kept a card that had been sent with a bunch of flowers. Written
in black felt-tip pen, it read: 'Dad, I love you, Rob.'

Friends continue to point out the similarities between Rob
and his dad but they tend to be superficial ones based on the
fact that many of Pete's mannerisms seem to have rubbed off
on his son. They both have great charm and a twinkle in their
eye. A friend once described Pete as wearing a smile even when

he wasn't smiling. Eileen Wilkes observes, 'Pete is Pete. He'll never grow up.' Kelly Oakes, who met Rob's dad when she used to appear in amateur dramatics with Rob, recalls that she thought Pete a bit self-centred: 'I think he liked being in the limelight.'

The great poet Philip Larkin famously wrote: 'They fuck you up, your mum and dad. They may not mean to, but they do.' Rob's parents have had an immeasurable effect on his life – one that he has, perhaps, been able to examine far too closely in his recent years of therapy. His father Pete is a Jack-the-lad character and a great companion whose presence and style clearly influenced the creation of Robbie Williams, the public performer.

Rob's bipolar personality is never better illustrated than by his chaotic appraisal of his relationship with his father. On the one hand there is the affectionate tone of his hit 'Strong', in which he says that when he gets drunk he dances like his dad and that he is starting to dress like him. Then there is the lyric to 'My Culture', in which he rages that he is the boy whose father reduced him to tears and who has been lonely for twenty-seven years.

The observations and recollections from those who knew Rob reveal a degree of emotional turmoil as he grew up. Intriguingly, it is the female of the species who noticed the sensitive side to his nature, certainly where his mother and father were concerned. He would never have dreamt of opening up to 'the lads', which would almost certainly have been considered a mark of weakness. Instead, Rob had to bottle up those feelings while maintaining a veneer of bravado for his mates at school. Under these circumstances, 'having a laugh' became a method of protection, a form of defence that he continues to use in public.

2

Dodger

The house in Greenbank Road was ideally placed for both the Mill Hill Primary School and the St Margaret Ward Roman Catholic High School. It was also a short stroll to High Lane Oatcakes, one of young Rob's favourite places. Oatcakes in this part of the world have nothing to do with biscuits for cheese. Instead they are belt-busting savoury pancakes filled with cheese and bacon and other goodies that have no place in the faddy diets of celebrities. Rob loved them – and as a youngster he wasn't slim.

When he was at Mill Hill, he took the lead in school productions, playing, among other roles, Fagin in *Oliver!* One of the teachers, Phil Rossiter, recalls that he was very keen on anything remotely to do with dance, drama and the choir: 'He wasn't very athletic. He was plump and short. He wasn't everybody's favourite and some of the other children found him a bit big-headed and pushy. But he definitely stood out as taking the main parts in our plays. I was amazed later on, when I saw he was in Take That because I remembered him as a podgy boy aged nine.'

Rob's mother may not have had show business at the top of her list of ambitions for her son but she realized early on in his life that it would be better to work with his dreams than to face the same struggles she'd had during her marriage to his father. When Rob was nine, they were watching television together when the dire eighties group Kajagoogoo came on. Jan suggested playfully that Rob must want to be famous like them but Rob surprised her by saying that he aimed to be an actor and had no interest in becoming a pop star.

She subsequently encouraged him to find an outlet for his interest in performing away from the classroom and that is how he met Zoë Hammond for the first time. Zoë was bright, vivacious and a chatterbox. She and Rob bonded from the start: 'He was one of the reasons why I loved the theatre so much. Wherever I went, he followed and vice versa.'

Their lovely ten-year friendship, forged on the boards of local amateur dramatics stages, is like a touching love story without the frisson of sex. Zoë never fancied her leading man. People who saw them out together could scarcely believe they had never had a real date. She explains, 'When I see him on the telly now and everyone is going "Phwoar", I can't because I've seen him as that podgy little lad with freckles. He was bloody fat when he was a child. To me he is just Robbie and I love him.'

Zoë and Rob first appeared together in a production of *Hans Christian Andersen* performed by the North Staffordshire Amateur Operatic and Dramatic Society (known as North Staffs), the biggest group in the region. They were just two of the chorus children who sat around listening to the fairy tales but the roles required a lot of singing and dancing, which Rob was not at all sure he fancied. When the children first had to jump in the air and clap, he pulled a face at Zoë as if to say, 'What's all this malarkey?'

Zoë recalls, 'I told him, "You've got two choices. Do you want to be in it or not?" But he did and he knew he did and he was dead good. It's the same with everybody who wants to be on the stage. Suddenly you've got a long skirt and dance shoes on and, as a little lad growing up, I think he thought, "Jeez", but he did it. By the time he had learned what to do, he had crossed that bridge and it didn't bother him.'

Rob and Zoë won their first juvenile leads at the age of eleven in a local pantomime company's production of *Chitty Chitty Bang Bang*. The Stoke-on-Trent Charity Pantomime and Drama Company had been formed for local children interested in music and theatre. Carole Banks, the company secretary, put a large advertisement in the evening paper, *The Sentinel*, inviting children to attend an audition at a hotel in Hanley. Jan dropped Rob off and he swaggered in to audition, along with thirty other boys, for the part of Jeremy. He sang the famous number from the show, 'Truly Scrumptious'. Carole recalls, 'The moment he opened his mouth, I knew he had got the part. And the other kids knew it as well.'

Zoë, who won the part of Jemima, was not so impressed with Rob's singing: 'He wasn't all that good at singing but, because he was so good at everything else, it didn't matter. He used to struggle with "Truly Scrumptious", which we sang together. I wouldn't say he was crap but he didn't stand there, deliver it and be spot on. I used to say, "You can tell me to shut up if you want but that line shouldn't be like that." He'd ask why and I'd show him. He did listen. I must have been a right bossy little madam because my mum used to say to me, "He's probably thinking who does she think she is!"'

Chitty Chitty Bang Bang was originally a children's story written by Ian Fleming, the creator of James Bond. It reached a wide audience following the 1968 film version in which Dick Van Dyke played the hopeless inventor, Caractacus Potts, who rescues a derelict car (Chitty) and gives it magical powers. The car helps Jeremy and Jemima to overthrow the government of a country that hates children. It was perfect panto fodder.

Eric Tams, who played Potts, would rehearse with Zoë and Rob: 'They hit it off so well. Zoë would have a smile from ear to ear. You get some kiddies of that age who resent each other but there was not an iota of that. They were brilliant together. If someone else was rehearsing, they would be sitting on a stair going through their lines together.' Zoë and Rob would always learn the whole script, not just their own parts, so they could act as unofficial prompters if anyone forgot a line during rehearsal.

They had no time for the 'little prima donnas', the children who would turn up to auditions or rehearsals and think they were going to sail through. The voice of Robert Peter Williams could be heard announcing loudly, 'There's a lot more people here without talent than there are with.'

Zoë had first-hand experience of young Rob's chubbiness when the script called for them to share a bed together because they were brother and sister: 'It wasn't a real bed because it was a set and it was small and not very safe. He was a stocky little bugger and when he was in the bed I could barely get in it. We were cramped together every night and we couldn't stop laughing.'

Rob managed to wind up the director, the rather grandly titled Nicholas D. Florey, a Bristol-based theatrical. Rob had the habit then of saying 'nuthink' instead of 'nothing'. 'It's "nothing will change me", Robert,' Mr Florey would say. He would then insist that Rob go away and practise quietly until he could come back and deliver the line properly. When Rob had perfected it, he would join Eric Tams and announce, 'I'm going to do nothing wrong, Eric.' He would then go out and do his line: 'And nuthink will change me . . .' Eric would invariably get a fit of the giggles at his young co-star's antics. Another of Rob's tricks was to hide Eric's shoes two minutes before he was due on stage, causing a mad dressing-room panic. He was a prankster. 'We used to call him Rob when he was good and Robert when he wasn't,' laughs Eric.

Every night Rob and Eric, who was like a father figure to the children in the cast, would clean and polish the car – the original one used in the film – making sure it was in tip-top condition. They would sing or go through their lines as they did it because there was such a lot to learn. It was hard work but Rob would often turn to Eric and say, 'I absolutely love the theatre.'

Eventually the first night arrived, attended by the Lord Mayor, Jack Dimmock. It was a triumph for Rob and Zoë, although not for the car. The sound effects failed when it was supposed to start up for the first time, which left Eric on stage feeling a bit stupid. Quick as a flash Rob piped up, 'Get a decent car!'

Eric was full of admiration for both Rob and Zoë: 'There wasn't one performance where they forgot any line. There was no hiccup at all. When they sang "Truly Scrumptious", it made the hairs on the back of your neck stand on end.' Afterwards they both came and said, 'Hasn't it gone quick, Eric?'

The Mayor went backstage after the show to congratulate all three. 'Well, Eric', he declared, 'all I can say is that the theatre is in safe hands with these children.' Zoë and Rob stood there, all smiles, absolutely overjoyed. The Mayor was not the only one who was impressed. David Ogden, who played the Toymaker, maintains, 'Everybody felt that they were better than the kids in the film.' Eric Tams thinks their success was because the mischievousness they needed for the roles came naturally to them.

Rob proved himself to be a trouper by not letting a stomach upset ruin his performance despite having to make frequent dashes to the toilet. One of the girls in the chorus still has her programme for the night signed by 'Robbie the Toilet Man'.

One of the disappointments of the night is that none of the cast has ever seen the video of the performance, much to Carole Banks's annoyance. She had arranged for a professional to video the show but Jan Williams insisted that her boyfriend could do it. Carole has asked Jan on numerous occasions to see it but with no luck. Perhaps it never came out properly.

Flushed with his success, Rob was keen to do more musicals. He turned up at the Theatre Royal in Hanley to join Zoë in an audition for *Annie* with North Staffs. She had to tell him that there were no boys in *Annie*. 'I can always wear a wig,' he countered, showing off his American accent. In the end, he stayed to support Zoë, who passed her audition, and even though he wasn't in the show, Rob would still join her at the theatre. 'He just loved it,' observes Zoë. 'He used to tell us ghost stories and he'd have everybody right there in the palm of his hand. It was like *Jackanory* but ten times better – even the adults would sit round and listen to him. He was brilliant.'

Rob kept his acting interests well away from his new senior school, St Margaret Ward. There was no school play and his school friends had absolutely no idea of his hidden talents. This was the start of the splitting of the Robert Williams personality. On the one hand there was the sensitive lad Zoë Hammond knew. He was still fun and a laugh but he was troubled by his parents' break-up and he was fuelled by ambition. And then there was Rob the class clown, always joking, up for anything, a boy who would while away his schooldays in aimless tomfoolery.

Rob the actor appeared in *Fiddler on the Roof* and *The King and I*, in which he was one of the children at the court. 'He always made an impact,' observes Zoë. 'He could have a two-bit part but you'd know he was there.' He wanted to play the title role in *Bugsy Malone* but, for once, failed to get the part.

He had better luck with *Pickwick* for North Staffs. For the audition at the splendid old Queen's Theatre in Burslem, Rob had to sing a song from the show, recite a piece of script and do some dancing in front of the society's committee of some twenty people. All that effort and at the end of it Rob was given the role of Fat Boy, a two-line part.

North Staffs was big news for a seriously aspiring actor, even one with just two lines. It was also very businesslike. Rehearsals started almost immediately and Rob had to attend two or three times a week – quite a commitment for a boy of his age. Ironically, Rob was a little slimmer by now and needed to be padded out to make a realistic fat boy. *Pickwick* played to full houses for ten nights.

The following year, when he was fourteen, Rob went to audition for what has so far proved to be the pinnacle of his acting career. He wanted to be the Artful Dodger in the North Staffs production of Lionel Bart's Oscar-winning musical *Oliver!* The role of the leader of Fagin's gang of pickpockets is one of the great children's roles in musicals and one that everyone agreed Rob was born to play. The competition to play the part was literally around the block but Rob's version of 'Consider Yourself' won him the day. Zoë Hammond, who was there, recalls, 'Nobody else was anywhere near his league. It was like lighting a firework.'

The rehearsals under the stern eye of the director Ray Jeffery were serious business and an ordeal. This was no 'Anyone for tennis?' type of amateur production. Jeffery treated both adult and child equally harshly. Brian Rawlins, who played Fagin and worked very closely with Robert, as he called him, maintains: 'Robert found it very difficult being bawled out by the director. Ray was a perfectionist in his work and he could be very hard on people and very scathing. If you didn't get the inflection just how he wanted it, he could be bloody rude in front of the whole company. Robert found that a bit hard to take. On a couple of occasions at least I found him outside really quite upset after he had been bawled out in public.' And if it was not the director giving the children a tough time, then it would be the chorus mistress: 'She was a huge lady and she would scream at them if they didn't get their words right. The song "Be Back Soon" was quite complicated for me and the boys. The trouble was that while they were concentrating on their feet, they were forgetting to sing. It was tough.'

Zoë Hammond says that both she and Rob hated the director: 'I used to think "that bastard". I used to want to tell him what I thought but I never dared to. Rob just took it – most of the time. I can't remember what Ray said once but Rob goes and puts his trainers on and says, "That's it" to me and I said, "All right then, see ya." And he started walking off and I said, "When am I going to see you again then?" I was upset but I wasn't really showing it because I thought, "You don't go running after a bloke, do you?" He walked all the way down to the door and turned to me and said, "I've had enough. He's not talking to me like that." I told him, "Calm down a bit, go and have a cup of tea and think about it." I knew he was the sort of person, if he was really upset, who would have just gone. He would have done it. If he had walked out, the show would have been crap without him. By the time he did Dodger, he was a star as far as I could see. He was just brilliant and everybody loved him. I loved him.'

Whatever the merits of Ray Jeffery's methods, he succeeded in extracting a fabulous performance from Rob as Dodger. He had the jaunty walk, the swaggering style, the cockney boy mannerisms, and he was wizard at pickpocketing – a skill for which he received special coaching and which enabled him to nick the wallets of fellow cast members. Zoë recalls, 'It was thrilling the way he did his lines. It's never left me to this day.'

The big first night arrived on 19 October 1988. Rob did suffer from nerves. Most people, who didn't know him that well, were impressed by his apparent confidence but, much more than that, he had 'bottle', the courage to go on. Only someone as close as Zoë Hammond knows that behind the bravado Robbie Williams can be just as scared at the prospect of performing as anyone else. 'There were times when he had nerves,' she explains. 'Then he would say, "Fucking hell. I can't fucking remember. Can you remember?" I'd tell him to calm down and take a chill pill, and then he'd find it. I told him he knew every last line but if he went on like that he would be shit: "Are you going to be good or are you going to be crap?" And then he'd go, "I'm going to be good." And I'd gee him up with, "You are going to be the best!"'

Rob has often needed a special person to spur him on: in those early days it was Zoë. He was also able to express his feelings to her. She would always sit and listen to what he had to say, confident that he would feel better if he had a talk about what was troubling him – often his mother and her boyfriends – until he was ready to pick up his bag, pack up his gear and declare, 'Right, what are we going to do next?'

That easygoing but close relationship continued away from the rehearsal rooms, when the two friends would meet up in nearby Newcastle under Lyme, where Zoë's family lived and where, at the time, Rob's mother ran a small coffee shop. Invariably, it was Zoë who would suggest doing something together: 'It was weird because he would never come up to someone and assume anything. In a funny way he was insecure. If I mentioned doing something on a Saturday, then he would ring me on that day and say, "Right, what time are we going?" He was a brilliant lad but he needed a bit of a shove.'

Often the two of them would go swimming at the local Jubilee Baths before going on to Jan's café. Their hair would still be wet and Jan would say to Zoë, 'Your mum will go mad with me.' On one occasion Jan gave them some gateau and asked them what they wanted to drink. Rob piped up, 'We don't want any of that cheap Coke.'

His mother, who always wanted him to speak nicely, said, 'I beg your pardon, Robert?' Zoë recalls that when Jan addressed him that way his eyes would roll upwards to the heavens.

A group of Rob's mates from school went to *Oliver!* to see

him perform for the first time. One friend, Giuseppe Romano, comments: 'This was the first time we had any real indication of him doing anything like this. I was really impressed.' Up until then Rob kept his acting ambitions quiet, on the grounds, he said, that his mates would have thought him a 'poof'. Perhaps, at last, Rob himself had realized just how good he was and wanted to show his friends what he had achieved.

Rob was so sure of his destiny as a youngster. He would play truant from school with his mates but, while many of them faced uncertain futures, he would say to Zoë, 'Who's going to make it big first then, me or you?'

Zoë would always answer, 'Me.'

The two friends would have that conversation time and time again over the years. Sometimes it would be: 'Who'd you reckon will have a number one?' When they were growing up, many thought Zoë had a better chance of stardom, especially when she reached the final three for a leading role in the Hollywood film version of *Annie*. But sometimes an extra ingredient of luck, or choosing the right direction on the career signpost, is needed to turn promise and potential into fulfilment.

As seventeen year olds, Rob was in Take That, while Zoë was working the Midlands pub and cabaret circuit as part of a singing duo. She appeared once at the Mill Hill Tavern opposite Rob's house in Greenbank Road: 'It was a dead ordinary night and he just walked in with his dad. I told him, "I really want you to go home!" He said, "Don't be silly. I've come to see you, mate." All I could say was, "This isn't really how I wanted you to see me. I wanted you to see me do something a bit good." He just laughed.'

A few months later Zoë tried her luck as a soloist with her first gig at the Greek Star, a small, clean and bright pub in Hanley. Just before the interval, she looked up and saw that Rob had slipped in to watch her. At the end of the gig Rob got up on stage and presented Zoë with a huge bouquet of red roses. She recalls, 'He said, "I'd like to say a few words about this girl" and went on to say some really nice stuff. I didn't have any clue that he'd come and there he was and it was just like "Wow!" Even with everything going on his life, he'd come home. I thought it was lovely of him.'

3

The Lads

Rob's teenage life revolved around what can best be described as a 'lad's culture'. He was desperate to be part of it, to be considered one of the boys, a paid-up member of the gang of schoolmates who had a 'life's a laugh and we don't care' attitude. It was a philosophy in direct contrast to his female-dominated domestic life at Greenbank Road or his acting life, where he was able to reveal his sensitivity and hurt to Zoë Hammond.

At home, his mum called him Robert. At school, he rejoiced in the nickname of Willwogs – occasionally Willywogs – a most un-PC moniker, which not surprisingly failed to find its way on to his Take That curriculum vitae. 'He is the junior captain of the golf club and he answers to the nickname of Willywogs' are not the sort of titbits that are going to encourage young girls to stick your poster on their bedroom wall. Everyone had to have a nickname at school. Rob's best mate, Lee Hancock, was Tate; then there were Giuseppe Romano (Gius), Peter O'Reilly (PO 2) and Phil Lindsay (Lino). Sometimes Rob would get away with being called plain 'Will' or, on other occasions, 'Swellhead' because he literally had a big head, although some thought the nickname suited him perfectly because he was so full of himself.

Rob unintentionally stood out when he first arrived at St Margaret Ward because he started school a few days' late – always a mistake because it becomes that much harder to be accepted once initial cliques have formed. The start of term had clashed with his appearance in *Chitty Chitty Bang Bang* at the Theatre Royal in Hanley. Phil Lindsay recalls seeing him for the first time in the school foyer sporting a ridiculous haircut: 'He must have had his hair dyed for the play because it was in streaks.' Rob did not tell the other boys then that he had been in a musical, preferring to suggest that he had been on holiday. The boys responded by nicking his BMX bike, which had Rob weeping and wailing that his grandma had bought him the bike but she was dead. 'We felt that sorry for him that we brought it back,' recalls Giuseppe. 'Then he legged it home.'

Lee Hancock confirms, 'He was full of that much crap!' Lee and Rob were not the best of friends at first because they fell out over a girl, the first real object of desire for pubescent young Rob. Her name was Joanna Melvin, a very pretty girl with mousy brown hair. 'We both fancied her. She was in my class. We were in the top band and Rob was in the dunces' class. I asked her out and she said no. Then Rob asked her out and she went with him for a bit, then she changed from Rob and went with me. She chose me over Rob. I ended up courting her for three or four years when we were about eleven to fourteen. I remember that she was the first girl in school to have one of those frizzy perms when they first came in years ago. Rob and I used to have fights over her – we hated each other! I would say, looking back, that our fights were even.' The rejection by Joanna obviously rankled with young Rob. Years later, when he was hugely famous, he told Phil Lindsay, 'I bet Joanna Melvin would go with me now!'

The conflict over Joanna obviously did not help Rob's efforts to break into the ring of friends in the lower years of senior school. Lee, Giuseppe and Peter were inseparable, although there used to be a 'massive gang' of boys they all belonged to. Rob and Peter were soon at loggerheads over another girl, Sharon Fernley. Once again it was Rob's precious bike that suffered. Giuseppe Romano recalls, 'We had decided to get revenge on him and let down the tyres. He kicked up this big stink about them being special tyres with special valves, which meant you couldn't just pump them up with any old bicycle pump. We all got into trouble with the headmaster, who made us run round the football pitch.'

Rob discovered that the only way he was going to be allowed into the lads' circle was by making them laugh. As a result, he swiftly gained a reputation for being a bit of a clown. He used to walk home with Phil Lindsay and his sister, Leah, who lived near Greenbank Road. Phil recalls, 'He was always messing about, being the class clown. At the time the Rambo films were really big and he used to put his tie round his head as if he were Sylvester Stallone. And we would always walk past this row of hedges and most nights he would dive over them pretending to be Rambo.' Rob also managed to fall out with Phil over a girl, Leanne Cox, whom they both fancied. 'We didn't actually fight over her but we had some serious arguments.'

Girls, in these early teenage years, weren't a priority, despite the odd masculine dispute. 'We used to take the piss out of them,' remembers Giuseppe. 'There was a big posse of us who would hang out and we would have a laugh at the girls' expense. We would speak to the girls and that was about it. There were a couple of fit girls – Joanna was all right. It was a lad's culture. I can't remember him having any birds at school. We just had a good time, really, and girls didn't come into that.' Lee can't remember Rob going out with any of the girls – certainly there was no steady girlfriend.

Rob, however, had a real crush on Kelly Oakes, who was in a class two years above. He wouldn't have wanted the lads to know that she brought out the soppy in him. Kelly was an athletic blonde who wanted to be a dancer and was in the chorus of almost all Rob's forays into amateur dramatics. Being in the same school as well meant that Kelly uniquely saw both sides of the teenage Rob: the sensitive and the senseless. Kelly liked Rob, who was amusing and persistent, but she was sixteen and more interested in young men with cars than in old Willwogs. He bought her flowers and chocolates and sent her little notes. On one Rob had written: 'You are my sunshine.'

Rob was secretive about Kelly and also about losing his virginity to a girl from Liverpool called Anne-Marie. He never told Giuseppe or Lee, for fear they might take the mickey out of him, but he did confess to Phil Lindsay as they chatted at his house the day after the deed was done: 'He said it was in his bedroom at home. I don't know if any drink was involved because they were never going out or anything like that.' Rob's recollection of it is that it was not his best performance and it was over too quickly, although he was delighted. He later immortalized the encounter, wittily, in the song 'The 80s' in which he recalls, 'she said "Fuck me" and I thought fuck me'.

Eventually Rob became accepted as one of the boys. 'He was still the show-off, even though he was now one of the gang,' observes Lee. Their own close bond was forged when they discovered they shared the same off-the-wall humour and, in particular, a love of the satirical Northern band the Macc Lads, a now defunct rock group from Macclesfield. Lee remembers, 'We used to sing all their songs, which had lots of swearing in and were degrading to women. We used to love them.'

Then there was Vic Reeves, who became Rob's schoolboy hero. Later the pair would become firm friends when Robbie appeared on Vic's *Shooting Stars* programme on television. At this time, in the late eighties, the 'in' show was *Vic Reeves Big Night Out*. Willwogs and Tate, like many a school friend before them, would laugh themselves silly recounting the previous night's show to each other, literally line by line. Lee observes, 'We were always reciting Vic. We just discovered we had the same sense of humour. We talked about Vic Reeves, Macc Lads, beer and football. We never talked about school work. We never worried about exams. It didn't matter and we didn't care.'

One of the reasons Rob was not too bothered about school work was because, academically, he was not the brightest apple in the barrel. He was in the lower stream and he never particularly shone. Lee recalls, 'He was that thick in French that the person next to him told him the answer to the French for "I am a boy" and Rob stood up and said, "*Je suis un jardin*" – I am a garden.' He did poorly in exams, never taking them seriously. The adult Rob is clearly not stupid, so perhaps he gave the impression of being thick at school or he became used to being told he wasn't bright and stopped bothering.

What the school did for Rob more than anything else was to give him a sense of belonging. There is the theme running through his life of someone with an enormous need for approval and acceptance. Clearly his ability to communicate through lyrics and humour was not something that could flourish in a school environment. Indeed, one teacher famously derided Rob, declaring that he would never amount to anything – a prediction that Rob took great pleasure in throwing back at him on his *Life Thru a Lens* album with a devastating poem that began 'Hello Sir, remember me?' Rob was never a candidate for sixth form college, which was something his mother and father had to accept.

Kelly Oakes observes, 'I don't think he ever had a plan in mind. He was just going to be an entertainer and that was it.' Rob told his dad he wanted to be an entertainer when he was twelve and never wavered.

Rob and Lee became Tunstall's answer to the Chuckle Brothers. When Jan Williams was running the florist's, the pair would go in and make a nuisance of themselves. On one occasion they sent jokes to all the other Interfloras on the fax machine, clogging up the whole system with jokes from

Bloomers, May Bank, Stoke-on-Trent. 'He got bollocked for that,' laughs Lee. They went babysitting for one of Jan's friends: 'We were smoking, as you do, and we decided to ring 1471 to see who'd phoned. Then we used to ring the people up and tell them jokes. We phoned up this chartered accountant and told him jokes on his answer machine for a quarter of an hour until his tape ran out.'

The two 'Likely Lads' would also ring up advertisements they saw in the paper: 'We once saw this car for sale in *The Sentinel.* It was for a Lada Estate. We rang it up and pretended we were funeral directors, as you do. "Hello," says Rob. "We're very interested in this car you've got for sale. The thing is we need it in a bit of a hurry 'cos we're undertakers and the hearse has broken down. What I need to know from you is will it hold a dead body in the back?" Rob was so brilliant at voices; we used to have great fun on the phones.'

Their *pièce de résistance* was repeatedly ringing up some poor bloke. Rob would run through his repertoire, including Frank Spencer and a loud black man, which Lee recalls was his particular favourite. 'Some bloke would answer and Rob would ask, in a voice, "Is Pete there?" The bloke would say, "No, never heard of him." Rob would put the phone down and then ring back, using a different voice, "Is Pete there?" "No!" This would go on for four or five times, one after the other. Then, finally, I would ring up: "It's Pete here. Have there been any messages for me?" We used to do stupid things.'

Occasionally Rob's own sense of humour would fail. A group of lads went back to his house after school and Rob set about cooking a large omelette. Giuseppe was chatting in the kitchen, chewing a piece of gum, which he proceeded to lob into the frying pan when Rob wasn't looking: 'When it was cooked he put it on the plate and started eating it. We were killing ourselves so I had to tell him it was a spearmint-flavoured omelette. He went right off it and chucked it outside in the backyard. He wasn't very happy.'

Now that he was a fully paid-up 'lad' Rob was able to participate in two of the favourite pursuits: football and curries. He joined games in Tunstall Park, just a kick-around after school. One of the boys who played, Paul Phillips, never knew Rob's real name until he was in Take That. He was just known as Willwogs.

Whenever it was one of the lads' birthdays, half a dozen of them would pile over to an Indian restaurant in Shelton called Al Sheiks. Lee remembers, 'There would be quite a few of us. We would go across the road to the Norfolk Inn and get all the beer because the restaurant didn't have a licence. We paid fifty pence deposit on the glasses and took them to the curry house. We always ended up drunk and throwing all the food about, as you do. I don't know why they used to keep letting us back in – we used to cause that much of a nuisance.'

Towards the end of his school years, Rob took up smoking with the rest of the lads. He would trot down behind the school water tower, where the hardened smokers would fill their lungs with their cigarette of choice. Rob's preferred schoolboy inhalation was Silk Cut Ultra Lights. Zoë Hammond recalls that he was smoking when he played Dodger in *Oliver!*: 'You could smell it on him. He was about thirteen when he started hanging out with his cronies and smoking. He would have smoked whatever he could have got his hands on, being a dead ordinary lad.'

There was always the hint that Rob was a lot less cool than he would have liked to be. He discovered rap music. His record collection read like a coffee shop menu: Ice T, Ice Cube and Vanilla Ice. He loved Vanilla Ice, a one-hit wonder whose number one 'Ice Ice Baby' is unlikely to find a place in any playlist that includes Eminem.

School was a bit like a holiday camp. Rob has always said how much he enjoyed it and it's true that he seldom got into any trouble, even though the headmaster, Conrad Bannon, had a fearsome reputation among his ne'er-do-well flock for being very strict. Giuseppe observes, 'He was pretty decent really, although we all had the cane. We just used to take the piss out of a lot of the teachers.' One favourite trick for Rob and Lee was walking behind the French teacher, Mr Openshaw, who had a hearing aid. The boys would start whistling, so the poor man would start tapping his hearing aid, thinking it was on the blink. Lee laughs, 'Rob loved all the messing around.' The whistles for the PE teacher, Mrs Gittings, were of a different variety because all the lads fancied her and admired her impressive rear.

Certainly Rob was doing his share of 'bobbing off', as playing truant was called. If there was a lesson they didn't fancy, the lads would scoot down towards the gates at the bottom of the school grounds where there were temporary classrooms and loads of trees in which they could keep out of the way, have a smoke and chat about things. Very occasionally they would talk about their aspirations. Giuseppe wanted to be an airline pilot, Lee an air traffic controller or stockbroker and Rob a Redcoat at Butlins.

The students were not allowed out of the grounds at lunchtime; instead they would eat chips and kick a ball about in the yard. Lee and Rob used to have a competition to put all their chips on a fork and see how many they could get in their mouth at the same time. The pair also had sweating competitions. The idea was to see who could get their shirt to smell worst by wearing it day after day. It got to the stage where they would sit next to radiators all day to get more of a sweat on and develop those lovely wet patches under the arms.

Giuseppe and Rob had a bet that involved shaving off their pubic hair. 'I remember it was very itchy. The bet was that we would each shave off half our pubes. It was something we arranged in the changing rooms after PE. We both did it, but the funny thing is I can't for the life of me remember what the bet was for!'

Occasionally the girls would get their revenge on the lads –

like the time they told them there was going to be a great party in a local community hall. The boys arrived, clutching alcohol and shouting out, 'Hey, we've got the beer!' only to discover that they were gatecrashing an evening karate class. The girls also ran a 'fit list' in the fifth year to determine who the 'fittest' boy in school was. Rob didn't win, nor did Lee, Giuseppe, Peter or Phil.

By the time Rob was fifteen, booze was a major part of his teenage life. A lot of his contemporaries would have parties and he and his friends would go round and get drunk. It was easy to get booze. The tallest of the gang, Richard Kirkham, would be designated to go into the local off-licence and buy it. If there was no party, they might sneak into the school gym and play on all the equipment: PE was a lot more appealing after a few cans of beer.

On a Friday or Saturday night the big thing was the disco. Jan used to drive Rob and a couple of his mates to the Zanzibar (now the Ritzy) in Newcastle under Lyme and another called Norma Jean's in Hanley. Sometimes there might be a fight, sometimes not. Phil Lindsay remembers a fight on a bus with some Stoke lads on the way back from Hanley. It is still fresh in his memory because he was the only one who got hit.

Giuseppe Romano remembers another time when they were chased through the streets by the boys from the rival James Brindley High School, known locally as Chell School, who had 'the biggest lad in the city' on their side: 'At the time we were probably more scared of our dads than the chasers – in case we got into any trouble.' Later, when he was in Take That, Rob remarked that this was one of the advantages of having parents who had split: 'If I get told off by my mother, I can go and tell my dad. And if I get told off by my dad I can go and say, "Mum, me dad's been telling me off."' Rob was always lucky to avoid fights because young men and boys getting involved in a spot of bother was pretty much the norm in Stoke-on-Trent. As the Elton John classic goes, 'Saturday Night's Alright (For Fighting)'.

St Margaret Ward was a Roman Catholic school where it was compulsory to take classes and a GCSE in RE (religious education). The school had its own chapel and Rob had to join the other pupils to celebrate feast and saints' days. Giuseppe says, 'The Catholic faith did play a significant part in the education.'

The most obvious religious link for Rob came when there was a weekend away to a Catholic retreat called Soli House in Stratford-upon-Avon. The then deputy-head, John Thompson, was impressed with Rob's contribution to a day spent discussing moral issues, including poverty: 'He always led the discussions and helped act out the playlets to illustrate the concerns. He thought very quickly and could ad lib well.' Mr Thompson's considered recollections of Soli House are a little different from those of Rob's mate Lee Hancock. 'It was a weekend away boozing – a day or two on the pop,' he observes. Another friend, Phil Lindsay, confirms, 'We used to sup beer until we fell asleep. You were free to do what you wanted.'

The schoolmates, however, were overawed by a glimpse of Rob's singing talent, which, up until then, had largely been hidden from them. On the last day, each of the fifteen year olds had to do a little turn – a mini talent competition with no prizes. Rob sang a song quite beautifully. It was 'Every Time We Say Goodbye', the haunting classic by Ella Fitzgerald and a slightly less inspiring hit in late 1987 for Simply Red.

The drugs culture at school was not huge. Rob's drug of choice then was Lynx spray deodorant. He and his mates would put a towel or tissue over the top, shake the can and bring the gases out gradually. They called it 'toiling over the nozzle'. Besides sniffing gas, the kids used to do some 'blow' and sniff amyl nitrate (poppers) in class. Phil Lindsay remembers, 'I don't know if the teachers knew but they never said anything. They must have noticed us with the bright red face on. We were lucky to get through it, I suppose.'

On the very last day at school, in July 1990, about ten boys and girls, including Rob, snuck away at lunchtime. They crept down to the back of the school, where the grassy banks swept down and hid them from view. There they all shared an end-of-school joint. Phil observes, 'We didn't actually get stoned. It was school kids' stuff but it was a nice way to go out of school.'

When school finished, Lee was waiting to start college and Rob was waiting for a break. They both got jobs selling double-glazing. The first ones were with a firm called Abacus Windows, just round the corner from Rob's house. They were paid £50 a week and it was money for jam. Lee recalls, 'The gaffer used to drop us off in the morning in one place and say, "Knock this area, lads", and we just sat on the wall smoking all day until he picked us back up. We didn't do any work. They paid you extra if you made a sale. I made one but I can't remember Rob making any. We did a few of the window companies – Staybrite was one – because it was dead easy money.'

When they were not working, Lee and Rob would raid Jan's drinks cabinet. They would get an empty two-litre plastic Fanta bottle and fill it up with everything they could find – gin, vodka, whisky, mixers – literally anything. They would then put the top back on and shake it all together, and go up to Tunstall Park for an hour or two to get 'rat-arsed'. 'We were big drinkers when we left school,' says Lee, who still remembers being sick on Rob's sister's bedroom carpet when he stayed over one night, too drunk to make it home after the two friends had made a night of it at the Ancient Britain. No wonder Jan was getting desperate to find something for her son to do.

Rob has often said that he felt he missed out on his teenage years because he joined Take That when he was just sixteen. That can be only partly true because all the evidence shows that he had a very full and happy time with his contemporaries. He may have had to play the fool initially to get accepted but that was always part of his nature – he had been a prankster from a very young age. Where Rob may have been different from his peers was that he always had something extra in his life. Being a 'lad' was only part of his day-to-day existence: there was also the Artful Dodger, the youngster who was so certain he could make it, and his friendships with Zoë Hammond and Jonathan Wilkes, which were completely separate from the world of sweating competitions and shaving off his pubic hair. He had a secret drive that would raise him above the norm.

One of the heart-warming things about discovering the real world of Willwogs is that the friends he left behind still have enormous regard and affection for him. When they heard him sing 'Mack the Knife' or 'Every Time We Say Goodbye' they thought it was 'absolutely fantastic'. They were knocked out by his performance in *Oliver!* They did accept him, both at school and in the local community, which is one of the reasons why Rob's roots have always been so important to him. The tricks they got up to still raise a smile and a laugh today without any hint of 'I went to school with a celebrity'.

Nothing better illustrates that bond than when Rob was famous and in Take That and he joined Lee, Giuseppe and the lads for their Monday night jaunt to the bars in Hanley. Lee recalls the night, 'Monday night was student night. It was fifty pence a pint in loads of places and most of them you could get into for free. Rob came out with us this one night. There were loads of people in this one bar giving him aggro because of who he was. So we put him in a taxi, which carted him off home. And then we had a fight for him outside the kebab house in Hanley. We won!'

4

The Sporting Life

In his younger days Pete Conway was a keen amateur boxer
and introduced his son to the sport. Rob didn't box but was
happy to join his father on nights out to the local fights. He
would sell programmes to make some extra pocket money and
roped in his mates Lee Hancock and Giuseppe Romano to
help, either at the King's Hall in Stoke or the Victoria Hall,
Hanley. The boys would also do the music and the lights when
the boxers made their 'grand' entrance. Afterwards they
would adjourn to the Wagon and Horses, which was run by a
friend of Pete, and Rob would get up and do a turn with his
dad. One night Rob got drunk and accidentally smashed his
picture of Muhammad Ali, a prized possession. He was
mortified and never forgot his clumsiness. Years later he was
able to replace it with an Andy Warhol print of the famous
sportsman.

Boxing was not the sport for Rob, although he was never
afraid to stand his ground at school. As a teenager, he was particularly adept at pool and table tennis, a product of whiling
away wet afternoons with his dad at the holiday camps of Great
Britain. At the pool table, Rob would mesmerize his opponents
by having one of the strangest grips imaginable – bridging over

the knuckles instead of the thumb. He would play ping-pong with his dad for hours at a time – matches that were always highly competitive although Pete usually won.

Rob was also keen on tennis but even more so on golf. The nine-hole course at Burslem Golf Club was only a five-minute walk away from the house in Greenbank Road, so Rob could easily pop in after school or during the holidays. His indulgent mother had bought him his own set of good quality clubs and he got plenty of use out of them. Sometimes he would play with his father, sometimes his mother, but more often than not he would muck in with Tim Peers and his fellow juniors.

Rob was a useful if cavalier player, always trying the daring shot. He was elected junior captain of the club when he was fifteen. It was 1989, the year before he joined Take That, and Rob was not yet a sharp-dressed young man. At the golf club, his sweatshirt was legendary. Tim recalls, 'It was a hideous thing, white with a sort of skiing scene on the front with lots of pine trees. He wore it all the time.' In the clubhouse, however, he could often be seen dressed more like a member of the Young Conservatives than a fashionable boy band. Tim remembers just how seriously Rob took the game: 'His persona on the golf course was nothing like the Robbie Williams we read about but it was still a good crack when we played.'

Tim's father, Jim Peers, who was responsible for organizing the junior team, recalls, 'Rob was responsible for the conduct and etiquette of the other juniors, particularly when they played other clubs in competitions. He was always very polite and had to wear a jacket and tie just as the senior members do after a competition. He also gave a speech at the junior captain's day.' The persona of a well-mannered young man was not something that would have been difficult for Rob to adopt; he was one of the most polite boys you could find in Stoke-on-Trent. Everyone remarked on it.

While there was a side to Rob that enthusiastically embraced the contemporary teenage culture of drinking, drug-taking and scallywag behaviour, the other, hidden Robert Williams was one who always treated people with courtesy. That element of his personality never formed part of his future image. Belonging to a golf club and observing the rules and traditions of the game is not going to bring street cred or working-class hero status.

To achieve that, you needed to play soccer. When he was young, Rob always had the dream of playing on the left wing for Port Vale and scoring the winning goal in a big match, often in the local derby with Stoke. He once listed this as one of his two youthful ambitions in life. The second was winning a Brit Award, something he would do many times. One suspects that, like many lads, he would have preferred to achieve the first. He used to sit in his bedroom playing the Sega football game hour after hour.

Surprisingly, despite his devotion to the game, nobody remembers Rob playing for the school team. Both Lee Hancock and Giuseppe Romano were in the team for their age but they recall that Rob was not picked, which must have been disappointing for him. Instead, he would kick a ball around with them in the playground at lunchtimes. Then there were the games after school in Tunstall Park, which were never organized but the lads used to roll up and there would always be enough people to have a game. In summer they would play three or four times a week, which everyone agreed was a much better use of their time on a nice evening than homework. The matches became quite serious if they were between the boys from St Margaret Ward and the nearby Chell School. Rob would always take up his customary position on the left wing. Phil Lindsay says, 'He was a bit of a show-off at football but he wasn't bad.'

Rob always used to practise little tricks in his back garden. Coco Colclough, who also played, assessed his ability: 'He's all right but he thinks he's a lot better than he is. He would always be trying something, little flicks and stuff like catching the ball on the back of his neck or juggling it with his feet.' On the pitch, Rob was always known as Willwogs too.

Rob could not fail to be a supporter of Port Vale. It was the local team, practically on his doorstep when he was born. He loved leading the obligatory chanting at Vale Park. 'Can you hear the goalposts sing?' he would shout to the rest of the crowd.

'No!' they yelled back.

When he was thirteen, Rob couldn't go to football as much as he would have liked. He had his commitment to amateur dramatics but he'd also become the Saturday boy at Signal Radio, the commercial station in Stoke-on-Trent. George Andrews, one of the best-known names in local football broadcasting, recalls that Rob's job was to get the coffee: 'He was just an ordinary kid. He was always polite and courteous and very enthusiastic. He liked his sport.' Rob would start at ten on a Saturday morning and finish at six, so there was no chance of catching a home game.

George remembers that Rob was just as keen on the broadcasting side of things as the Saturday afternoon sport. He says, 'Rob was always interested in the mechanics. He would always be sitting there, watching how it was done. He had a broad Potteries accent and I suspect he could still slip into that even now. Sometimes he would go into the studio and DJ by himself and you could tell he really enjoyed that. But we didn't see a musical side to him – he didn't go round the office singing!'

Rob stayed at Signal for a couple of years and had more time for watching football once he'd left. Lee Hancock was a Stoke fan but he would join Rob to watch the Vale because they were guaranteed to have a laugh. They used to go in the Railway Stand and keep everyone amused on damp and grey December days by making up songs, or more precisely chants, from the advertising hoardings. Lee's favourite, which they would do every time they went, involved the board for the Langport Fish Bar. The whole crowd would join in: 'Langport Fish Bar', *clap, clap, clap*; 'Langport Fish Bar', *clap, clap, clap*. It must have been a little disorientating for the opposing teams. Another was 'High Lane Oatcakes', *clap, clap, clap*. 'It was crazy and great fun.'

Rob has never shouted it from the rooftops but, at the time, he was also a big fan of Manchester United. Coco Colclough explains, 'If you are a lad living in Stoke-on-Trent you have two teams – Stoke itself and Port Vale. You support one or the other. But everybody's fickle and you've also got the big famous teams that you support. Rob's – and mine – was Manchester United.'

To his great delight, Rob was introduced to the captain, Bryan Robson, at Haydock Park racecourse and had his picture taken with him. Rob could not have looked any squarer, wearing a buttoned-up shirt and a jumper with lurid horizontal stripes that only your mother could make you wear. It makes a vivid contrast with another photo opportunity a couple of years later when Take That met Robson as part of a charity event and were pictured posing with the Premiership trophy that Manchester United had just won. The now cool Rob had evidently binned the stripy jumper in favour of a leather jacket and sideburns.

Rob never bothered with pictures of scantily dressed girls or rock gods like Jimi Hendrix or Jim Morrison on his walls. He was a lad and preferred his sporting heroes, such as Bryan Robson and Muhammad Ali. He also had a picture of himself taken with Neil McNab of Manchester City after he and Lee Hancock had gone up to Maine Road, Manchester.

Rob has never lost that innocent, schoolboy love of football and respect for the men who play it. It partially explains why, in the future, he was so starstruck when he met David Beckham. Rob went bright red and started doing his telltale nervous walk – he moves his right arm and right leg followed by his left arm and left leg. Rob is a great admirer of Beckham as a footballer and also as a celebrity who could handle the pressures brought on by fame, including keeping cool when people abuse you because they are jealous of your star status and the material benefits that brings.

5

Gary's Gang

Ambition counts for nothing if all you are doing is smoking your days away, sitting on a wall, while you're supposed to be selling double-glazing to some hapless punter. Rob had determination, guts and an absolute certainty that he was going to be somebody in the entertainment industry but he needed something to happen. Fortunately for him, his mother shared his belief in his abilities and she understood that her 16-year-old son was unlikely to make much of a life for himself if he stayed in Tunstall. Not surprisingly, it was Jan who spotted the story in *The Sentinel* in which a Manchester-based talent agency was seeking a candidate for a newly formed boy band. She pressed Rob, who, at the time, was more likely to be reading the back of a fag packet than the local newspaper, to send in the details of his experience on the stage and try to get an audition.

The agency in question was run by a thirty-something go-getter called Nigel Martin-Smith. He had established a foothold in the entertainment world in the early 1980s working as a casting agent in Manchester, where he was determined to challenge a London bias in the entertainment business. He began to build a name for himself promoting local actors and talent through his Boss Agency, although he also harboured ambitions in the music industry.

His initial venture was managing a local singer called Damian, who had a top ten hit in 1989 with 'The Time Warp', an energetic and flamboyant cover of the song from the hit musical *The Rocky Horror Show*. It was not a big breakthrough but it did illustrate a persistence that would serve his next music venture well. 'The Time Warp' had been released in two earlier versions before finally making the charts. Damian Davey had one more minor hit with 'Wig Wam Bam' before disappearing off the radar. He had, however, appeared on *Top of the Pops*, which back then was still a key ambition for most music wannabes and an achievement with which Nigel could impress new acts.

Nigel needed some inspiration and he found it when he saw the latest American teen sensations New Kids on the Block at a television studio in Manchester. He didn't actually like what he saw. He told the pop columnist Rick Sky, 'I couldn't help but feel how obnoxious they were. They seemed to be very big headed, strutting around the studio as if they owned it.' Even though he was unimpressed by the group in person, Nigel was very taken with its enormous success.

It was a rare bedroom wall that was not filled with a poster of the band from Boston – Jordan, Jon, Danny, Donny and Joey. In 1990 alone – the year Take That was formed – they grossed a reported £861 million, making them the highest earning boy band of all time. That year they had eight top ten hits in the UK charts. No wonder Nigel felt there was room for a home-grown band to share some of the action. Fortunately for him, by the time Take That were trying to make a name for themselves playing small clubs around the country, New Kids were old news.

The decisive meeting in the story of Take That had nothing to do with Rob. It was when Gary Barlow, a young Northern musician, turned up at Nigel's offices in Chapel Walks,

Manchester, for an afternoon appointment. Gary was nineteen, three years older than Rob, but a generation older in terms of musical experience. He had been brought up on a close-knit council estate in Frodsham, a small town in Cheshire about twenty-five miles from Manchester. His grandparents lived round the corner and his dad, Colin, kept pigeons in the back garden.

When he was ten years old, his father offered him a choice of Christmas present: some new wheels for his BMX bike or a keyboard. Gary chose the keyboard after being mesmerized by Depeche Mode performing their synth classic 'Just Can't Get Enough' on *Top of the Pops*. Within a couple of weeks, Gary was displaying a precocious talent: he was able to hear a tune on television and play it on his new Yamaha. His father decided to buy him a proper synthesizer and sacrificed his holiday pay to buy a £600 version – quite an investment in an eleven year old. Gary literally spent every waking moment playing what he called 'this bloody organ'.

The irony is that, for all the animosity of future times, Gary and Rob were quite alike in that they shared the same inner certainty of success and were prepared to work at it even at a very young age. They were both fortunate that they also had mothers who realized early on where their sons' talents lay. Unlike Rob, whose ambitions were vague within the broad parameter of entertainment, Gary was always completely focused on being a singer- songwriter.

A year later and Gary was ready for the big time. He entered a talent contest at the Connah's Quay Labour Party Social Club in North Wales and came third performing 'A Whiter Shade of Pale'. The club chairman, Norman Hill, was impressed and offered Gary a regular Saturday night residency, playing from 8p.m. to 10.30p.m., for £18 – a fortune for a lad who'd just turned thirteen.

By the age of fourteen, Gary had moved on from the Labour Club to the more prestigious Halton Royal British Legion Club near Runcorn and therefore much nearer home. He did four gigs each weekend, finishing at 2a.m., and picked up £120 a night – a very fair wage for someone just discovering the joys of acne.

This was exactly the sort of venue where one might have expected Rob's father, Pete Conway, to be plying his trade. Gary recalls that Ken Dodd, Jim Davidson and Bobby Davro were three of the 'household names' whose acts he would accompany. Gary was becoming a seasoned performer of a style that would not have seemed out of place in *Peter Kay's Phoenix Nights*. Gary would later say, 'No wonder I felt that I was fourteen going on fifty.'

When he was fifteen, Gary entered a BBC Pebble Mill competition called 'A Song for Christmas'. He wrote a ballad, 'Let's Pray For Christmas', his first proper song, which his mother thought too slow and dull but Cliff Richard would have loved. He was invited to London to record the track at the Hampstead studios of producer Bob Howes. Gary made the final of the competition but would later acknowledge that meeting Bob was far more important. Bob encouraged him to keep writing songs so that, amazingly, Gary had written two of Take That's finest, 'Why Can't I Wake Up With You' and the memorable 'A Million Love Songs', before he had reached his sixteenth birthday.

In many ways Gary had an idyllic existence as a teenager. He had a steady girlfriend and was working at something he was passionate about. He also had wads of cash. When he left school at seventeen, he was earning roughly £600 per week from gigging, comfortably more than the average wage of the working men in his neighbourhood. It would have been easy for him to settle for that easy, cheesy life. In addition to the money he made performing, he made pirate tapes of himself singing popular songs and sold them at his gigs. He had never had to go out and sell double-glazing to earn some beer money.

Gary's efforts to make the record companies sit up and take notice, however, were getting nowhere. They thought him too young. And, anyway, Rick Astley was from 'up North' and the thinking seemed to be that there was room for only one singer with a Northern accent in the charts. The difficulty for the young Gary Barlow was that he was not cutting edge in any way. He admits that he was the squarest teenager in the world: he was podgy, boss-eyed and couldn't dance. He also had one of the least cool names in the history of the charts. Gary Barlow sounds more like the name of a Northern comic – Gary 'Chubby' Barlow appearing nightly at the Legion Club, Runcorn. When he travelled down to London to try to drum up interest in his songs, he wore a suit and carried a briefcase. In a now legendary incident, one publishing agent listened to his demo, which included 'A Million Love Songs', then calmly took out the tape and threw it out the window.

Gary Barlow came across as too nice and polite so it is ironic that he revealed in his memoir *My Take* that he was a teenage love rat, two-timing his steady girlfriend with a brassy blonde in a short skirt. The ménage came to an abrupt end when girlfriend number one rolled up at his home, where he was enjoying the company of girlfriend number two, and it all ended in tears.

While he continued to send out publicity packs to almost everyone he could think of, Gary laid plans for the future by securing a job on a cruise ship for a year. And that was when Nigel Martin-Smith got in touch. The first meeting was low key, with Nigel explaining he was putting a group together and Gary saying he was interested – nothing more than that, but Gary did leave behind a demo tape, urging Nigel to listen to it. Surprisingly, he did and he liked it. He was even more impressed when Gary told him on the phone that he had written all the songs, sung them, played all the instruments and made the recording. Later that day the foundations for Take That were laid.

When they met for the second time, Nigel played Gary a tape of New Kids on the Block – Gary had never heard of them – and told him that was the sort of sound he was looking for. Nigel also wanted his group to be a more modest bunch. He was looking for boys who were down-to-earth, ordinary lads, perhaps unemployed but likeable and definitely not big headed. He obviously had no idea that one of Rob's nicknames at school was 'Swellhead'.

Nigel realized right away that he could build the group around Gary and his songwriting talents. He had found someone who could write the music for his Northern New Kids, thus generating a much greater income from music publishing royalties. Gary recalled, 'I told him I was crap at dancing and could only do a few hand movements. But I was very keen to be a star.' Gary's heart had been set on making it as a solo performer but Nigel managed to persuade him that it was too soon. The lad from Frodsham was desperate to follow in the footsteps of his hero, George Michael, who had used the teen-friendly eighties duo Wham! as a stepping-stone to becoming a solo superstar. That was the path Gary dreamt of following. It would be him and four Andrew Ridgeleys. The problem was finding the right four.

When Nigel Martin-Smith met Jason Orange and Howard Donald, they were already a double act. They were athletic, muscular and six-pack heaven. They were also two of the best break-dancers in Manchester. Every young man in clubland aspired to master the high-energy gyro-technics that were hugely popular at the time. Rob was no exception. He loved it. At weekends, he would go down to Ritzy's nightclub in Newcastle under Lyme with a bunch of mates to polish up his technique.

Zoë Hammond, who used to see him down there, recalled, 'Everybody used to clear the floor because they were bloody good, I tell you. Rob was amazing and I always used to stand on the edge of the dance floor. He used to say, "What do you think of that move? I've just learned that." I'd say, "It's great."' These days, Rob and his pals would have put together a group of street dancers and applied for *Britain's Got Talent*.

While Rob was an enthusiastic amateur, Jason and Howard were professionals. Jason was the son of a Manchester bus driver and one of six brothers, including his twin, Justin, in a Mormon household where alcohol and caffeine were banned. He had little interest in school but was always mad keen on dancing. While working on a YTS scheme as a painter-decorator, he started busking as a dancer in the city centre.

Howard was also from a large Manchester family, with three brothers and a sister. He had bunked off school regularly to practise his dancing, including getting into 'awful trouble' for absconding for five weeks in a row. He was following in the nifty footsteps of his father, who was a Latin dance teacher. When Howard left school, with zero O levels, he, too, had a YTS painting job as a vehicle painter.

The boys met up in the Manchester nightclub the Apollo, when they were dancing with rival crews; both considered themselves to be the best of the bunch. They decided to team up and formed Street Beat to enter competitions and dance professionally at clubs. This background would be invaluable when they set about working out the steps for the flamboyant Take That dance routines.

Jason and Howard went to see Nigel Martin-Smith to try to interest him in professional representation. They were not seeking to be in a boy band. They were not singers. They were dancers with male model looks. Howard had done some modelling and left Nigel a model card that he'd already had made up. Jason handed over a video of himself dancing on the nineties TV show *The Hitman and Her*, hosted by Pete Waterman and Michaela Strachan. Nigel was impressed and quickly decided they would be perfect for his group.

Legend has it that Gary Barlow and Mark Owen had met and become friendly before they met Nigel. They had chatted at Manchester's Strawberry Studios, where Gary was given some studio time as part of his BBC songwriting prize and where Mark used to hang out with a friend of his sister, making tea. He and Gary found they got on well together and Mark would trail along to Gary's gigs, carrying equipment and making a brew. Eventually they formed a half-hearted band called The Cutest Rush to perform a mixture of Gary's own songs and some corny standards. The problem with the story is that it's not true – it was part of a fictional history created by Nigel to make his band appear more interesting.

Mark was a very good-looking prospective model whom Nigel thought would be perfect to attract young girl fans. He met Gary, as the others did, for the first time at Nigel's auditions. The manager had recognized that Mark's cuteness was a quality very important to the development of Take That. Girls wanted to pick him up and cuddle him. Mark, to his credit, has always loathed being described as 'cute'.

Mark, who was brought up in a small council house in Oldham near Manchester, was only two years older than Rob and the member of Take That who became closest to him. Like his mate from Tunstall, Mark went to a Roman Catholic school, loved acting and was mad about football. While Rob was practising Frank Sinatra, Mark was an Elvis fan, even dressing up as The King, which must have been quite funny to witness because he was always a wee lad.

As a teenager Mark had wanted to make it as a professional footballer but trials with Huddersfield Town, Rochdale and even Manchester United failed to provide the career breakthrough he had hoped for. A groin injury put paid to any long-term ambitions and he had to settle for a job in a local boutique, Zuttis of Oldham, where he was well known for being fashion conscious and spending most of his wages on clothes. One of his schoolteachers, Fred Laughton, observed, 'He was very good at soccer, but he was a little bit of a poser. He used to prepare his looks and comb his hair before he went on the football pitch.'

This, of course, was before David Beckham introduced Armani underpants to the world of football.

After the boutique, Mark worked for a while as an electrician's mate before moving on to a job in Barclay's bank. He was restless though and saw a boy band as a possible means of escape.

And so there were four ... Nigel Martin-Smith deserves enormous credit for putting together a band almost by instinct. He had an idea of what he wanted and, with a great deal of luck but also professional intuition, he found the nucleus of the group without the great nationwide search that would later characterize the formation of the Spice Girls or the reality show winners Hear'Say and Girls Aloud.

Crucially for the future career of Robbie Williams, New Kids on the Block had five members. If they had had just four, then it might all have been different because Nigel could have stopped there and never placed the advertisement in the press: *Singers wanted. Singers and dancers wanted for a new boy band. If you have what it takes, call Nigel Martin-Smith ...*

In reality, Nigel needed only one more band member. He had two brilliant dancers to obscure the fact that Gary was hopeless in that department, a babe magnet in Mark and, in Gary himself, a highly promising singer-songwriter. His Northern New Kids was almost complete. The missing ingredient was 'on the knock' in Stoke-on-Trent.

Rob was excited and exuberant about his upcoming audition. On his way home from school he spotted Joan Peers in her garden. He shouted across to her: 'Mrs Peers, I am going to an audition tomorrow for a group.' Joan laughingly replied, 'When you become famous, come back and give us an autograph.' It would take a while but Rob never forgot the conversation. When Take That were finally number one in the charts, Rob knocked on her door. He had an autograph in his hand and announced to a surprised Joan: 'I hope I'm famous enough for you now.'

That was two years in the future. For the present, Jan arranged cover at the florist's so that she could drive Rob to the audition at Le Cage nightclub in Manchester. Nigel had invited one other hopeful to attend but he did not last the course. The other four were there; it was the first time they had got together. Gary introduced himself with a 'Hi, I'm Gary Barlow and I'm the singer', which did little to impress Rob, who told everybody his name was Robert. After all, his mum was there.

Nigel had asked Rob to prepare the Jason Donovan song 'Nothing Can Divide Us', a piece of chart fodder from Stock, Aitken and Waterman. It had been the Australian soap star's first UK hit in 1988, when he came to Britain following the success of his *Neighbours* love, Kylie Minogue. Rob had the priceless advantage of being an old hand at auditions and he managed a very passable interpretation. He clearly could hold a tune and, in any case, it would have been very difficult to be worse than the original. Nigel said he chose the song because it was a hard one to sing and he wanted to see how Rob would stretch himself.

Meanwhile, Jan buttonholed Nigel to find out exactly what the band was all about and what he intended to do. Jan's astute sense of business would prove invaluable to Rob as his career and his wealth have grown. She was not going to let him sign up to something dodgy. Nigel admitted, 'She fired twenty questions at me and gave me the hardest time.' Jan was reassured by the size of Nigel's own personal investment in the band – £80,000 – and by his very businesslike demeanour. The audition concluded with Nigel treating everyone to lunch at British Home Stores.

6

The Man in the Mustard Suit

Rob's O Level results were, according to his mother, Jan, 'dreadful'. He didn't get any. Rob 'celebrated' their arrival by drinking Fanta bottle cocktails and playing drunken bowls on the bowling green all afternoon with Lee Hancock. He was out, therefore, when the phone call came from Nigel Martin-Smith; the news had to wait until he and Lee staggered back to Greenbank Road in the early evening. Jan couldn't contain her excitement. 'Nigel says you're in,' she shrieked when the lad himself opened the front door. Lee recalls, 'His sister Sally ran down to Bargain Booze to get some beers.'

That was the easy part over. Rob, however, had 'absolute certainty' that this was the start of his success. When a photographer came round from the local paper, he leaned out of the window of his bedroom and shouted to the world that he was going to be a star. Not everyone was so convinced. On the day before he was due to leave to start his training in Manchester, he was shopping with his mother in the Trent Vale branch of Tesco, when they bumped into Brian Rawlins, who had played Fagin to his Dodger.

Brian recalls, 'He told me what was happening and that he was off to join this group. I can remember saying, "Do you think it's wise?" I wouldn't have let him go and I remember saying that.

'At the time I was running a youth theatre group and I saw so many kids go off and think they were going to be a star. I told him that. I worked in education and I would have preferred him to stay on in school. I remember asking Jan, "How well do you know these people you will be handing him over to?" and she said she hoped it would be all right because she had made quite an investment in it all. She had bought him some new clothes and that sort of thing. And she would have to pay for his accommodation in Manchester.'

One of the first things Rob did when he started spending time away from home was get a tattoo on his left leg, the first of many illustrations. He told the Peers family, 'I've had a tattoo and I daren't tell me mum.' Jan has never been that fond of her son's tattoos. He waited until she was in a good mood in the local curry house, the Kashmir Garden in Tunstall High Street, before he revealed his now famous Maori tattoo on his upper left arm. They were having dinner with the Wilkes family when he took off his sweater and waited for a reaction.

Jan sighed, 'Oh Robert, why do you mark your beautiful body?'

Rob grinned at her before replying, 'Don't worry, Mum, when I'm sixty I'll still have a beautiful bird on my arm.'

Long-suffering Jan would end up funding her son's ambitions for some two years before Rob would be able to provide for himself. Some weeks it might be £100, another week she might have to find £200. 'I paid for hotels, transport and things like that. I told him I would buy the essentials like his trainers.' And it wasn't just Jan who helped. His nan, Betty, also opened her purse to help her beloved grandson.

His mates in Tunstall were always enthusiastic for Rob. Lee gave him a letter to sign which, trustingly, Rob did. When he turned it over, it read: 'I, Robert Williams, being of sound mind and heart declare half my earnings to Lee Hancock.' Lee kept the letter and laughs, 'He owes me forty million quid.'

Just when Rob was finally one of the lads back home, he left them behind. Looking back during an interview with BBC Stoke, Jan Williams made a telling observation about Rob's teenage life that provides some explanation for his future problems. He lost two years' growing-up time when he joined Nigel's group. She said, 'He was a very young sixteen. The lads he ran with at school were absolutely delightful lads but they weren't streetwise really. When he joined the group, he missed a block of his "normal" teenage years, of running with his peers. He was in this controlled place with management. You don't grow but remain the same in lots of ways as when you were sixteen, so it became very difficult to cope with a lot of things.'

Rob, in effect, stopped growing up when he joined the group. He was cocooned in a Neverland where he was neither given nor took responsibility. Instead, all his youthful energy was applied to the task in hand – making it. Around him, others shaped his destiny. One of the first things he had to become used to as a boy band member was a new name, Robbie.

His Tunstall mate, Coco Colclough, observes, 'His manager named him Robbie and, I must tell you, he hated it himself. It surprises me a bit that he has kept it. I imagine it is because it has made him so successful. And I suppose changing it now would be impossible. If he walked past you in the street and you called him Robbie, he wouldn't take any notice. But if you went "All right, Rob?" he would turn around straight away because he would know it was one of his mates.'

Right from the start, being called Robbie meant that the entertainer Robbie Williams became separated from Rob Williams, the lad from Stoke-on-Trent. Robbie Williams is such a boy band name, conjuring up an image of floppy fringe and toothy grin, summer camps and first loves. It's an innocent name. There was more to come.

Robert Peter Williams also acquired an extra forename – Maximilian – a total invention but one that still pops up in under-researched newspaper articles as being one he was born with. Rob went along with everything, swept along by the excitement of it all, but also because, as he has admitted, he was a little scared of Nigel and, despite his weekly efforts at Ritzy's nightclub, he was well behind in the dancing department – more on a par with Gary than with Howard or Jason. He recalled, 'I was terrible. I kept getting everything wrong.'

The dance training seemed to last an eternity. Rob was under strict instructions to get fit and stay fit. The fags and boozing mentality of Tunstall Park was, at least temporarily, out the window. Even when he was back home for a spell, he was under strict instructions from Nigel to go to the gym. Coco, who used to accompany him to the Powerhouse Gym on the Newfields Industrial Estate, laughs, 'It was always like a muscle man's gym. Rob was not really a big lad although he had a good physique. We used to go down there and there were all these blokes with veins popping out of their heads, really giving it some with all these big chunky weights. Rob and I had to search around just to find something we could pick up!'

Even as an active teenager, Rob was developing hang-ups about his weight, which would shoot up the moment he had a bag of chips and a couple of oatcakes with bacon and cheese, nicely washed down with a couple of cans of lager. Zoë Hammond recalls seeing him one weekend after he had evidently been having a difficult time in Manchester. He turned to her and said plaintively, 'I'm not a fat bugger, am I?'

On another occasion when the going was particularly tough, he told her, 'It's not hard but there are times when you could just sling your hook and walk out.' Zoë advised him, 'Just promise me that you'll count to ten before you do or say anything you don't need to.'

Originally, Nigel called his new kids Kick It but luckily the name failed to catch on. Instead, the group came upon Take

That by accident. They were sitting around killing time when they came across a sexy picture of Madonna in a magazine with the caption 'Take That'. Mark Owen explained, 'We thought it was snappy and had a punch to it. We wanted to make sure our name was original.' First of all they called themselves Take That and Party but dropped the extra two words when they heard of a minor American group called The Party. Instead, *Take That & Party* would become the title of their first album.

Rob wasn't doing much partying in these pre-pop star days. He just wanted to fit in. He was the last to join the group, just as he was the last boy to start senior school. He needed to be accepted at St Margaret Ward and it was a similar story in Take That. Coco Colclough observes, 'I think they must have been a bit cliquey in Take That. Rob always felt like he was an outsider.'

One of the great imponderables about Rob's progress in Take That is how much of the resentment he would clearly feel was developed in retrospect – the wisdom of twenty-twenty hindsight? Here was a teenage lad living his dream of becoming a star. How much did he hate Nigel Martin-Smith during these early days? Clearly he did not respond well to too much control but did he really think of him then as 'Satan's son' – his memorable description of his former manager, which popped up in his book *Feel*, written by his friend Chris Heath, published nine years after he left the group?

Nigel had just as much antipathy towards Jason Orange as he had towards Rob – perhaps more. Gary Barlow hints in his book that Nigel fancied Jason. And then there was Gary himself, who would become a focus for Rob's feuding nature. Gary was only nineteen when the band was formed but, as he pointed out, when you are that age there's a huge gap to someone who is sixteen.

Gary inadvertently revealed the true patronizing order of things in Take That in his autobiography. It was Gary, the old hand, who 'prepared' the others for recording. At the first practice, he noted that it was Rob who made him think,

'There's my other vocalist.' Clearly Gary thought of Take That as his group. There's nothing to suggest this was malicious or an attempt at empire building. He just was, as Rob later pointed out, always eighty. Gary admits that he thought of Rob as the young one of the group and concedes it must have been hard on him. These early days of Take That would sow the seeds of a bitter feud between the two.

Rob's perception of himself as a bit of an outsider was not helped by niggling little things, not least by being dropped off at junction 15 on the M6 motorway whenever the boys were on their way back North from a personal appearance. It would drive him mad that they would never listen when he explained that it was not out of their way to drive through Tunstall and continue on towards Manchester.

Going home to Stoke was, in these early days, a welcome break for Rob. He was able to join his friends and still act normally. On an evening in May 1991 he put on a sharp mustard suit and sauntered down to Regime's club in Newcastle under Lyme. He didn't know it but he was about to meet an important person in his life.

It was Rachael Gilson's sixteenth birthday and she had a double reason for celebrating, as it was also her last day at school. One of her best friends, Kay Wilkes, had helped arrange a night out at the club and told Rachael that her cousin Rob was going to be with her and that he was really 'charming'. Kay always called Rob her cousin because he was so close to her family and always had a soft spot for her.

The club was over-18s only but the girls had no trouble getting in as they were all dressed up and looked much older. Kay introduced Rob to Rachael, who was much struck by his mustard suit, which seemed to be several sizes too big for him. Rachael was a stunning girl, tall and lean like a young Kate Moss, and Rob took an instant fancy to her. They danced with each other in the time-honoured way of young people.

Rachael's mother, Margaret Heath, whom she told about that first evening, recalls, 'They were dancing like kids do and just ignoring each other and playing it cool. Later on in the night, Rachael went over to the bar. Rob suddenly appeared by her side and asked her if she wanted a drink. Rachael told me no one had ever asked her before if she would like a drink. She had only just turned sixteen so she didn't know what to say. She heard someone in front of her order a white wine spritzer. She didn't have a clue what that was but went ahead and told Rob she would have one of those. She hated it and didn't drink it.'

Rob had broken the ice and soon he and Rachael were chatting happily together and didn't leave each other's side for the rest of the evening. They discovered they had much in common – not least being brought up by their mothers after their parents had split when they were very young. Rob took Rachael's phone number when they said goodnight and said he would call. Rachael went home and told her mother, 'I have met someone tonight, Mum. He was wearing a mustard-coloured suit and he is going to be famous.' Margaret's reaction was sceptical, along the lines of 'Yeah, right' because 'Kids tell you these things, don't they?' She was intrigued, however, and said she would like to meet him some time.

Clearly, Rachael made a big impression on Rob because he phoned the very next day and asked her to his mum Jan's birthday party. She had to turn him down because she had already arranged to go to a christening but they agreed to meet up for a game of tennis later in the week. Kay Wilkes had told Rob that Rachael was a keen tennis player. They met up at the tennis courts in Endon, a village about five miles from Tunstall, where Rachael's family had lived when they were all together. She and her mother had moved from Endon to a small house off the Leek Road but she had remained on good terms with her dad. According to Rachael, she let Rob win at tennis. Rachael's father taught physical education and both she and her brother were very sporty.

After tennis, she and Rob caught the bus home, sat in the back and snogged the whole way. It was definitely time for Rachael to introduce Rob to her mother. Margaret has never forgotten her first meeting with Rob: 'He walked in, said, "Hello", went straight through to the kitchen, opened the fridge door and asked for a cheese sandwich. "Oh," I thought, "that's fine", made him his sandwich and we went to sit in the living room. I sat with them to talk. Rob sat next to Rachael on the sofa with his hand on the inside of her thigh. I was horrified! Rachael just sat there frozen with massive big eyes.

'He had to get the bus home so I offered him a lift. He was very polite and said thank you when I dropped him in Greenbank Road. When I got back home, I said to Rachael, "You shouldn't let him do that; you shouldn't let him put his hand there." She told me that he didn't mean anything by it.'

Margaret echoes the view of Rob's mother about Rob being young for his age: 'Both Rachael and him were a bit green in those days. They were just naive really and I think all he was doing was making the point that "This is my girlfriend and I am going to look after her."

'Of course, he came round many times after that and I really warmed to him. But he never put his hand on the inside of Rachael's leg again – not in front of me, anyway. He still always came in, opened the fridge and made himself a sandwich.'

One of the first things Margaret learned about Rob was that his father was Pete Conway, which brought back memories of when she herself was a sixteen year old. Then, she was a bit of a rock chick and liked Jimi Hendrix. She was dating a musician in a rock band and used to travel with them in a tatty old van to gigs in working men's clubs. On one occasion, they gave a lift to a comedian who was also appearing that night. Margaret recalls, 'There was a terrible thunderstorm and I was terrified in the back and this bloke was cracking jokes like we were all going to die or whatever. He had us in stitches. I had forgotten all about him until I met Rob. It was Rob's dad.'

Laughter proved to be the bond that cemented the relationship between Rob and Rachael. They were boyfriend and girlfriend at an age before life and relationships became too serious. Rob still didn't have money so, if he was coming round in the evening, Margaret used to leave them a few pounds to rent a film: 'Rob was just an ordinary lad, full of enthusiasm. I used to hear them laughing, you know, when they were walking back from the video store. I could hear them laughing as they walked up the street. It was just lovely.'

Rob was always quick to play the clown – especially if he was hiding a temporary embarrassment, usually caused by his clumsiness. One evening at the store he knocked over a life-size cardboard cut-out plugging a new film. Of course, he pretended he had done it on purpose and proceeded to dance around the shop with the cut-out as if they were Fred Astaire and Ginger Rogers. Rachael was left weeping with laughter.

Rob was the sort of lad one could never be mad at for long. In those days, Margaret used to run an evening exercise class for local women. She would come in at about ten o'clock and would often find Rob there: 'I would go straight into the kitchen to make us a cup of tea and the kitchen would be a bomb site. Neither of them could open a bottle of tomato sauce without it ending up on the ceiling or on the walls, you know, and all they had done was make a cheese sandwich.

'Another evening, he had come over in a huge pair of steel toe-cap boots and had left them by the front door because I had just had a brand new carpet fitted. When it was time to leave, he told me about this new dance he was learning and he wanted to show me. I said OK so he went straight over to put on his boots. So I said to Rob, "Can you dance in those big, heavy boots?" He said, big eyes staring back, "Yeah, of course I can, that's the idea." You can imagine what happened . . . Robert Williams owes me for a new front room carpet.

'It wasn't all bad, though. The next evening I thought I

would try using the move in my class, so I tweaked it a bit and I've used it ever since. I used to call it my "Take That move".

'He used to sing to me sometimes when I was driving him home – just the early Take That songs. And he used to say, "What do you think of that?" And he would just sing, so natural and so keen. He was very focused and enthusiastic. He really did give it everything he'd got. He always used to tell me that they were going to make it one day. His eyes used to light up because he so wanted to do it. And Rachael was right behind him. She would say, "He is going to do it, Mum, he is going to do this."'

By this time, Take That were making some progress. They had played their first gig, a low-key affair at Flicks in Huddersfield where a couple of dozen unenthusiastic people made up the audience. They underwhelmed the crowd for twenty minutes. It wasn't the exhilarating start they had hoped for. Perhaps it was just as well the fanfares were kept subdued, as the boys were far from the finished product.

The first incarnation of Take That was very camp. Nigel, who had told the boys early on he was gay, dressed them up in tight black leather so they all looked like the biker guy in Village People. They even performed the Village People's 'Can't Stop The Music' in their act. He began booking the boys into gay clubs, which proved to be a shrewd move. From this humble, small-time beginning, the group was able to build up a substantial gay fan base. Nigel also arranged for them to perform or make personal appearances at under-18 discos and sixth forms. Nigel was proving to be a canny manager, forever looking to give his band an edge.

The gay impression given by Take That was further emphasized by the group's early television appearances. Nigel was friendly with a former *Smash Hits* journalist, Ro Newton, the producer of a short-lived music show called *Cool Cube* that aired on the now defunct BSB channel. He persuaded Ro to see the boys, who impressed him with their dance routines and singing voices. They performed a couple of Gary's original songs and went down well enough to be asked back a few times. For one show they wore red velvet bomber jackets and skintight black cycling shorts that left little to the imagination and that Ro admitted to being 'a little dubious about'.

Nigel was trying hard to secure the boys a record deal but there were no takers. So he decided to set up his own label, Dance UK, and bring out their first single himself. Gary had written a catchy disco track called 'Do What U Like', which had a very eighties feel to it.

The first Take That single was released in July 1991. The boys all crowded round the radio the following Sunday to hear the chart rundown position and started getting excited when they had reached the top ten and their song had yet to feature. It turned out to be because not many people had bought it and it was way down at number eighty-two in the charts, which was disappointing.

At least the accompanying video achieved notoriety and did more to get the boys noticed than the song. It was a camp classic and became known as the 'jelly video'. It was co-produced by Ro Newton and Angie Smith, who had worked on *The Hitman and Her*. The boys did an energetic dance routine dressed in their leather gear but Nigel was keen for the video to get the boys noticed. It was originally intended to end with a close up of one of the band member's bare bottom surrounded by some wobbly red jelly. The problem was which bum to choose. The boys, always competitive, started to argue about who had the most photogenic derrière. In the end, Angie decided to audition each behind: 'I have never seen five people strip off so quickly in my life. Robbie was very keen!' The choice proved too difficult, so all five naked bottoms were pictured slopping about in the jelly.

They shot the video at a studio in Stockport and, afterwards, Nigel treated everyone to a meal at nearby Bredbury Hall. Gary, being the talented one, got up and serenaded the guests with some of his cheesy favourites, including songs by Lionel Richie and Barry Manilow. Afterwards Angie remarked that even the waiters thought he was great. 'I realized what a talented singer and musician he was,' she gushed. While Gary was Mr Talent, Rob continued to develop his classroom persona as band clown.

The video, which had adults' and children's versions, was seen for the first time on *The Hitman and Her* just ten months after the band had been formed. Rob's sister Sally admitted to Rick Sky that she and Jan were rather shocked by what they saw. Although the final chart position of 'Do What U Like' was very disappointing, to put things into perspective: Rob was only seventeen and he had a record out; he was appearing on television even if it wasn't yet *Top of the Pops* – and more people than he could ever have imagined had seen his bare bottom.

His girlfriend, Rachael Gilson, was also not standing still. She had been waiting to start sixth form college in Fenton, Stoke-on-Trent, where she wanted to study sport with the aim of becoming either a physiotherapist or a PE teacher. One day, she travelled down to London to visit a friend when she was spotted on the train by a woman from *The Clothes Show*, who told her, 'You could be a model. Go for a casting.' When she returned home that evening, she told her mother, who recalls, 'She said to me, "Guess what happened to me today?" When she told me, I thought, "Over my dead body." Anyway, she got the job.'

Unlike Rob, who had always been certain what he wanted to do, Rachael was genuinely unsure. When she was a little girl, her parents' friends used to say she was so pretty she would be a model when she grew up. The idea had been with her since then but she had not pursued it. Instead, modelling found her. She joined the Respect model agency in Manchester and started to combine modelling assignments with college. It didn't work. Margaret explains, 'She came home one day, really confused and asked me, "Who do I let down? I'm letting the college down and I keep saying no to jobs." In the end, she went to her tutors and they told her, "Go for it, Rachael. You can always come back to education." So she became a full-time model.'

In many ways these were the best times of Rob's life – full of innocence and expectation. He was bursting with enthusiasm for Take That, yet he loved the house in Greenbank Road, coming home to see his mum, having fun with Rachael and taking time away from the relentless rehearsals and the uncomfortable van they used to travel to appearances and gigs. All his mates liked Rachael. Lee Hancock, recalls, 'She was really nice looking, Rachael; a nice person as well.'

Rob still didn't have any money. He was so broke he sold his golf clubs, which resulted in a severe telling-off from Jan. He went round to see Rachael that evening. Margaret was there: 'He was really upset. The thing was that Rachael had done the same thing – selling her flute – so I knew exactly how Jan felt because Rachael had done it.' The incident, quickly forgotten, does reveal Rob's enduring sensitivity.

He was always complaining to his friends about his lack of funds. Coco Colclough recalls, 'He used to tell us he'd been paid £25 for a gig. And he was only getting something if they had done a bit of a gig. It was paper round money. Three hundred miles up the road, three hundred miles back, dance your heart out and whatever, all for twenty-five quid. Half the time we'd go out and we'd have to give him the taxi fare home. I used to say, "Rob, you're mad."'

At least he did not have to travel three hundred miles when they appeared at the Ritzy in Newcastle under Lyme, memorably described by one of Rob's friends as a 'really shitty place'. Rob and Rachael had split up after a tiff but he was really keen for her to go. Kay Wilkes told her that he wanted her to be there but Rachael was being stubborn and refused to go 'just because he wants me to'. She went, of course, but did not tell Rob that she would be there.

During the gig, the boys were engaged in one of their energetic dance routines, which included one of their best-known moves, where they spin round and kick their legs in the air. Rob caught sight of Rachael standing with Kay, looking down on the stage from one of the balconies. It put him off – just as it had done when he'd seen his father in the front row during the first night of *Oliver!*. He completely missed his steps and kept on spinning round. Rachael told friends, 'It was very sweet.' Afterwards they met up and decided to start going out together again.

7

No Girls Allowed

One of Nigel Martin-Smith's unbreakable rules was that the boys were not to have girlfriends. They also were not allowed to take the phone number of any girl they met on the road. He wanted to make sure the young girl fans thought that Take That were available. The thinking behind it was that every girl could dream of being 'the one' who would steal the heart of their idol. They would quickly switch to another act if that were not the case. Twenty years later the rules of the game have changed and nobody seems to care about that. Justin Timberlake, for one, has never suffered a backlash from having a beautiful girlfriend. A desirable partner only makes the star more appealing. Media gossip fuels notoriety and the love lives of the rich and famous are its oxygen. Everybody needs their daily fix of Cheryl Cole and Britney Spears.

Nigel was adamant, however, and so, to avoid his suspicion, Rachael was always introduced as Rob's cousin when she turned up at one of the small gigs around the country. She would go on to the hotel afterwards and give the password so that she could be admitted to the inner sanctum. The other band members liked her. All five signed a card, which she kept.

Jason Orange had written: 'When you've finished with Cousin Robbie, let me know and I will take you out.' Nigel would have had a fit.

All the graft of going to small gigs eventually paid off when a forward-thinking A&R man at RCA Records, Nick Raymonde, heard about them. He decided to take a trip out to a small club in Slough where Take That were supporting Right Said Fred, the over-the-top duo who had a big debut hit with 'I'm Too Sexy'. He was impressed. He loved the boys' blend of sexy and camp. Back at his office, he already had an ally in Nicki Chapman, who would later become a judge on *Pop Idol* but was then an up-and-coming PR. She had already spotted the band's picture in a magazine and told Nick about them.

Nigel was able to negotiate a record deal for £75,000, which the band signed in September 1991, one year after the official birth of the group. Nigel took 25 per cent, which left Gary, Robbie, Mark, Jason and Howard to split £50,000. They each received £10,000 minus Nigel's deductions for things he had bought for the band. It didn't leave much for a year of hard graft but it was probably more cash than Rob would have made selling double-glazing – at least it would take the pressure off his mother.

An equally significant deal was sealed four days later. They all signed the contract with Virgin Music Publishing but, in effect, it was just Gary who was wanted. He was the songwriter and he alone received an advance of £150,000. The seeds of later discord were sown there and then. Gary was rich and Nigel was doing well but the other four were picking up loose change. From that moment on, Rob knew that the real money was in writing songs. He wasn't wrong. They would all eventually make a million from the band's success, but Gary later revealed in his autobiography that he made *seven* times as much as anybody else.

Rob had never played an instrument at school. He could carry a tune but any musical talent had lain undiscovered.

Rachael, however, was very musical. She used to play the family piano in the front room and compose her own songs. She could also play guitar, so whenever Rob came round she would help him get his fingers round the chords to some of his favourite songs. She tried to teach him the timeless 'My Girl' by The Temptations, which had one of the classic guitar riffs, but Rob could never quite get it. He did, however, master 'The Cross' by Prince, a three-chord number. Rob improved with practice but his gift would prove to be in his quick wit with lyrics, especially raps.

Gradually throughout 1991 young girls began to notice Take That, thanks to a concerted media blitz in teen magazines such as *Jackie* and *Just Seventeen.* Their first press officer, Carolyn Norman, made a conscious effort to promote the band as fan friendly, always happy to give interviews – with Rob usually making everyone laugh – or participate in competitions. One teenage girl, who won a day with Take That, was forbidden by her father from going when the lads turned up at her house driving a rickety old yellow van. It took all of Carolyn's powers of persuasion to cajole him into allowing his daughter to go, saying it would be all right because they were only going to Alton Towers. The important thing was to keep the band's name in the columns. It did no harm to the band's reputation, for instance, when girl fans smashed a plate-glass window at a nightclub in a bid to see the new teen idols – at least that's the story that kept interest running high.

Take That were now being firmly marketed to an audience of under-18 girls. The first thing to be ditched on signing their deal with RCA was the Village People leather look. Instead they wore hunky string vests on their whistle-stop promotional tour for their debut single with RCA, which was released in November 1991. 'Promises' was another Gary song, a lack-lustre, overproduced disco track that entered the chart at number thirty-eight – better than 'Do What U Like' but still nothing to get excited about. The boys were thrilled to make the charts at last. Everyone thought it was a good start until it disappeared out of the top forty the following week.

The year 1992 began disappointingly. The third single, 'Once You've Tasted Love', was a flop, failing to make even the lower end of the chart, peaking at a dismal forty-five. Behind the scenes, a knock-back for Rob proved to be another brick in his wall of resentment towards Gary. He wrote a rap that was recorded and put on the end of the song. Rob was chuffed to bits. He asked for a credit for his contribution but Gary, when he heard, was not willing to share billing and always protected his territory. Rob would not forget this.

Take That were not going forward. If it had been 2010, this probably would have meant an inglorious end for the group. The patience of record companies today is notoriously short, but they had already recorded their first album, which was a size-able investment for RCA. There was, however, little point in releasing it when the band was 'cold'.

Nigel hit upon a brilliant strategy. He joined up with the Family Planning Association and sent the boys on the Big Schools Tour, preaching a safe sex message and plugging the band relentlessly, sometimes with as many as four mini concerts in a day. It proved to be a ground-breaking success, with the band getting the message across to 50,000 youngsters before the release of their next single.

Take That were in danger of being the best-known group in the land never to have a proper hit. Fortunately, that changed with 'It Only Takes A Minute', a cover version of an old Tavares song from the seventies. While this was still more *Saturday Night Fever* than New Wave, it did have the benefit of familiarity. The track entered the charts at number sixteen but this time continued to improve its position, ending up a highly creditable number seven. This was more like it. They celebrated at a restaurant called La Reserve in Fulham where – a sign of good things to come – a mass of girl fans gathered outside with their noses pressed up against the window.

Take That were on their way up. Rob met royalty for the first time when Princess Margaret was the guest of honour at the *Children's Royal Variety Performance* at the Dominion Theatre, London, in May 1992. She told them she enjoyed their dance routines.

In June 1992, they appeared on *Top of the Pops* for the first time, fulfilling an ambition for the band. Rob was astonished that nobody else was as excited as they were: 'Everybody else looked so bored. I couldn't understand why they weren't excited to be working on *Top of the Pops.* I was!' The show's producer, Jeff Simpson, was impressed by Take That's enthusiasm and described them as a 'godsend': 'At last there was a buzz about music again. They regularly delivered what the show desperately needed – excitement.'

Rob had the chance to sing lead vocal for the first time on the next single, 'I Found Heaven', which had a similar feel to 'It Only Takes A Minute' but was not as strong a track. It peaked at number fifteen in the charts. Better news came when the first album, *Take That & Party*, was released and went in at number five. Again, it was a false dawn and it went down to number nineteen before disappearing altogether the following week. The video of the album achieved much better results: it was number one for fourteen weeks. At this stage Take That, it seemed, were more pleasing to the eye than the ear.

The group embarked on a nationwide tour of HMV shops but the thirst for publicity was satisfied early on when several thousand girl fans created madness and mayhem at the first couple of appearances. In Manchester, where 5,000 turned up to see their idols, the boys had to be smuggled out of the shop disguised as policemen to avoid being torn to bits. HMV cancelled the rest of the tour for safety reasons, which did the band's growing reputation no harm at all.

Tucked away on the album were two tracks that would transform the fortunes of the band: 'A Million Love Songs' and a cover of the Barry Manilow favourite 'Could It Be Magic'.

Whenever *The X Factor* contestants perform on Take That night, it's certain that these two songs will feature. Until them, Take That records were largely unmemorable. The band had bags of energy and had built up a loyal following but there was absolutely nothing to suggest longevity or hint at the songwriting abilities of Gary Barlow.

The beautiful ballad 'A Million Love Songs' changed all that. It was a mature song, complete with a mellow saxophone introduction and a powerful chorus. Some critics thought this was Take That's attempt to copy the feel of George Michael's first solo number one, 'Careless Whisper'. There is nothing like a classic ballad to change public perception and expand appeal. Gary acknowledged that the song changed the band's career: 'A lot of people thought it would be the kiss of death and there were a lot of rows but in the end we got our way and it was released.' The track reached number seven in the charts.

This was the perfect time for Take That to abandon the small gay venues and school classrooms and go on a proper tour, starting in Newcastle upon Tyne City Hall. Nobody seemed to notice that Rob had a bad throat and had made a speedy trip to the doctor before the concert. The *Daily Mirror* review was ecstatic, declaring that the boys 'could give Michael Jackson a run for his money when it comes to dancing.'

Take That's approach to a concert – one that Rob would embrace as a solo artist – was to regard it like an important football match. Nigel would get the boys in a huddle as if he were a manager about to send them out on to the pitch at Old Trafford: 'Work for each other and take no prisoners.' Sometimes that enthusiasm went too far, however, as was the case when Rob accidentally got his finger caught in Howard's nipple ring, which was complete agony for the body beautiful. Howard spent the entire concert trying to kick Rob very hard during the dance routines.

Rob was gradually coming to the fore within the group. He again took the lead vocal on 'Could It Be Magic', a track full of verve and optimism, and one that probably best represented Take That in the early years. It sold more than 250,000 copies, reached number three in the charts and won the group a silver disc for sales.

Rob sported a newly grown pair of sideburns on the video and the five were filmed giving it 110 per cent in an aircraft hangar that had been made to look like a huge garage full of cars. At the start, a girl turns on a light switch. She had won the role by writing in to *Jim'll Fix It* – it was just another small illustration of how fan-friendly Take That were.

Rob was still travelling home as often as he could. He bumped into Brian Rawlins on the train from London. Brian didn't recognize the young man, wearing a 'silly woolly hat', in the queue for the buffet, so Rob piped up, 'It's Robbie.' Brian had to apologize for not recognizing him: 'I remember being surprised he called himself Robbie. We went back to the carriage together and talked the rest of the way back to Stoke, much to the amazement of the man sitting on my inside, who clearly recognized him and was listening in intently.

'He was already quite famous but he was still travelling second class on the train up to Stoke. Famous people don't travel second class on a train in case ordinary folk annoy you.'

Brian had not realized that Rob, at the time, craved to be ordinary himself. He would travel home, as he was that afternoon, to relax and try to maintain a grip on normality. Rob likes to tell the story of having a kick-about with some young kids on the green outside the house. Suddenly his mother opened the window and shouted out, 'Robert, it's time for your tea.' Rob was so chuffed at this that he told his mum that he would go out and play again later so she could call him in for bed.

He would play pool with his old golfing buddy Tim Peers in

the Ancient Briton. Tim recalls the time he popped in with Mark Owen for a game on their way to play a gay club in London. 'They had a helicopter standing by but they wanted a game of pool first. Mark Owen was a very small fellow but a good lad.' Rob would take his father up to Burslem Golf Course for a round before they enjoyed a couple of pints together. He went to karaoke nights at the Talisman. He would rollerblade round the familiar streets of Tunstall. He would go out to local clubs and bars with his mates.

That would amaze Zoë Hammond: 'He'd just turn up and I'd say, "I don't think I'd dare" and he just said, "Well, most of these people know me", because it was Stoke-on-Trent, but I used to think there's still dickheads about who would glass you. I said, "You're braver than me."'

He liked to go out dancing. One time, when his mates went to pick him up to go to Shelly's in Newcastle under Lyme they were astonished by the sight that greeted them. Coco Colclough recalls, 'He was wearing a little black vest top, black cycling shorts, and black Reebok boots with his socks rolled down. He looked like the dancer off *The Hitman and Her*. He was going out to dance!'

These were happy days but Rob's life in Stoke was in transition. It was still his favourite place in the world but he was leaving it behind. The excitement Rob felt as a fully fledged pop star was being tarnished by what was happening when he returned to Greenbank Road, which he still considered to be home. His efforts to carry on as a normal Tunstall lad were gradually being thwarted. The easy friendships and sense of belonging were beginning to disintegrate and a vital piece of the bedrock that contributed to his personality and well being was eroding as well. He went from being a member of the cast of his home town to becoming a guest star.

To begin with, relatively insignificant things happened. He went to put sounds on the jukebox in the Talisman pub in Furlong Road and someone shouted out, 'Don't put on any of that Take That rubbish!' If he went out with his mates, he would often run the risk of getting a tough time from the Stoke City fans. They would threaten him with all sorts of bodily harm. Giuseppe Romano recalls, 'When he was in Take That, he was out for the evening with a friend of ours and got chased through Hanley by a group of Stoke City fans. I think it was pretty much the last straw as far as going out was concerned.'

One weekend Rob bumped into Zoë Hammond's dad, Tony, outside a club in Newcastle under Lyme. They knew each other well and had always had a laugh. If Rob saw him in a bar, he used to say, 'Hey, Mr Hammond, what are you doing in here, you old crony?' This night, however, Rob was not feeling light-hearted: 'Do you know what, Mr Hammond? I've got a problem here. This dickhead won't let me in. They've said no trainers and no jeans. He knows very well who I am but he was on my back, saying, "Not tonight, sunshine" before I had even opened my bloody mouth.'

Tony went up to the doorman to try to plead Rob's case: 'Just let the lad in. Just because he's doing all right. He's come a long way.' But the bouncer, a classic example of a bonehead, was not budging.

Tony suggested the two of them should find another bar for a drink but Rob said, 'No, you're all right. It's knackered my night now.' With that, Rob took off his coat, swung it over his shoulder and swaggered, whistling down the street with an 'I don't give a damn' attitude. Tony Hammond, however, thought differently: that behind the bravado Rob was really thinking, 'I've popped in to see my mum and I can't even go for a ruddy pint.'

At least Rob was finally making some decent money. He decided to surprise his mum on her birthday by giving her a special present. He went up to her florist's shop in May Bank when she was not expecting him. He surreptitiously set off all the alarms so that she came running out of the shop in a panic to see what was going on. There, parked outside, was a gleaming white BMW with a great big bow tied on the bonnet.

Nigel had warned everyone right at the start that when they broke through their lives would become unrecognizable, privacy would be out the window and they would have to make sure their whole life was ex-directory, not just their phone number.

Changing his own phone number every couple of months was just the start for Rob. What do you do when the telephone operator is a fan or some fan's father is a policeman? It becomes impossible to keep it a secret. Even his nan had to change her number.

Friends who used to see Rob happily whiling away his time rollerblading around the streets of Tunstall would now witness him speeding down the pavements at breakneck speeds pursued by a small army of frantic girls. He received sackfuls of mail simply addressed to Robbie Williams, Stoke-on-Trent. Girls from all over Europe and beyond would turn up outside his home. They would trawl the telephone book to phone up people at random and ask them if they knew where Robbie was. Or, failing that, they would try the dialling code for Stoke-on-Trent and then add a random number in the very slim hope of getting Rob.

One evening, Rob was in the Cheshire Cheese pub in Tunstall when the phone rang behind the bar. The barman answered, then shouted over to Rob's table: 'There's a phone call from Italy and they're asking for you, Rob.' Everyone was amazed that the Italian girl had achieved a million to one shot by ringing a random bar just as the object of her adoration was enjoying a pint with his mates. 'I don't want to take that,' he said firmly.

Elsewhere in Stoke-on-Trent, taxi drivers were celebrating an unlikely lottery win, as fares asked to be taken to Robbie Williams' house. Then, if the cabbie were really lucky, the fan or fans would want to be driven on to Oldham to see if Mark Owen was mowing his lawn. The wall outside Rob's house in

Greenbank Road resembled a piece of urban graffiti, as girls' names, messages of undying love or lust and accompanying phone numbers were scratched into the brickwork for all the world to see, much to the delight, no doubt, of their mothers.

Rob did not find it easy to adjust to becoming public property. He was annoyed at the pressure it put on his family, especially his mother, Jan, who was feeling like a prisoner in her own home. Sometimes there might be as many as 300 girls camped outside her front door. Jan would complain bitterly about the nuisance, especially when the bolder ones came and knocked on the door. She was forced to put up a handwritten notice asking them to keep away. Even on a slow day, she would come home from the florist's and there would be thirty or forty fans outside.

The way Rob dealt with it then remains the way he deals with it now. If he is being Robbie Williams, then he embraces stardom and the inconveniences it brings. If, however, he is plain old Rob Williams from Tunstall, he hates it, especially if fans start asking him for an autograph while he is having a pee. One male fan put his arm round an astonished Rob when he was in mid-flow. A supermarket manager once closed his store so that 'Robbie Williams' and his mother could buy their groceries without getting hassled by the public. In this case, even Rob found it funny: 'It was hysterical because it was a Monday morning and there wasn't a soul in there anyway.'

When Robbie Williams is working, he will go out of his way to speak to the fans and engage with them but if it is a 'day off' they have little chance of a friendly greeting. He has been that way since fame took over his life. He would ignore the girls outside his house hour after hour and go about his life as normal inside his home in Greenbank Road. When he eventually emerged, he would refuse to have his picture taken or sign any autographs. Instead he would tell them gruffly he was not 'at work' and they should go away. The fans would never understand that Rob was not Robbie.

His aloofness belies the occasions when Rob has a soft heart. One evening, he was supping a pint or two in the Ancient Briton with his mate Tim Peers. They decided to carry on drinking with some girls they knew at Tim's house round the corner. Tim recalls, 'Rob went home at about one o'clock and everybody else went soon after. About half an hour later, I was getting ready for bed when there was a knock at the door. It was Rob. I said, "What's up, mate?" and he said, "Do you know any bed and breakfasts, Tim?" I told him I thought there was one at the bottom end of town but wasn't sure. I asked him why and he said, "There's these girls asleep in the driveway and I want to fix them up." He made sure he found them a place before he called it a night. And he paid for it. People don't get the right idea about what he's like.' Rob had to keep that particular good deed very quiet or else every teenage fan of Take That would have been sleeping in the driveway of his home in the hope that he would rescue them.

At least he could always count on Rachael for a laugh and a sympathetic ear. One of the last times life had been completely normal had been the previous summer just before the release of the album. They had both come back to spend a day or two with their mothers. It was a really hot sunny day and Rachael rang Rob to see if he wanted to join Margaret and her to swim and catch some sun at the nearby open-air brine pool in Nantwich.

Margaret recalls, 'We went to pick him up and he had slept in a bit and was running late. And his mum had left him some washing to hang out, so I hung it on the line while he was getting ready. We arrived at the pool and, fortunately, it was very quiet. Rob looked ever so lean and handsome and I remember he was wearing a leather thing around his neck. I sat on a sunbed at the corner, reading, while Rachael and Rob were swimming and fooling around in the pool. They were splashing and holding hands, like you do. Suddenly the young lifeguard blew his whistle and shouted, "No petting or else you go out. You will leave the pool." You should have seen Rob's face.'

Rachael was not pining for Rob. She was not stuck at home in Tunstall in a dead-end job. Instead her own life as a model had become exciting and glamorous. To begin with, Margaret would often travel with daughter: 'I was so worried about her but I soon learned she was really grounded and she had got a business head on her shoulders. I watched how she handled people. You always worry when your daughter goes into that business that she is going to be a bit exploited or get into the wrong hands but she handled it really well, so I left her to it.' When she was not modelling, Rachael would do little gigs around Manchester, performing her own songs and accompanying herself on piano and guitar. She had no plans to be a singing star like Rob but performed because she enjoyed it.

Inevitably, Rob and Rachael became too busy to have a proper relationship. Sometimes they would get the same train from Manchester home to Stoke-on-Trent without even realizing that the other was on it. Rachael was under no illusions that Rob was living his dream and enjoying all the temptations that accompany it. She told her mother that she wasn't 'stupid enough not to know what he was doing, for God's sake!' They would regularly split up and get back together again until they drifted apart when they were nineteen. Margaret recalls, 'It was a gradual thing because of their work.' Rob would still call Rachael, for the next five or six years, if he was feeling down or if he had a massive decision to make or if he just needed a friend to talk to.

Rob and Rachael had a very innocent, uncomplicated relationship. They had a strong and genuine bond, which many would call an enduring love. She has turned down many lucrative offers to talk about Rob, happy with her own memories and feelings – memories of how things were before real life got in the way. She prefers not to read about him. In the book *Feel*, Rob admits that he is still very fond of Rachael: 'She's just the sweetest, unassuming, nice-natured, good-hearted, prettiest thing in Stoke-on-Trent.'

Some years after they had broken up, Rob played an acoustic gig in the round at the Granada studios on Water Street, Manchester. Rachael was there with a friend. This time Rob was not surprised to see her and he appeared to sing the whole concert to her. Even her companion said, 'Do you see what I'm seeing?'

Rachael replied simply, 'He's just used to singing to me.'

8

Drugs, Rock 'n' Roll and Sex

Whenever Take That were interviewed, it was Rob who was the most entertaining. Rick Sky, who wrote a book about the band, recalls meeting them for the first time: 'I thought he had charisma by the bucket-load. He was just a show-off really. You have to have a lot of arrogance. You could see he had great personality. I would say he had one hundred times more charisma than the rest of the group.' It was really no contest.

When they were doing press interviews for 'Why Can't I Wake Up With You', they were asked about the video, a rather dull one of the boys looking wistful in a sparsely furnished mansion. Mark observed, 'It's a bit dreamy and you can get taken in by the dream.' Jason volunteered, 'It's so sensual and sexy looking.' Robbie said, 'An essential part of the video was finding the dead stoat in the middle of the lake, don't you think?' Another question asked if a film or book had ever changed their lives. Gary said, '*Star Wars.*' Mark went for *The Outsiders*, 'which is about friendship and staying loyal'. Rob said, 'My life as a male prostitute by Robbie Williams.' Rob had a winning combination of the quick wit of his dad, Pete Conway, and the zany, off-the-wall banter of Vic Reeves.

The much-sought-after Take That number one finally came

with another Gary Barlow song, the uplifting up-tempo 'Pray'. It went straight to the top of the charts as the band began their first sell-out arena tour at the Manchester G-MEX Centre in July 1993. The song was the first of a new style of Gary song that has been a feature of his work ever since: you wanted to shout the chorus as loud as you could. Gary had written it during the previous year's tour when taking a break from the hard work of rehearsal. 'Pray' stayed at number one for four weeks, cementing Take That's position as the UK's premier boy band.

Songwriting was always Gary's preferred method of relaxation. He used to sit at Mark's keyboard and find new melodies to work on. He knew the keyboard well because he had sold it to Mark so that he, too, could learn how to play. The only problem with the transaction from Mark's point of view was that Gary continued to use it as if nothing had changed.

This was a period in Rob's life when sex, drugs and rock 'n' roll began to blend seamlessly together. Rob snorted his first line of cocaine just before he went on stage at the G-MEX. It was the opening night of Take That's first arena tour and Rob spent the entire performance flying. Up until this point, Rob had not indulged much in drugs. His was very much a drinking culture. He had sniffed gas and smoked a few joints with the lads at school. He had tried acid with his mates in Shelly's nightclub in Newcastle but had subsequently seen the devil in the mirror of the gents' toilet, which put him off.

Rob soon discovered that sex as well as booze was on tap now that he was famous. It didn't matter whether he was on tour with Take That or back home having a drink or two in the Ancient Briton. The latter was a happy hunting ground for Rob. He went back over the road with one girl and they became so enthusiastic in the bathroom that they knocked a load of tiles off the wall, which took a little bit of explaining to his mum.

One night his mate Coco Colclough walked into the pub

and saw Rob with a girl: 'He had obviously been drinking because he was quite slaughtered. I don't think he had a clue who she was but she had her hand down his trousers. His eyes were, like, half open. He just sort of whispered, "whisky", so I did the usual and went and bought him a drink. I was, like, talking to him and he was going, "All right, Coke, how are you going?" And I said, "Rob, you look like you're hammered," and he said, "I'm all right, mate, just having a bit of a blow out." I said to this girl, "Excuse me, love, do you mind if we just have a chat for a bit?" But she just carried on what she was doing. I thought, "Leave him alone for five minutes and come back to him." But she didn't.'

Rob never had a proper girlfriend at school. He was brought up in a matriarchal household and put his mother on a pedestal – a position she continues to occupy. The other two most important women in his life were his nan and his sister. These were women to be loved, admired and protected. He wanted the same in return. He admits that he craves love and affection from women, liking nothing more than them putting their arms around him and giving him a hug. It was this type of relationship he enjoyed both with Zoë Hammond, when he was younger, and later with Rachael Gilson.

Rob and Rachael shared a genuine and long-lasting affection. It was very different from the mentality of the lads at school, where the big question in class was whether a girl put out. When Rob found fame with Take That, there were literally hundreds of girls willing to do that. Nigel Martin-Smith's ban on relationships only encouraged Rob, with teenage hormones flying in all directions, to persist in the schoolboy view that women were to be treated as slags and that sex was a loveless exercise undertaken in planes, trains, automobiles and lavatories.

Rob certainly had little moral restraint. When a groupie thrust a room number in his hand, he would tuck it away in his pocket in case he felt horny later. On one occasion at the

Robbie leans out of his bedroom window in Tunstall to tell the world he is going to be a star, after signing with Take That, aged sixteen.

Left: Zoë Hammond as Jemima in the local pantomime company's production of *Chitty Chitty Bang Bang!*

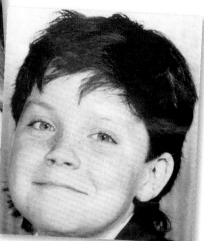

Right: Robbie as Jeremy in the same production, the first time the two friends worked together in lead roles.

The role he was born to play – as a 14-year-old Artful Dodger in the North Staffs production of *Oliver!*

St Margaret Ward class of 1990. Rob is grinning in the back row, fourth from the right. His best friend Lee Hancock is second left in the fourth row. Giuseppe Romano is next to him on the right, Phil Lindsay is in the row behind them second from the left and Peter O'Reilly is next to Rob on the right. Joanna Melvin is in the second row second from the right.

His girlfriend, Rachael Gilson at sixteen. Robbie called her the 'prettiest thing in Stoke-on-Trent'.

Robbie revealing the suave charm that so impressed Rachael.

Camp beginnings – Take That, posing in 1991.

Robbie and Gary Barlow on stage in Manchester in 1993. Guess which one took everything seriously.

The Fab Five in tribute to the Fab Four, the Beatles, at the Brit Awards in February 1994.

A kiss from Liam Gallagher at a memorable Glastonbury Festival in June 1995.

This lot are better looking than Take That. After leaving the group, Rob was paid £100,000 to pose for a 7up Light advertisement.

The feud continued – luckily Denise Van Outen stood between Robbie and Gary at the Concert of Hope in December 1997.

Robbie's first adult love, Jacqui Hamilton-Smith, came at a time when he was not ready to settle down.

His alliance with songwriter Guy Chambers was an important factor in the making of Robbie Williams. They won an Ivor Novello award in 1999.

Robbie enjoying the best five minutes eleven seconds of his life, on stage with Tom Jones at the 1998 Brits.

Loew's Hotel in Monte Carlo, he discovered the girl's hotel room was on the same floor, only half a dozen doors away. And so, like a tipsy Milk Tray man, he made his way outside his hotel room window and, with the water lapping the shore below, crossed the balconies until he found the right room and tapped on the window. It was quite a surprise for the young woman in question because Rob had decided to remove all his clothes before embarking on his night-time adventure. Sometimes his nocturnal antics did not go so smoothly: Nigel walking into his hotel room when he was pulling a topless girl through the window was not part of the plan.

During these mad, hectic times, a one-night stand was a long relationship. The newspapers knew nothing of Rachael, and instead concentrated on Robbie the stud. He was a hormonal bull in a china shop, able to 'shag anything I wanted to'. Sometimes it ended up in the pages of a tabloid newspaper when the girl, often a lap dancer, would tell all about their passion. Rob tends to be quite relaxed about these revelations, providing the girls are quite complimentary about his physical attributes and stamina. One Bournemouth lap dancer revealed that Robbie had taken her virginity when she was sweet sixteen. She had given him oral pleasure and kept thinking, 'Bloody hell, don't get any bigger.'

Rob had been to so many places he could have written his own *Rough Guide* to the world. He and Mark would stick together on tour, playing football on Acapulco Beach one day and checking out the remains of the Berlin Wall the next. Rob was living his life at breakneck speed, hardly pausing for breath it seemed.

Getting to the top is such a fantastic adrenalin buzz that nothing else seems to matter. It is only when you get there and draw breath that the enormity of your position dawns on you. Kylie Minogue once said, 'I climbed the ladder of success. Now I'm right at the top but when I look down from the dizzy heights there is no one there except me.'

Rob was only nineteen and it was a bit too early for him to become spoiled by success. The girls, the coke, the Brit Awards – what was not to like? And he was a star. More pertinently for the future, he was clearly becoming *the* star within the group. His local paper in Stoke, *The Sentinel*, declared after the G-MEX concert: 'Robbie is undoubtedly becoming the star member. He possesses a cheeky, almost irritating self-confidence and star quality.' This was just the sort of observation that would *not* be music to the ears of Gary Barlow.

The concerts themselves were more overtly sexual than before, with the boys finishing their encore of 'It Only Takes a Minute' by bending over in their underpants on which the letters in Take That were spelt out. Each of them had two letters of the band's name on their pants – Rob had TH – except Gary, in the middle, who just had a star on his. At least the letters were not written in felt tip on their bare bottoms. Banners in the audience proclaimed 'Robbie – I want your babies' and 'Robbie I want to be your babe'.

Rob's popularity had grown since he had come into his element on stage, where his theatrical training was of enormous benefit, even when he made a cock-up. At the Wembley concert he launched into his lead vocal of 'Everything Changes', the title track of the second album, and proceeded to sing it completely flat, much to his discomfort. He admitted that it was made even more embarrassing because he knew Elton John was in the audience. At the after-show party he asked Elton if he had heard his horror. Unfortunately, he had. Elton invited the boys over to his mansion near Windsor for dinner the next night and gave them all a stern lecture about the perils of taking drugs. 'Stay away from fucking cocaine,' he said, apparently looking hard at Rob the whole time.

At the end of 1993 Take That claimed eight *Smash Hits* awards. The following February they won two Brits for 'Pray': Best Single and Best Music Video. They performed a spectacular tribute to The Beatles, whom they were being compared to, perhaps a little unrealistically. They probably looked better in their sixties suits than the Fab Four had ever done.

The second album, *Everything Changes*, went straight to the top of the charts and they began a run of four consecutive number one singles – the first act to achieve that since The Beatles. Nothing, it seemed, could go wrong. It was mildly annoying when they were knocked off the Christmas chart top spot by Mr Blobby, proving that television could always sell the most dreadful garbage. Blobby continues to haunt Rob but for very different reasons these days: it's the nickname the media gives him when he puts on weight.

Rob sang the title track on the album – the third and last time he sang the lead on a Take That single. Originally he had been given the lead on 'Relight My Fire', the follow-up number one to 'Pray'. But, according to Gary's memoir, Rob was in the studio for two nights and just could not get it right. On the third night, Gary went in to sing it so Rob could copy his vocal. Gary says that everyone loved his version so much that it ended up on the final recording.

Pete Conway, meanwhile, was finding it easier to adjust to being the parent of a famous pop star than his ex-wife. He never seemed to mind being the dad and did not set about making a career out of it. He continued on the holiday camp circuit as before. The first and last time he bragged about his son was when chatting to some Take That fans in a bar where he was appearing. The DJ was playing 'I Found Heaven'. 'I'm Robbie Williams's dad', he announced proudly. The girls looked at him sceptically before one of them replied, 'Are you? Well, I'm the Queen Mother', and with that they marched off.

Jan put the house on Greenbank Road up for sale at the end of 1994 for £57,950. She described it as 'a kind house' but she wanted a place where she could put the washing on the line or the bins out without fear of them being rifled through. Rob bought her another home on the posh side of Newcastle under

Lyme where she had always fancied living. It didn't change her. Lee Hancock recalls that he would still see her knocking around in Tesco: 'She always used to speak. She was always down to earth, just the same.'

When she moved, Jan was nearer to her daughter Sally, who had moved out of the family home before Rob joined Take That. She lived in Newcastle with her partner, Paul Symonds, a local golf professional, which was handy for family golf lessons. Sally helped to run the Take That fan club, which at its peak had 70,000 members.

Jan moved house not just to escape the headlamps of celebrity. She was beginning to realize that her son was drinking too much and she did not want the photographers to have an easy opportunity of catching him drunk whenever they happened to be passing. She gave up the flower shop and set about fashioning a new life for herself, which, inevitably, would revolve around her son.

She enrolled at the Stoke-on-Trent College in Shelton to do a social studies course that would enable her to act as a drink and drugs counsellor. She didn't train to be a counsellor because of Rob but because it was something she had wanted to do ever since she had run a pub, the Red Lion in Burslem: 'I didn't go back to college to help Rob because I didn't have a clue that he had a problem at that stage. My children had to be solvent, because I was the only breadwinner, before I could pack in the business and do what I wanted to do. I went to train as a basic therapist and then decided to specialize in drugs and alcohol. I worked at the Stoke-on-Trent Alcohol Advisory Service for about six years while I was at college and it was during that time that Rob hit real problems.'

Rob was concealing his problems from the world. He had to – it was the Take That way. If Jan had been at the annual Glastonbury Festival in the summer of 1994, however, she might have been amazed at the state her son was in. The rock, pop and New Age jamboree had established itself as the premier summer event for Rob's generation, a three-day extravaganza of drinking, drug-taking, fabulous music, police arrests and mud. It represented the antithesis of everything Take That stood for. To be seen at Glastonbury would be the ultimate transgression for a member of the band. Rob was left in no doubt that under no circumstances should he go – so he went anyway. He wasn't yet at the point where he was brave enough to flaunt the rules entirely, so he spent the duration of the event hiding in a tent getting drunk with the Irish singer Feargal Sharkey. He had sniffed the air of freedom. It was a start.

Here, according to the publicity machine, is a typical Take That day on tour. Half past seven: get up, breakfast and chat about last night's gig. Pack up. Half past nine: get on the coach for what might be a couple of hundred miles to the next hotel. Discuss business, play cards. Three o'clock: check in and have lunch. Half past four: sound check at the venue. Half past five: local interviews and photographs to plug concert and any record out at the time. Half past seven: meet and greet fans backstage. Half past eight: Take That on stage. Ten forty-five: back at the hotel, late supper and a few beers. Midnight: lights out.

Maybe the younger fans believed this boring, monk-like routine but, in Rob's case, it failed to mention the lines of cocaine or the blow jobs in the toilets. From the very beginning he felt constrained, a prisoner cut off from the outside world. He had learned a harsh lesson early on when he gave his phone number to a pretty actress who caught his eye and was told off like a naughty schoolboy all the way home. He became more and more oppressed by the joyless professionalism on which Take That prided itself. He was assigned his own security guard on tour, specifically to keep an eye on him because he was such a handful. He spent most of his spare time trying to give his minder the slip.

Rob was becoming more difficult to control. Rick Sky observes: 'Robbie Williams is a natural rebel, just like Liam

Gallagher and Keith Richards, in that he likes to buck the rules. Things were being made very hard for him within Take That.' Rob's rebellion started off small. The band was staying at a hotel in Dunadry, near Belfast, and, as usual, a large group of teenage girls gathered outside, shouting their names for them to come out and make an appearance. Rob suddenly appeared at an upstairs window or, more accurately, his bare bottom did. Once again the least mysterious bottom in the world made an appearance as Rob mooned his fans. At least everyone knew it was his. The press coverage, a nanny reaction, suggested everyone was deeply shocked. The gesture almost certainly made it a day to remember for the fans. Another time, he plunged, drunk, into the fountain in the lobby of an Italian hotel and cut his head open, resulting in the scar he now bears just above his forehead.

The most exposed bum in the history of popular entertainment was out again in May 1995. Rob turned up to the MTV show *Most Wanted* with a new bleached blond hairdo, and proceeded to take over. When the presenter, Ray Cokes, asked the band if they would ever pose naked, Rob immediately piped up that he would do it for a tenner. A female member of the audience promptly brandished a ten-pound note to call Rob's bluff. Mark Owen loyally tried to stop things getting out of hand by saying Robbie would only do it for ten old pounds but Rob, now with the bit between his teeth, was having none of it. 'No, I'd do it for ten new pounds,' he said. 'As long as it's ten pounds, I don't care.' And, with that, he dropped his trousers and pants, showing his backside to several million viewers. It was deliberately provocative, although it was little more than an extension of the behaviour of 'the lads' back in Stoke-on-Trent.

The fans may not have been aware of it but, if you chose to look, the signs were clear that Rob was being marginalized within the group. He did not sing a solo on their third album, *Nobody Else*, which sold 250,000 copies in its first week of release in May. Rob countered questions by saying that he was concentrating more on the writing side of things. According to Gary, Robbie had been given twelve songs but did not learn any of them. The reality was that Rob's untrained voice had cracked up under the abuse of late nights, boozing and cigarettes. He would later admit, 'I abused my voice and I paid the price.'

The first single from the album, 'Back For Good', was the biggest Take That record to date, selling nearly a million copies in the UK alone. It also made the top ten in the US, a sign that perhaps they could make headway in that lucrative but notoriously difficult marketplace.

Rob, however, was getting progressively more fed up. By the time Glastonbury came round again in June 1995 he appeared to be past caring what anybody thought and there were strong hints of the decadence and debauchery to come. He travelled there by himself, armed with a case of champagne, hoping to be admitted to the inner sanctum of rock. He walked in to where Oasis were having a drink. Liam Gallagher turned round, took one look at Rob and declared, 'Take fucking what?' These days anybody seems welcome at Glastonbury but in the mid-nineties it was still a bit precious, an exclusive club for those who thought themselves cool. The last thing you would expect was a member of Take That off his face but there was Rob in sublime drunkenness, peroxide blond hair and a front tooth blackened out with marker pen, making a spectacle of himself by jumping on the stage where Oasis were performing a set.

At this point in his life the Gallagher brothers represented everything Rob aspired to in music and pretty much everything Take That were not. They were true Manchester lads with edge and bottle, not prancing about like refugees from Copacabana Beach. Rob gave every indication that Liam Gallagher was a bit of a hero to him – a role model and drinking buddy and the rock star he wanted to be. Of course, that didn't stop Rob from doing a brilliant impersonation of the Mancunian headcase. When Liam pulled him on stage at Glastonbury, he was happy, beer bottle in hand, to be their dancer for the night like the peerless Bez from Happy Mondays. *Face* magazine memorably described the event as the day Robbie Williams 'leapt from being popcorn to pop idol'. Rob might have been excited about that if he could have remembered anything about the night.

Gary and the boys were less impressed. The bond between the five Northern New Kids had been one of ambition. In the beginning it had been a laugh sharing a room in a bed and breakfast. Now they could barely stand being in the same room as one another. Jason, in particular, had a thinly concealed antipathy to all things Robbie Williams. Rob was threatening the whole secure, reassuring cocoon that had bred Take That's success. He was simply becoming too dangerous for the band.

Rob's divisive presence within Take That was nothing new in pop music. The same thing had happened, for instance, in the sixties when Brian Jones of The Rolling Stones was famously jettisoned after drugs and psychological problems escalated to such an extent that he threatened the fabric of the band.

Rob thought everything was 'cool' with the others. He made sure everyone knew he would not be able to exist under the Take That regime for another two or three years but he said he would be there until Christmas and thought, with a big tour coming up, that would keep everyone happy for the next six months. He could not have been more wrong.

9

Melon

No single reason led to Rob splitting from Take That. It was a combination of things over five years. First, there was the money. Rob was a wealthy young man compared to double-glazing salesmen in Stoke-on-Trent but he was nowhere near as rich as Gary Barlow, who had recently bought a huge country mansion. Rob's only songwriting credit on a Take That hit was as one of the co-composers on the 1994 number one 'Sure': he and Mark had written the rhyming rap in the middle of the song.

He felt he had much more to offer and resented the fact that Gary seemed to have a God-given right to receive all the plaudits while he was perceived as nothing more than the group clown. It was Gary Barlow who received four prestigious Ivor Novello Awards for songwriting; it was Robbie Williams who would feature under headlines about the crazy things he said. He would easily have won any 'Daftest Member of Take That' Award. He admitted, 'I was the one who'd sit back and take the piss out of the others or the situation. I wasn't expected to say anything serious.' Rob would much rather have won an award for being the most talented, the richest or the most famous. It is ironic that the man who could only boast of winning 'Best

Haircut' at that point would become the awards king of modern times.

After money and envy, the third thing that ate away at Rob was the iron discipline within Take That. Of course there were many ways around it but he had tasted sex, drugs and rock 'n' roll and wanted a lot more of all three. He was a little boy in a sweet shop unable to reach the best flavours on the top shelf. Amazingly, considering the success of Take That, the band was actually becoming too small for him.

Gary Barlow revealed a conversation he had with Rob in early 1995, when the subject of leaving the group first came up. In his book *My Take*, Gary recalls Rob saying he wanted to leave because he was bored. Rob apparently astonished Gary by saying that he would have been a success with or without the group. At the time, this may have appeared outrageously arrogant but Rob has regularly felt he is not given enough credit for his talent and resented the suggestion that others were more responsible for his success than he was.

Rob, perhaps naively, thought everyone in Take That was friends. He told Piers Morgan in 1993: 'They're like my best friends. There's not one I couldn't tell my problems to. I suppose that's good because a lot of bands have friction between themselves, and I couldn't cope with that sort of tension.' It was all a bit sad. Rob needed to have friends, he wanted mates and he wanted them to tolerate his bad lad behaviour, pat him on the head, say he was a laugh and carry on.

It wasn't just the drunken shambles of Glastonbury, however, but a progressive isolation that was destroying his place in the band. The older pair, Howard and Jason, had little to say to Rob. Gary remained focused on his own ambitions and tended to socialize, as always, with them. Mark, too, had less time for Rob's youthful antics and was absorbed in Buddhism. Gary observed, 'Mark grew up and became a very truthful person. He got into Buddhism and became very interesting. I think he left Robbie behind and Robbie resented that.' Ironically, we know today that Mark was not the saint he then appeared to be.

It may seem indulgent of Rob to be so self-obsessed when he was only twenty-one and had achieved his dream of stardom as well as become a millionaire but it doesn't make his anguish any less real or significant. He would later reveal that he would often knock back a whole bottle of vodka a day from the age of nineteen: 'I was so depressed, going back to my hotel room in Manchester, and I'd just drink myself to oblivion, wailing like a banshee in my room by myself.' As far as the other members of Take That were concerned, Rob had simply lost the plot. He was out of sync with them and oblivious of the need to pull together.

The Cheshire Territorial Army barracks in Stockport was the unlikely setting, on 17 July 1995, for one of the most famous events in UK pop history: the day Robbie Williams left Take That. Nobody died – but don't say that to Take That fans.

The boys were there to rehearse for their summer tour promoting the *Nobody Else* album, which was scheduled to start two weeks later. Rob's heart may still have been in a field in Glastonbury but he started to knuckle down and learn the dance steps. After a morning practising steps, Rob slipped out for a healthy lunch at McDonald's. On his return it was clear something was up when he had word that the band wanted to see him. They wanted to talk. It was a court martial. They were clearly unhappy with him dictating at what point he would leave the band. Jason Orange told Rob, 'If you are going, go now so we can get on with it.'

Rob reacted just as he always did, just as he had when he was refused entry to the club in Newcastle under Lyme: he swaggered. He grabbed a melon from a pile of fruit on the table, asked, 'Is it OK to take this with me?' and, with a spring in his step and a smile on his face, he left. He made straight for his car, with its rock star blacked-out windows, and was driven home to his mother's house in Newcastle under Lyme. He kept up the façade the whole way – this was Robbie Williams. Only when the driver asked what time he wanted to be picked up tomorrow did he tell him, 'You won't be picking me up tomorrow. I'm not coming back. I'm not in the band any more.'

Rob, who, as his real friends know, can be extremely sensitive and vulnerable, waited until he had shut the front door before shedding many tears. Still clutching his melon, he told a concerned Jan that he had lost his job and was out. It was a momentous event in the life of a twenty-one year old. For five years he had eaten, slept and breathed Take That but the following day he would have to wake up knowing that he no longer belonged. He confessed to 'feeling abandoned and totally alone'. Later he was able to laugh at the fact that he did not even like melon.

In the mayhem that ensued, it became very difficult to unravel the truth as everyone tried to find an acceptable version of events. Some Take That fans took it really badly. It was reported that a female fan in Berlin had even tried to commit suicide, so distraught was she at the news. Conspiracy theorists had a field day. Did he walk or was he pushed? Technically, he wasn't sacked because that would have been a legal and financial minefield, although the legal ramifications of his departure did enrich the lawyers for several years to come.

In many ways he had constructed his own dismissal by revealing a death wish in relation to the group that had made him a household name. The *Sun* carried the story of Robbie's departure as their front-page splash the following day. It quoted Rob as saying that he 'had decided to call it a day' and that 'everything was entirely amicable', which, of course, it wasn't. His departure, announced officially the following Monday, even made *News at Ten.*

The following day, Rob issued his own statement and the game of tit for tat in the pages of the newspapers began. Rob's utterances tend to be either personal, chummy and encouraging of a sympathetic response or off-the-wall and slightly dark.

This was the heart-on-the-sleeve, little-boy-lost version: 'At the moment I am very scared and confused. I read the press statements yesterday and feel it is of great importance that I must apologize to everybody who feels let down by a decision for me to leave the band. I still love all the boys and I'm sure there is also a lot of love for me. But things have changed and I need to do something else for my own peace of mind and health.' The key phrase was 'a decision for me to leave'. He did not say 'my' or 'their'. It was left vague.

Jan Williams is at her best in a crisis and before Rob could find the time to wallow in self-pity, she was in London talking to lawyers on his behalf. Rob was most angry about missing out on the tour. It would have meant he could have left the band later on a high and from a position of strength. The circumstances of his departure left him in limbo. It was especially galling because Take That were just about to have a big hit in the United States and Robbie Williams was not going to be part of that either. In fact, when the album *Nobody Else* was released there a short time later, Rob had already been airbrushed from the cover.

The group's summer concerts that year were very well received, with some critics saying that as a foursome they gave their best shows yet. All four sang Rob's vocals on 'Everything Changes' and 'Could It Be Magic', as well as two covers that had been earmarked for him, 'Smells Like Teen Spirit' by Nirvana and Pink Floyd's 'Another Brick in the Wall'.

Something unexpected happened when Robbie Williams and Take That parted company: the sex appeal left with him. The youngest female fans might fantasize about their favourite – usually Mark Owen – but it was never a heavy, sexual thing. A couple of adolescent girls might take a poster to a Take That concert suggesting lewd behaviour – Rob particularly liked 'Rob from Stoke, Give Us a Poke' – but they were more than likely to run a mile if he tried to take them up on it. The older girl, past the legal age of consent, would, nine times out of ten, pick Rob for a romp. He was a bad boy not a bland boy. Without him, Take That was very tame.

The tour to the Far East, Australia, Japan and the USA was a huge success but things had changed. The fact that Rob was stealing some of their thunder was getting under their skin, and Gary, in particular, was tiring of the boy band format. He wanted a better showcase for his talent and that meant leaving the boys behind. There was also a complex financial arrangement that meant Rob would have to be paid if they continued to perform under the name Take That. Rob wrote to the *Sun* suggesting they should reunite for one last charity concert in order to say goodbye properly to the fans. Nigel Martin-Smith gave the idea short shrift, claiming it was a 'cheap trick to get sympathy and public support'.

Take That's demise became official on 13 February 1996 – coincidentally, Robbie's birthday. At the press conference Gary was asked: 'Have you got a birthday message for Robbie? It's his birthday today.'

Gary replied, 'Is it? Oh.'

PART TWO

THE MAKING OF
ROBBIE WILLIAMS

10

The University of Nights Out

Rob was in limbo when he departed from Take That. He literally didn't know what to do with himself, so he moved to London, where he was at the mercy of drinks, drugs and depression. Jan was doing her best but she couldn't keep too close an eye on him when he was fifteen junctions down the M1. For a good while relations between mother and son were strained. Rob began to live a life completely different to any he had known before. During a subsequent court case against Nigel Martin-Smith in July 1997, the Take That manager's barrister rather primly said that Robbie Williams had developed 'a taste for glamorous and flamboyant company, alcohol and narcotics'. A 'taste' does scant justice to Rob's appetites at the time.

Rob put on two stone on a diet of Guinness and kebabs – although sometimes he would forget the kebabs. His party trick was lining up five pints of Guinness in a row and downing all of them in a disgusting, gobbing movement. He allegedly once drank twenty-five pints of the black stuff in one day. He would go to the opening of an envelope and became known as the biggest 'ligger' in town. He was snorting enough cocaine to keep the Colombian economy afloat. A record company executive recalls the 1996 vintage Robbie Williams: 'He was just a fat schizo – a fucked-up boy.'

The 'fucked-up boy' was pretty hopeless at being by himself. He admits it. The self-loathing sets in and, as he puts it, he does not trust himself in his own company. With nobody to tell him to stay in and have a quiet night in front of the telly, he was always going out. He was able to go to the fashionable Met Bar and mix with the show business company he enjoyed at that time. He became friendly with footballers like Jamie Redknapp and David James. He socialized with his teenage hero, Vic Reeves. Rob would go and stay down at Vic's farm in Kent and, on one memorable night, joined him to serenade his prize pigs with a version of 'Lady Marmalade'. The pigs were deeply unimpressed by the rural karaoke and promptly charged them. Rob enjoyed drinking sessions with his new best friends, Oasis and the Geordie duo Ant and Dec, who had just moved down from Newcastle. He joined some of the Oasis entourage on the picket line with striking Tube workers, singing 'We Shall Overcome'. Rob, it seemed, was everywhere.

All the time, he was at the mercy of cocaine. Surprisingly, however, he found work almost straight away. While he might have been expected to do nothing, he signed on to a stint as the guest presenter on Channel 4's *Big Breakfast*, the show that was for a decade a lively and welcome alternative to the jumpers and cosiness of mainstream schedules. Despite paying him a reported £2,000 a day, employing Rob was anything but a gamble. Viewing figures went up by 600,000 per day while Robbie Williams was on. More than a thousand fans would gather outside the studio in the East End where the show was filmed just for the privilege of cheering on their favourite. Rob loved it and played to the crowd, shaking hands, planting kisses and signing autographs. He enjoyed playing Robbie Williams, the big star, at times.

Rob was originally hired to do the star interviews on the Big Bed that had been made famous by Paula Yates. His performance was riveting and hilarious, as he gradually took over the show by the sheer force of his personality. He asked Gary Lineker if, when he was the most famous footballer in the country, he ever dreamt that one day he would be advertising crisps. He tried to enlist the help of actor Stephen Baldwin in fixing him up with his sister-in-law, Kim Basinger. He donned a pair of Mr Spock ears to interview *Star Trek* fans. Rob was proving to be an absolute natural and a career in television seemed a good bet. When he was asked if he might go back and present again in the future, he replied, 'Only if you change the name to *The Big Dinner*.' Rob had never been a morning person.

He was keeping himself busy and in the public eye. He appeared as an extra in *EastEnders*, talking on the phone in the Queen Vic. He reportedly made £100,000 for shaving his legs, stripping off to his white Y-fronts and putting on a black wig and high heels to plug 7up Light surrounded by a group of bikini-wearing girls.

At least his love life was becoming a little more grown up. To begin with, it was the same old randy Rob. When he left Take That, two young women were quick out of the traps to reveal their nights of passion. A hotel receptionist in Stuttgart claimed he had been up for it five times in one night of unbridled lust. She said he was 'unbelievably passionate' after downing pina coladas, which did not sound like Rob's kind of drink. She also recalled that he had told her how lonely he was and that he had no friends. Then a former model reported that he had bedded her in a hotel in Glasgow, a typical on-the-road rock 'n' roll assignation. She gave Rob eleven out of ten as a lover which, when he read her account, cheered him up immensely. The most amusing thing about her story, however, was that having told all to millions of readers, she announced: 'My mum will probably kill me.'

One of the more unusual stories involved Rob and a mother of two more than ten years older than him. Her distraught husband claimed he knew about their fling only when he saw her in a newspaper pictured with Robbie coming out of a trendy bar in London. Soon the headline 'Take That Star Has Taken My Girl' appeared, although the reality was that she was part of a group of people whom Rob enjoyed a drink with from time to time.

The first well-known face to declare an interest in Rob was Samantha Beckinsale, a star of the television series *London's Burning*, who arrived with him at a Take That end-of-tour party in Manchester. 'I love him to bits,' she declared and Rob wrote a song for her. Rob can afford to buy a girl any present but a song is probably the most personal gift he could give. The song was the haunting 'Baby Girl Window' on what would be his first album, *Life Thru a Lens*. Rob, who has a very spiritual attitude towards death, wrote it about her father, the popular comedy actor Richard Beckinsale, who died when she was twelve. Rob imagined that he would be watching proudly over her now – it was a theme he would return to in his songwriting.

Rob fell in love for the very first time not long after the shackles of Take That had been cast aside. At first glance, Jacqui Hamilton-Smith was an unlikely girlfriend. He might have been expected to have a trophy girlfriend, a pop bimbo, an aspiring soap actress or footballer's wife. Instead, Jacqui was a make-up artist working on fashion shoots for magazines and a daughter of a peer of the realm. That always sounded slightly grander than it actually was. Her father, Lord Colwyn, was a Wimpole Street dentist, who occasionally made the gossip columns because the jazz band in which he played trumpet was in demand at society events. He played at Prince Andrew's twenty-first birthday party and at the Queen's fortieth wedding anniversary celebration. Jacqui, tall, elegant, with streaky blonde hair, caught Rob's attention when they met by the way she said the word 'lovely' in a 'dead posh accent'.

Much more importantly, Jacqui, who bears a passing resemblance to Tara Palmer-Tomkinson, was, at twenty-eight, more than six years older than Rob and well equipped to handle the rather immature, rumbustious ex-member of the country's top boy band. As a young man, the majority of the important women in Rob's life were older than him, able to help him through difficult periods – which, in his case, was almost all the time.

The world of celebrity is a tiny universe. Rob and Jacqui were introduced by one of her best friends, Patsy Kensit, at a party in London given by record producer Nellee Hooper, who happened to be one of her ex-boyfriends. They shared a good laugh at the party and kept in touch by telephone over the coming weeks before finally meeting up again in Manchester. At a time when Rob was at a low ebb, indulging in far too much drink and drugs, Jacqui was a godsend and she seemed much more interested in him than in telling the world about it all. To her great credit, Jacqui has never spilled the beans on her time with Rob.

Rob accompanied her to the funeral of her grandmother in Cheltenham. Jacqui was brought up in some style in a village in the Cotswolds and after the funeral she and Rob stayed the night at the home of her mother, Lady Hamilton-Smith, and stepfather, John Underwood, who said, 'He struck me as a very pleasant young man.' They popped into the local pub for a drink but, being the country, no one recognized Rob or, at least, nobody admitted to knowing who he was. When the media found out about Rob's first real affair, it substantiated the feeling that he was someone with plenty of mileage left as a celebrity. The rough, working-class pop star and the posh totty is tabloid heaven.

They went on holiday to Barbados and the rest of the world was able to witness their obvious delight in each other's company when the photographs appeared in the *Sun*. The ruse of checking into their hotel under the names of Lord and Lady Tunstall didn't fool anyone. Putting aside any cynicism about celebrity pictures, it is abundantly clear that Rob is very happy and pleased to be in Jacqui's company. They rubbed noses, splashed each other in the swimming pool – fortunately there was no lifeguard to shout out, 'No petting!'– and indulged in smoochy kisses in the natural manner of two young people in love. The rest of the world did not exist for them. For the first time Rob felt able to tell a woman other than his mum that he loved her. Rob found the romance very liberating after finding it impossible to have relationships in Take That.

Jacqui shared his home for a while but it was at his most troubled time of drink and drugs. Sometimes he would disappear for three or four days with no word about where he was. Sorry, on these occasions, was the easiest word but it quickly proved insufficient, as Rob showed no signs of wanting to change his ways. He did take Jacqui back to Tunstall to meet his family and they liked her. Rob and Jacqui stayed together for most of 1996, but it was her bad luck that at a time when she was ready for some stability in her life, Rob was involved in his 'lost year', the period post-Take That when his self-esteem was at its lowest and where he had lost track of the important things in life in a fog of cocaine and alcohol. Jacqui pushed very hard for Rob to seek counselling and treatment for his problems.

He was lost until October 1996, when he was persuaded by a combination of Jacqui and a concerned Elton John to go and see Beechy Colclough, counsellor to the stars. Sir Elton may well have seen some of his own problems mirrored in the young man from Stoke. He, too, suffered from waging a continual war with his weight and having a poor self-image – in his case, of a fat boy with glasses and thinning hair. He also had a tricky relationship with his father while adoring his mother. Elton eventually owned up to twenty years of substance abuse so, hopefully, it would not take Rob that long to confront his problems.

Beechy Colclough, who helped stars like Michael Jackson, Kate Moss, Paul Gascoigne and Elton himself, did not believe in treating celebrities differently from ordinary folk: 'They're just people with addictions.' It was not a cure for Rob, or even half a cure, but it was a start. He saw Colclough every day for a month and said at the time it helped him 'enormously'.

Rob managed to retain a sense of humour amid his soul searching, observing once that he had left his mother's house on New Year's Eve 1995, and returned with the same overnight bag on 1 January 1997, a year and a day later. 'That was some party, Mum,' he shouted as he came through the door.

Sadly, by that time, he and Jacqui had called it a day. Perhaps she felt she was facing a losing battle with Rob or was simply looking for a greater commitment than he could offer at that difficult time. Jacqui soon started dating rugged actor Sean Pertwee, the son of former Doctor Who John Pertwee, and within eighteen months they were engaged. A year later they were married at the House of Lords, a celebrity wedding attended by two people Rob would later feud with – Noel Gallagher and Nellee Hooper.

It might have been different if Rob had been older but Jacqui was ready to settle down and start a family. Ironically, on that holiday in Barbados, she had asked him to marry her. It was Leap Year Day, when women are traditionally allowed to request a hand in marriage. She was joking but Rob was convinced that she would have gone through with it if he had accepted. What would have happened to Robbie Williams if he had said yes?

After Jacqui, Rob took up with Anna Friel, the very attractive former soap star and media darling. She, too, was coming out of a longer relationship – with TV personality Darren Day. She and Rob had a laugh together and genuinely enjoyed each other's company but this was a celebrity romance in that it garnered far more column inches than it deserved. The difference between Anna and a number of other young women Rob saw after his break with Jacqui was that she was newsworthy. They made a great 'celebrity couple' but they were never really a couple at all. She spent most of the two months they were supposed to be together making a film in Ireland. Rob received some terrible publicity while she was away because he was seen partying, going on a 72-hour bender and allegedly getting off with a blonde bearing a seahorse tattoo on her breast. Anna was only twenty and, just like Rob, was going out and enjoying herself on location in Dublin (although not on 72-hour benders). The newspapers took the hysterical line: 'How could Rob betray poor Anna?'

11

Finding Team Robbie

Rob's very public embrace of the sex, drugs and rock 'n' roll lifestyle was all very well but he was missing one vital ingredient – the rock 'n' roll. Rob found himself in a legal minefield that brought his singing career to an abrupt halt. Somehow sex, drugs and breakfast television did not have the same whiff of danger.

There was no music from Robbie Williams because of his contract with RCA, Take That's record company. Two weeks after Take That announced they would be splitting up, Rob was due in the High Court to argue that he should be released from the agreement because of the conflict of interest the company – controlled by BMG – would have trying to represent both his best interests and the other members, who would now be pursuing their solo careers. He withdrew the action before it reached court and left it to his new manager, Tim Abbott, to broker a deal. His career effectively became frozen for six months while the terms of that deal were sorted out and while negotiations to find another record company were proceeding.

Abbott was Rob's second solo manager. He ran a company called Proper Management and took over the handling of Rob when he split from his first solo manager, Kevin Kinsella. In those rudderless days, everything Robbie touched seemed to leave legal footprints. Kinsella pursued him for four years for unpaid fees totalling £184,000 before an agreement was finally reached in 2000. Kinsella's was just one of several legal battles that would drag on through the nineties. None would be particularly significant unless he secured a record deal.

Over the years Kinsella has had plenty to say about Rob's sexuality and drug-taking. At least Abbott has had some kinder observations. His first impression of him was that he was a 'no-hoper'. After all, everybody knew the talented one in Take That was Gary Barlow. And surely nobody could take him seriously hanging out with the Gallagher brothers. Abbott recalls, 'Here was this cheeky chappy doing his duck walk, and there was just something about him that was incredibly engaging. I wasn't sure if he was going to be the next George Michael or the next George Formby.'

Robbie got lucky, however. A knight in shining armour arrived to rescue him from limbo in the shape of a maverick executive at EMI/Chrysalis called Jean-François Cécillon, known throughout the record business as JF. A company insider explained, 'He signed Robbie when many in the business wouldn't have touched him. He saw something in Robbie, the naughty rogue, that he wanted to take a chance on. JF fought for Robbie, who has always appreciated that.'

The other important figure was Chris Briggs, who was responsible for Rob's A&R at EMI: 'Briggsy was a major force because he made a concerted effort to get Robbie cleaned up.' Briggsy has always been quick to defend his biggest name: 'There's a difference between a prat acting the rock star, and a talented, sensitive person going into meltdown.'

At the end of June 1996, a press conference was called to announce the EMI/Chrysalis deal to the world – a three-album record deal worth a reputed £1 million. Rob was still enjoying his 'lost year', so the whole thing was a considerable gamble. What Rob said at the Royal Lancaster Hotel neatly sums up the importance of the deal: 'I've got a new family now. Thank you, JF, and everybody at EMI/Chrysalis.'

Rob had to pay BMG to free himself from that contract. Although the figure has never been confirmed, it was strongly rumoured to be in the region of £100,000, which is on the low side and perhaps indicative of the fact that Robbie Williams was not considered too valuable a proposition for the future. It was also whispered, but never proven, that the agreement barred Robbie Williams from releasing a solo single before Gary Barlow. The figure Rob was allowed to reveal was the amount he had to pay the lawyers – £400,000.

As part of his agreement with BMG, Rob had agreed to a confidentiality clause barring him from revealing its terms or from sounding off any more about the breakdown of his relationship with his former record company bosses. His mother, Jan, would subsequently sit in on interviews to try to stop her son's mouth from running away with him and breaking the terms of that agreement.

Somewhat surprisingly, shortly after the £1 million three-album deal with EMI had been signed, Rob left Tim Abbott and joined IE Music, based in West London, not far from his new record label. He said he felt it was time to move on and that he wanted 'total artistic freedom in the creative direction of my album'. It was a vital final piece in the jigsaw that led to the creation of Robbie Williams, the biggest entertainer of his generation. Tim Abbott was less than delighted and yet another court case sparked into life.

In all, Rob had four different managers in a little over a year, if you include Nigel Martin-Smith at Take That. He ended up having to pay a great deal of money to the first three. Abbott filed his proceedings in October 1996 and the case took nearly two years to be settled out of court. He claimed more than £1 million in unpaid commission and finally agreed a sum in compensation, reported to be several hundred thousand pounds. It would have been a messy court case at just the wrong time for EMI. Rob had maintained that he had signed the contract with Proper Management when drunk and without proper advice.

The legal process involving Nigel Martin-Smith was a long drawn-out saga, with his first manager eventually winning a case for unpaid commission on Robbie Williams' royalties. The cold logic of the law was against Rob. Some estimates put the final figure he had to pay Nigel as high as £1 million.

IE Music has been ideal for Rob. The company, based in Shepherds Bush, is run by two ex-public school, country gentlemen types, David Enthoven and Tim Clark. They are in no way flash wide boys on the make but senior and respected figures in the music industry, where they have both been influential for more than thirty years. They are sane and sensible businessmen who have skilfully moved Robbie Williams to the centre of British music. They are both survivors who have seen it all.

When he first met Rob, David Enthoven thought he resembled a horse that had been abused to the extent that he had lost his faith in himself and in other people. He tried to show him that there was a better place, free from hangers-on who just wanted to be his friend because of what they could get out of it. Enthoven, a witty and urbane old Harrovian, has been a father figure in Rob's life, particularly where drugs are concerned.

A friend describes him: 'He dresses a bit like a Californian rock star but the truth is he would not be out of place in a gentleman's club in St James's. He is a very kind man and his staff loves him. He will be as tough as anyone in a business situation but then take you out for an excellent dinner afterwards.' He has great experience in the music business through looking after such legendary acts as King Crimson, Roxy Music, Emerson, Lake and Palmer and T. Rex. It was David who came up with the user-friendly name T. Rex because he had trouble spelling Tyrannosaurus.

His partner, Tim Clark, who took over marketing Robbie Williams, had an equally impressive music history. He is the former managing director of Island Records, where he signed Bob Marley, Stevie Winwood, Free and many others.

David, in particular, knew and recognized the dangers of drugs and alcohol in this world because they had almost ruined his own life. As a result he has been a teetotal abstainer for more than twenty years and acted as a calm mentor for Rob as he tried to come to terms with his addictions. He was non-judgemental and did not blame Rob for any temporary lapses; the important thing was to start afresh the next day. Instead, he would be there with a nice cuppa and a pack of playing cards to try to keep Rob occupied and happy.

Rob now had a solid team behind him, backed up by his mother, who had also learned a great deal about the problems of drug and alcohol abuse. She was even able to take it in her stride when Rob tried to persuade her that it would be a good idea if she tried cocaine so she knew what it was like. She told him not to be so silly.

Everybody in the music business seemed so sure that Gary Barlow would be the next big thing. Tilly Rutherford, then general manager of PWL, Pete Waterman's label, commented just after Robbie had left Take That, 'Gary has got so much talent and he's the only one who can sing.' Gary's coronation had the air of smug inevitability that might not appeal unreservedly to the great British public, who traditionally like an underdog. The whole saga of Rob and Gary unfolded like a modern version of the tortoise and hare fable: Gary was the hare, the corporate darling of RCA about to zoom over the horizon with his first number one; Rob, the drugged-up tortoise, meanwhile, was going round and round in very small circles.

Take That officially ceased to exist on 3 April 1996, following a round of contracted promotional work that they had to honour even though they had announced their split in

February. The very next day Gary began work on his first solo album. He also shed a stone and a half in weight and looked fitter and better than he had done when he had four other fit guys to take the attention on stage. At that point Rob's record deal had not been finalized. Gary's debut record, 'Forever Love', was released in July 1996 and went straight to number one. Surprisingly, however, it stayed there for only one week; it was knocked off the top by the Spice Girls' first hit, 'Wannabe', which would be one of the biggest singles of the decade. Gary's ballad was, in truth, a little boring and was not as memorable as some of his Take That classics.

Rob's first single, released eight days after Gary reached number one, was a cover of the George Michael song 'Freedom', which had been a minor hit in 1990. Rob was celebrating so many areas of liberation with the track: freedom from his contract with BMG; freedom from Take That; freedom from the rules of Nigel Martin-Smith; freedom to party; freedom, in effect, to do whatever he wanted. The song was a statement, if a rather unsubtle one. Rob declared, with a nod to an Oasis lyric, that he was now 'free to do whatever I want and to do whatever I choose'.

One of the things he chose to do was to talk about Nigel at a press conference in June 1996, one year after his break from the band: 'I'd like to meet up with the manager in a fork-lift truck, souped up to go 150 miles per hour non-stop with no brakes!' A month later in the gay magazine *Attitude*, there was no doubting Rob's attitude to his former manager: 'I don't even have words for that c**t,' he declared, which was not strictly true as he has never been short of words about him unless restricted by a legal agreement.

Another of the things he chose to do was to slag off Gary's single, declaring it to be 'awful!' He also called him, personally, 'selfish, greedy, arrogant, thick' and a 'clueless wanker'. He saved his best barb, however, for Jason Orange. When asked how many of Take That would succeed, he responded, 'It just depends what they succeed in. Jason's going to make a brilliant painter and decorator.'

Gary was completely bemused by the gratuitous insults flying from Rob's mouth, saying that he did not understand how Rob could say the things he did. He thought Robbie had changed a lot in the relatively short time since his departure from Take That. Perhaps, in hindsight, it might not have done Gary any harm to say in public what he was thinking in private. That was not his style, although in his memoir he finally revealed the depth of his outrage, declaring that he had detested Rob for the awful things he said.

The success of the Spice Girls also meant 'Freedom' rose no higher than number two, although sales of 270,000 were respectable. After the massive publicity surrounding both singles from the ex-Take That boys, it was perhaps disappointing that they were swamped by 'girl power'. Would the Spice Girls have made such an impact if Take That were still the idols of the teeny-bop audience?

'Freedom' was never intended for Rob's first album but simply to mark a point in time in his life and career. The fact that it was a George Michael song made it an even more apposite choice because George was a role model for Rob, not only as a solo artist, but also in the way he had stood up to his record company and upheld his own artistic integrity.

Rob needed to get cracking on his album but that proved to be more difficult than expected. The beauty of releasing a cover as his first single was that he was still a blank canvas. The problem now was that he needed to show the public what sort of artist he was going to be. He could come up with anything. He could evolve his own sound.

One of the first tasks for David Enthoven and Chris Briggs at EMI was to find a musician with whom Rob could write songs. Rob, with Jan's help and influence, is quite shrewd about business. It did not take a financial genius, however, to understand that publishing was where the money was. He had seen the royalties that Gary enjoyed from Take That and he did not want to pass on that particular goldmine. It was not as easy as it looked and Rob made several false starts before stumbling across the right formula and, more importantly, the right man to help him create it.

He first started writing with Owen Morris, the producer of Oasis and friend of Tim Abbott. The partnership foundered when Rob and Abbott parted company, although one guitar-led number, 'Cheap Love Song', made it to the B-side of one of Rob's early singles, 'South of the Border'. He then hooked up with Ant Genn, the former bass player of Pulp whom he had met at Glastonbury in 1995: while Rob danced away on stage with Oasis, Genn took off his clothes during a performance by Elastica and dashed on stage. They wrote seven songs together but none saw the light of day until the album *Rudebox* eleven years later. Rob admired Genn because he was 'cool as fuck and Northern and funny.'

There was talk of Rob working with an American country music star, Mindy McCready, who had crossed over into the mainstream in the USA with 'Maybe He'll Notice Her Now', a duet with Richie McDonald, the former lead singer of rock band Lonestar. The idea was that Rob would take over Richie's part for the UK version. Mindy flew over to the UK but at the time her personal life was in disarray and she didn't want Rob to become embroiled in that so she decided to fly home again.

Next came an ill-advised trip to Miami to work with two established American songwriters, Desmond Child and Eric Bazilian, who both had impeccable rock credentials working with Bon Jovi and Aerosmith. Rob realized then that American music doesn't really get 'irony', a key ingredient in the even-tual sound of Robbie Williams.

He was also uneasy about the materialistic values. He cer-tainly didn't like the conversation he had with Desmond after recording: 'When we'd finished it we were sitting in his pool in Miami when he turned to me and said, "Do you like this house?

You helped me pay for it!" He ruined it for me and I'll never work with him again.'

Rob flew back home with several songs but only one, 'Old Before I Die', which he truly liked, although he wanted to re-record it with a more Brit Pop feel. By the end of 1996, Rob had worked with four co-writers and had only two possible tracks to show for it. The first album looked a little ambitious.

Lyrically, Rob could work fast, his poetry coming out in a rapid stream of consciousness. Much of the lyrical content for what would become his first album, *Life Thru a Lens*, he committed to paper in a week. It was a series of reflections on his life at that point in time, in particular his attitude to stardom and his battle with alcohol and drugs.

Rob was introduced to various possible collaborators but the one he clicked with was Guy Chambers, who had enjoyed a few minor hits in the early nineties with a band called The Lemon Trees. Guy was ten years older than Rob, and had a strong musical background that even Gary Barlow might have found impressive. He had written a string quartet by the age of eleven and written and performed a rock opera by the age of fifteen. He studied composition at the prestigious Guildhall School of Music in London, where he started to write and record his own songs.

When he left college, he toured as a keyboard player with eighties acts Julian Cope and The Waterboys. In the latter, he replaced Welsh songwriter Kurt Wallinger, whom he would subsequently join in the band World Party. Wallinger wrote the ballad 'She's The One', which would become a number one hit record for Robbie Williams. In the small world of music, the band also featured Chris Sharrock on drums, a role he would fulfil in Robbie's own band.

Guy moved on to form The Lemon Trees in 1992. By a happy coincidence, Rob had never heard of the group until his mother's boyfriend at the time mentioned them in passing. When Guy's name came up, Rob immediately thought it was a sign. David Enthoven gave Guy two pieces of advice about meeting Rob, which everyone would do well to remember. They were: 'Don't call him Robbie and don't try to be his friend.'

Guy first met Rob at the Capital Radio Road Show, when his band was also on the bill. Rob had the shakes, was overweight and looked like death warmed up. Despite that unpromising start, the two gelled. When Rob went round to Guy's flat in London, he listened to one of his Lemon Trees' songs and loved the melody. With a change in lyrics it was to become 'Lazy Days', Rob's third single.

Chris Briggs told *Music Week* that the early demos from Guy and Rob were very encouraging: 'They confirmed we had found a direction. But it had to come naturally.' Guy confessed that he wasn't sure what was going to happen: 'Can we get through this year without him killing himself?'

The last piece of the Robbie Williams musical jigsaw brought Steve Power, a friend of Guy's, into the mix as co-producer. A Liverpudlian like Guy, Steve had moved to London in the mid-eighties and worked as an engineer at Battery Studios on hits such as 'World Shut Your Mouth' by Julian Cope and 'Because of You' by Dexys Midnight Runners. His breakthrough as a mainstream producer occurred when he masterminded Babylon Zoo's 1996 number one 'Spaceman', which was then the fastest selling debut single of all time. Then he produced Babybird's 'You're Gorgeous', another huge hit. He candidly admits that they were both records that everyone hated.

Steve is well known in the business as a perfectionist. He will spend three days on a vocal take to 'make Rob sound like God'. He is adept at constructing the sound so that a song 'can reach its maximum potential'. He needed to be patient because both Guy and Rob were easily bored, eager to get on with the next song. They would write songs on a conveyor belt and had thirty-five ready for the first album by the time Steve was involved. He quickly helped them chop that down to a dozen or so possible tracks. He was as responsible as Guy for mould-ing the sound that so surprised those expecting Robbie Williams to be a son of Take That.

Where Guy Chambers arranged, Steve Power mixed. He is the third ear of the Williams/Chambers team. Together Guy and Steve won Producer of the Year at the 1998 International Music Managers Forum. They shared the award and, most of the time, they shared the priceless ability to handle Rob at his most mercurial.

Rob's well-documented troubles at the time of recording *Life Thru a Lens* made it extremely difficult for Guy and Steve to get out the record they wanted. Rob famously spent most of the time lying underneath the mixing desk sipping cans of Guinness. Steve explained it in football parlance that Rob was like an out-of-form striker, unaware of his capabilities, but that changed as his confidence grew. As Rob felt better in himself, the music improved.

In April 1997, Robbie Williams released a second single, 'Old Before I Die', an ironic title considering his excesses. The influence of Brit Pop was clear but the reaction from the public seemed uncertain, although again it reached a respectable number two in the charts, kept off the top spot by 'I Believe I Can Fly' by R. Kelly.

Gary released his second single, 'Love Won't Wait', the follow-ing month and once more reached number one. With hindsight Gary and his advisers made a bad decision in not releasing his debut album sooner. He had, in fact, gone to America to re-record much of it and, as a result, was keeping a low profile while Rob was busy entertaining readers of the tabloids with his exploits.

Rob could not continue on his downward spiral if he was going to have any sort of solo career. During this 'lost year' his nemesis was cocaine but alcohol was not far behind. The prob-lem was that booze does not have the same taboo. Rob was brought up in a working-class community where alcohol was the drug of choice and nobody would jump to judgement. His dad liked a pint, as did his mates. Nothing wrong with that, one might argue, nor with Rob propping up a bar continuously – he was simply a lad blowing off steam. The problem with this attitude to alcohol is that it takes much longer to recognize that someone has a serious drinking problem.

At least he stopped short of becoming a heroin junkie. He tried the drug on just one occasion but did not enjoy the experience and spoke out robustly against it, much to the delight of anti-drugs advisers. He declared, 'Heroin is evil – nobody should ever go near it. It was the worst experience of my life and I will never do it again.'

It was June 1997 when Rob made a major decision that he needed proper rehab and checked himself into the Clouds House clinic near Salisbury, deep in the heart of rural Wiltshire. Although he was urged to take that step by his mother and his management, he acknowledges that he alone could make that choice. His narcotic abuse had reached the point where he imagined furniture racing around his bed. He admitted, 'I don't have a switch that I can turn on or off in my head. I don't think you can get through frequent drug-taking and then have the sense to take it or leave it.' He arrived at Clouds, drunk and clutching four bottles of Moët in his hands. He had been to a party for the group Sleeper and, after spending most of the night sober, decided that he might as well go to rehab in a blaze of glory.

Clouds is not a half-hearted holiday camp for celebrities recovering from last night's bender. There are no penthouse suites. Rob had to share a dormitory with other addicts but found he quite liked the sense of camaraderie. He had to join the others to help cook and wash up after dinner – never something he much cared for. He was not allowed books (he hardly ever reads books anyway), magazines or even a radio or television. At a time when he would normally be enjoying his pop star sleep, he was up for his morning run. Rob responded well to having his life organized in this manner. It encouraged the sense of belonging that has always been so important to him.

He had to endure the humbling experience of group therapy, where his status outside the clinic counted for nothing. He was also introduced to the 'programme', the twelve-point plan for life known as the Minnesota Method, which is favoured by Alcoholics Anonymous. Step One is to admit to yourself and to others that you are an addict: 'My name is Rob and I am an alcoholic.' Step Two is to believe that a higher power can restore you to sanity. That may or may not be God. Despite being brought up in a Roman Catholic family, Rob is not a churchgoer and admits to being an atheist. He is, however, prepared to accept the existence of a 'force higher than yourself that you have to give in to'.

He stayed in the clinic for six weeks, and emerged fit enough both mentally and physically to promote his first album. He had not mastered all twelve steps, which include making amends to people wronged by your addiction, but he did recognize two important aspects of his problem. First, his addiction had made him very selfish. And, secondly, he should never look further than staying 'clean' for one day. Beechy Colclough observes, 'I think rehab can be harder for celebrities because of the added pressure of being known. They find it difficult to trust anyone when they are getting treated because of what might then get into the papers.'

Rehab, as any addict will tell you, is not a cure. It is a respite. Your addiction goes into remission but without care and diligence can resume at any time. Rob would sporadically and spectacularly fall off the wagon in the coming few years.

12

Angels

Peter Lorraine, then editor of *Top of the Pops* magazine, observed that no one had a clue what kind of music Robbie Williams was going to produce. That was not strictly true because his third single, 'Lazy Days', complete with jangly guitar intro, was leaning heavily towards Brit Pop. It could almost have been Oasis without Liam's trademark vocal sneer.

It was quite uplifting but there was little for Rob to cheer about. When it was released at the end of July 1997, it peaked at a disappointing number eight but that was sensational compared to 'South Of The Border'. Written on a platform at Stoke station, it limped to number fourteen at the end of September, selling a paltry 40,000 copies. One of the problems at the time, according to Chris Briggs, was that Rob could not promote the singles properly because of his rehab treatment.

The prospects for the album looked bleak. It hadn't helped that Gary's album, *Open Road*, had eventually been released at the end of May and, yet again, he was celebrating a number one. In no time at all the slick and smooth release had racked up sales of 350,000 copies. Then, curiously, it stalled, as if everyone interested in Gary Barlow had bought it and then there was nobody else.

Robbie's debut, *Life Thru a Lens* – originally called *The Show Must Go On* – was finally released on 29 September 1997, and sold slightly less than one tenth of Gary's sales in the first eight weeks – just 33,000 copies. This was an absolute crisis. It was an open secret that his record company was becoming disillusioned and seriously considering dropping him after only one of the three albums specified in their deal.

At EMI's 1997 autumn sales conference Robbie pulled himself together and sang a couple of songs before an invited audience of mainly disinterested media. Then he sang a track called 'Angels'. A former executive recalls the moment: 'We were about to drop him. But everyone was saying, "Oh my God! 'Angels' is such a hit!"'

If ever a song transformed a career, 'Angels' did that for Robbie Williams. It was an instant classic, albeit firmly in the middle of the road. Pete Conway already knew it was a great song. Rob had sung it to him in the car one afternoon. Pete told him it was extra special and went round telling all his mates, 'You wait until "Angels" comes out.' Pete was convinced it was up there with Paul McCartney's 'Yesterday'.

In truth, it was more like a classic from Elton John, with melancholic piano chords and Rob's voice sounding more mid-Atlantic than before. Some of Elton's great songs, such as 'Candle in the Wind' and 'Sorry Seems to Be the Hardest Word', are, however, a little downbeat lyrically. 'Angels' is unusual for such an introspective ballad in that it is unashamedly uplifting and, crucially, can mean something different for everyone. For Rob, it described his feelings about the death of his mother's sister, Auntie Jo, who had died when he was fifteen and, also, of his granddad, Phil Williams, Pete Conway's father.

The impetus for 'Angels' came on a bender in Dublin when he was supping Guinness and gazing at a fountain on a pub patio. He thought of a waterfall and the song's chorus took shape. He thought of it again during the second songwriting session with Guy Chambers and the famous song was the result.

The origins of the song would become the subject of dispute when an Irish songwriter, Ray Heffernan, claimed that he wrote the lyrics about his unborn son who had died. He met Rob in Dublin at Christmas in 1996 and the pair got drunk together before going back to Ray's mother's house where they started writing bits and pieces. Ray says he played Rob the verse and the melody to 'Angels' on an acoustic guitar and the two of them drunkenly sang into a Dictaphone. When he returned to England, Rob was not pleased to see Ray when he showed up on the doorstep of Jan's house and that was the last time they met. Rob has always disputed his claim to a co-writing credit. Ray was subsequently paid a modest £7,500 to give up any claim to future royalties.

'Angels' is a song about guardian spirits and personal rescue and, as such, rather aptly rescued Rob's career. It could even be said to have begun the career of Robbie Williams as we know him today. The video, almost as importantly, revealed a post-rehab Robbie to the world: strong-featured yet vulnerable, the famous eyes and a new close-cropped haircut with a shaved parting. And the package was wrapped up in an impossibly big overcoat that looked as if he had nicked it from army surplus. Gary Barlow was impressed when he saw it. The jellied buttocks of Take That were light years away.

Life Thru a Lens went straight back in the charts with the pulling power of 'Angels' on its side and ended up selling a million copies and more. It became the fifty-fourth bestselling UK album of all time, the first of four Robbie Williams albums in the top one hundred. It would be the first of many number one albums. Within a year, Robbie Williams would be the biggest selling British artist.

His next single, 'Let Me Entertain You', had originally been intended for release before 'Angels' but Rob had felt he lacked the confidence to project a song with such a brash title. By the time it finally made the shops in March 1998, all the old swagger had returned.

A couple of years later Rob and Jonathan Wilkes were guest presenters on Capital Radio in London and, unsurprisingly, 'Angels' was one of the songs they played. Rob introduced it by saying, 'Shall we play the song that transformed my career from a mere boozing, fat ex-boy band member?' Joking apart, Rob is well aware of the debt he owes this song.

'Angels' became so popular that it detracted from the rest of the album, which, in hindsight, is a fascinating example of Rob's conflicting personality of sensitivity and showmanship. He wrote 'One of God's Better People' about the 'most important person in my life – my mum Jan.' He sang it down the phone to her and she started to cry. The lyric to 'Killing Me' describes the tough time he was having as a result of drugs and alcohol. These are not tracks of a light and airy nature. They reflect Rob's real emotions – not least in the bitter bonus track in which he berates his old schoolteacher who said he would never amount to anything.

The thank-you list on the sleeve notes reflects a little of Rob's life at the time. The first is to Nigel Martin-Smith: '. . . my past is something I find difficult to accept, especially the part with you in it.' Of his former bandmates he asks, 'What the fuck happened . . .' He thanks the Kinsella family and Tim Abbott – clearly before he had to pay them six-figure sums in legal battles. He mentions the Gallagher brothers, Anna Friel and Clouds. He also says that if he has forgotten anyone, then the cheque is in the post.

The critics were mainly impressed. They enjoyed the lyrics – who but Robbie could rhyme 'needy' with 'in-breedy'? John Bush for *Allmusic* described it as an 'uninhibited joyride through all manner of British music' and continued that it was 'utterly enjoyable pop music'. *Vox* magazine loved it: 'A glossy, bold, funny, frolicking, lollipoppy, shiny, lovely, gurning pop album.' That was decidedly not the view of *Melody Maker*, in which Robin Bresnark wrote: 'Robbie Williams is as fascinating a hapless goon as we're ever likely to come across. But this album feels more like a press release than an album – and that's not what I call music.'

The success of the album laid a firm foundation for what might be described as the 'Robbie Williams formula': presenting himself as a cheeky, sarcastic, funny, sensitive showman. He declared after reading his album's reviews: 'I love listening to good music and I can't stop playing my album!' He could get away with such conceit because of the twinkle in his eye. All the smart wisecracks and wistful words would, of course, have counted for nothing if the music had not been so well crafted.

The Robbie Williams formula works just as well in concert as it does on record. A music fan who has seen him ten times on stage says, 'He has never *been* shit – even if he was feeling shit.' Two years after his departure from Take That, he was live on stage in the UK singing the band's biggest hit, 'Back For Good', in a form that Take That fans would not have recognized. He began quietly enough before launching into a pogo-dancing frenzy that would have made the late Sid Vicious of the Sex Pistols proud. It was totally unexpected but the corruption of the boy band classic was typical Robbie at that time – almost shocking. The banners in the crowd displayed rhymes that could have come from the pen of the lad himself: 'Rob – we want your knob' and 'Point Your Erection In My Direction' were two of the best.

He told his audience, in matey fashion, 'I've wanted to do this for two fucking years.' Everybody knew the words to everything, a feature of Robbie concerts throughout the years. When it came to 'Angels', Rob just pointed the microphone at the audience and let them indulge all their best karaoke dreams while he stood there with tears in his eyes, genuinely moved. A record company executive observed: 'He gets such an incredible high out of performing. How can you follow it?'

Rob was able to follow it at the Brit Awards ceremony in 1998 when he appeared with one of his musical heroes, Tom Jones. Rob has always loved the singer's classic, 'Delilah', believing it to be the all-time best song to get you out of bed on a Sunday morning when suffering from a Saturday night hangover. The only problem for a Port Vale lad like Rob is that 'Delilah' is a favourite terraces' anthem of arch rivals Stoke City. Rob used to study old footage from the sixties and seventies of Tom performing his hits and seek to emulate him. When they finally appeared on stage together in 1998, it was as if they had been performing together for years.

Their duet of songs from the film *The Full Monty* was the best thing to have happened to that tired awards show in years. Rob was prancing about the stage in black leather and Cuban heels, having the time of his life. He began with a version of the Cockney Rebel classic 'Come Up And See Me'. Then Jones the Voice arrived to sing the film's biggest hit, 'You Can Leave Your Hat On', which featured Rob dancing like a clockwork toy that had been overwound. It was a tongue-in-cheek tour de force.

Tom gave Rob substance and in return Rob made Tom appear up to the minute. It is a formula the Welsh star would subsequently milk to the limit in collaborations with Wyclef Jean, Catatonia and the Stereophonics. It did wonders for Rob's confidence when Tom told him he thought he was a great singer. Afterwards Rob declared, 'Those five minutes eleven seconds on stage with Tom Jones were the happiest of my life.'

The performance was almost as big news for Tom as it was for Rob. His stock soared and *Reload,* his album of duets, produced coincidentally by Steve Power, was a huge hit. Rob joined him to record 'Are You Gonna Go My Way', a Lenny Kravitz song. Rob was understandably nervous about joining the great man in the same vocal booth, so he did what he has always done. He revealed how he handled it in a phone-in with fans: 'I thought, "I know, I'll do an impression of him", so I did and I think I pulled it off.' The first time Rob had sung the complete song was their first run-through. After they had finished, Tom announced, 'That's it, then. Shall we go to the pub?'

Football, meanwhile, provided Rob with a welcome diversion through good times and bad. Flushed with the success of 'Angels', he agreed to play in the testimonial match for one of the Port Vale favourites, Dean Glover, against Aston Villa. Word had quickly spread that Rob would be playing and the crowd, mainly young teenage girls, was bigger than for any run-of-the-mill home game.

The rain was lashing down and halfway through the first half some joker in the crowd shouted out, 'Come on, Robbie, entertain us!' Just after the interval, he had his wish when Vale were awarded a penalty. Rob, wearing the number nine shirt, stepped up and scored with a sweet left-footed shot that gave the goalie no chance. Minutes later he got involved in an argument with the referee, who showed him the red card for 'foul and abusive language'. Rob bowed theatrically to the crowd and marched off. It was all pre-arranged because a Mercedes was waiting to whisk him back to London. Dean recalls, 'It was probably the only sending-off ever when the player wanted to go.'

Coco Colclough, who was at the game, observed, 'It was ever so funny. There was probably more of a police presence for that match than there was for the Vale–Stoke derby.' After Rob left the pitch, Coco went back to the dressing rooms to say hello and was told Rob would be out in a few minutes: 'By this time there were two or three girls there. They were from Crewe. And they said, "Do you know Rob?" Within ten minutes there were 500 girls there – and me. Rob comes out and says, "Excuse me, excuse me. I've got someone here I want to speak to." And they just cleared a path for him. He comes up and says, "All right, Coke?", puts his arms around me and says he has to shoot off to London. He says, "Give me your new address and phone number." I said, "Rob, do you seriously think I am going to give you my address and phone with all these girls here? I'd be having hundreds of phone calls every day for a month asking, 'Is he coming up?'" He just paused for a second and looked at me and said, "I understand."'

After the game, Vale manager John Rudge, tongue firmly in cheek, said, 'He's not the quickest in the world. His agent is talking about a £5 million signing-on fee but I'd really need another look.'

During the next season, Rob interrupted a promotional trip to the US to fly back for a game in honour of another of his favourite players, the Vale skipper, Neil Aspin, who had been with the club for ten years. The opposition was Leicester City. Rob scored one and made one and he even managed to find time to drop his shorts for the benefit of the crowd. After the match, Rob kept phoning Neil up to find out if he had got the video of the match yet because he wanted to see his goal again. Neil recalled, 'He kept saying, "Did you see my goal Neil? It was a good goal." I just felt that Rob had done really well for me.'

13

Never Ever

Robbie Williams is continually asked about love, marriage and family, as all celebrities are. It is standard, predictable fare for a media obsessed by their glossy world. Sometimes Robbie lets Rob reply. In May 1997, before he had met Nicole Appleton, from the girl group All Saints, he was asked in an interview if he ever thought about settling down. He replied that having a family was a major thing in his life and that he had even written a song, the never released 'If I Ever Had A Son.' He added, 'I want to stop going mad because I want to be a good role model for my kids.'

Nicole Appleton brought out the best in Robert Williams. They were both born in 1974, Nic, as her friends call her, on 7 October, making her a Libran to Rob's Aquarian. Like him, she came from a broken home. Her parents first split up when she was five and the other famous Appleton sister, Natalie, was seven. They were the two youngest of four daughters. It was a traumatic time because the family was literally split down the middle. Nic went to live in London with her father, a car salesman, and another sister called Lori, while Natalie stayed behind in Canada with the eldest, Lee. After two years their mother came to London and they resumed a relatively normal family life but that lasted only a few months before she returned to Canada, this time leaving all four girls in London. It was a very disorienting time, especially when their mother returned again within the year. They made the best of it, crammed into a small flat in Kilburn.

Nic and Rob were destined to be soulmates, sharing an understanding of the loneliness and confusion of having their home life divided and of dreaming of a glamorous world of show business as an escape route. She was a superb dancer as a child and passed the audition to attend the recently opened Sylvia Young Theatre School in Camden Town, along with Denise van Outen, who would later also date Robbie Williams. Her sister Nat joined her there but after four years their unhappy mother left once more – this time to live in New York. Both Nic and Nat went with her, part of a relentless merry-go-round as they tried and failed to settle in either London or New York.

Their new stepfather worked as an entertainments manager for a big hotel. He was almost an American equivalent of Pete Conway. The sisters would be like Butlins Redcoats, helping guests with fun activities and then getting drunk in the evenings. If Nic and Nat had lived in Tunstall, they would have been honorary lads, drinking until they threw up or passed out.

Nic was a slower starter than Rob in the music business. She joined Melanie Blatt and Shaznay Lewis in All Saints when she was twenty, the age at which Rob was seriously considering life after the most successful boy band of the time. Rob would be able to understand what Nic was going through when she began having major problems within All Saints. He would also have understood the effort involved in trying to get that first record deal and how the perception of girl bands was very much the same as for boy bands – usually neither are treated seriously. As in Take That, there was meant to be only one with talent in All Saints: Shaznay was their Gary Barlow.

In the beginning, Rob and Nic kept their relationship a secret. They met for the first time on a television show when All Saints were performing their most famous song, 'Never Ever', written by Shaznay. Rob was polite and complimentary to Nic about her music. In *Together*, her joint autobiography with sister Nat, she describes how he seemed 'very famous'. It was an insightful observation. There is nothing nerdy, introspective, geeky or apologetic about Robbie Williams. He is a 24-carat star with the charisma to match.

They met again in December 1997 during rehearsals at Battersea Power Station for the Concert of Hope in aid of the Diana, Princess of Wales Memorial Fund, the first time Rob and Gary Barlow had clapped eyes on each other since the demise of Take That. Gary had lost none of his cheesiness, beckoning everyone over to the piano for a singalong. It was Rob who lit up the room for Nic. He did not seek attention, she thought: he demanded it.

One of the intriguing aspects of the Appletons' autobiography is that they reveal so much of their vulnerability and personal insecurities. Nicole Appleton is a celebrity, albeit when she met Rob a very minor one, but she behaves like an uncertain schoolgirl whose knees turn to jelly at the sight of the football captain. She keeps looking over and then looking away quickly. She wants to talk to him but is worried she will be at a disadvantage if he knows she fancies him. She invites him to her birthday party and is ecstatic when he is the first to arrive. She treasures a Polaroid snap they have taken together. And she is secretly upset when she opens the paper and sees he has been out on a date with Denise van Outen.

Perhaps, inevitably, considering Rob's history, they got so drunk on Guinness the first night they spent together that they both passed out. A more worrying foretaste of what was to come in their relationship occurred when Rob called her in a dreadful state from a house in North London asking for her to come and get him. It was the morning after several nights before and Rob was at his lowest, most vulnerable and guilt-ridden.

In many ways, Rob and Nic found each other at exciting, make-or-break times for them both. Nic and All Saints were just grasping success for the first time, while Rob was at the cross-roads of success and failure with his post-Take That career. His first solo album, *Life Thru a Lens*, was released in late September 1997, a few weeks before he attended Nicole Appleton's birth-day party. He released his pivotal record, 'Angels', while 'Never Ever', All Saints' second release, was creeping relentlessly up the charts.

Nic describes a wonderful scene in Rob's bedroom one Sunday morning just after New Year 1998. His manager rings to give him the new chart position for 'Angels'. He sounds pleased and excited, puts the phone down and announces, '"Never Ever" is number one.' Amazingly, it sold 770,000 copies *before* it reached the top – a record. Rob even rang his mother to tell her the good news. Jan always liked Nic.

Rob and Nic's relationship became public property on 2 January 1998, when she was seen by photographers leaving his place in Notting Hill. The paparazzi had almost certainly received a tip-off that if they hung around outside Robbie Williams' home for a day or two they would spot Nicole Appleton. Or perhaps they were expecting to catch Denise van Outen. Or just any old lap dancer Rob may or may not have spent the New Year with. The next day the newspapers had their story. From that day on Rob and Nic would have to con-duct their own private tragedy against a backdrop of superficial media fascination, especially when it came to ques-tions about starting a family.

For a while everything went well. All Saints were increasingly perceived as an antidote to the Spice Girls: cooler, less noisy and producing better music. Rob and Nic were together at the Brit Awards when All Saints won two for 'Never Ever' and he came away with a disappointing zero. He had been nominated for four – his first post-Take That recognition – so, although he was his usual life and soul, Nic knew he was very upset. He had stolen the show, however, with his three-song medley with Tom Jones.

The following week, an exclusive interview appeared in the *Sun*, in which Nic spoke for the first time about their relationship, saying how much he made her laugh, although she warned that they were much too young to be committed yet. Nic was ever present during the filming of a BBC documentary about Rob entitled *Some Mothers Do 'Ave 'Em*. Rob is obviously happy, revelling in the relationship with Nic. He tells the camera that it has given him a lot of security and a lot of love and happiness but that he is learning to cope with the difficult as well as the great times.

The difficult times, which he did not chronicle, began in March 1998 when Nic rang from Vancouver to tell him that she was pregnant. Incredibly, considering the goldfish bowl in which they both lived their lives, they managed to keep what then unfolded entirely secret.

Rob was absolutely thrilled at the prospect of becoming a father. He started making plans, buying a new flat with enough space to have a room for the baby. He took Nic to Tunstall to see his beloved nan, Betty, who was eighty-three; she was happy at her grandson's news. In her book, Nic recalls that Rob put his hand on her belly and told her, 'This baby is saving my life.'

At four months' pregnant, Nic had an abortion in New York, with Rob waiting in the next room to support her as best he could. In her version of events, Nic blamed enormous pressure from everyone connected with All Saints. She maintains that she did it for the band – even though Melanie Blatt, who was pregnant at the same time, went ahead and had her baby. It was also impressed upon her, so she says, that Robbie Williams was bad news. Afterwards, she was consumed with guilt that she had let Rob down.

To this day Nic does not know if and to what extent Rob

blamed her for what happened. During the coming months he became more difficult to handle, unable to offer the sympathetic ear she needed over her troubles within All Saints, telling her she should just leave the band. Yet, paradoxically, he would trail along with her on the frequent doctor's appointments she required after the operation. It was as if he had no time for the world of celebrity, of entertainment and of 'Robbie Williams', but he was doing his best to do the right thing according to the standards of Rob Williams, an ordinary lad from Tunstall who understood the importance of personal loyalty and family.

Rob asked Nic to marry him in June 1998. The newspapers called it a whirlwind romance, unaware that the pair had packed more into six months than many couples do in a lifetime together. More often than not the romantic nature of Rob will win out over the 'love 'em and leave 'em' lad's attitude. He was proud of being in a grown-up relationship and wanted to do everything properly. He proposed on bended knee with an exquisite antique diamond ring proffered from his hand. The slightly less conventional aspect was that it was five in the morning and Rob had been sound asleep in bed when Nic came round to his house, having jetted in from an All Saints visit to Japan. Rob had to get out of bed in order to get down on one knee.

Unlike the pregnancy and the abortion, the good news of the engagement was, in true celebrity style, a secret for a couple of seconds. Both of Rob's parents were in London to see him perform an important solo concert at the Royal Albert Hall. They were pleased with his news. If they had not been in London, they could have read all about it in the press the following day. Nic was quoted, footballer style, as saying that she was 'over the moon'. Jan, normally so reticent about discussing her son, was just as pleased: 'I am very proud of him and his choice; she is a lovely lady. I was aware the engagement was coming up – they are just so in love and so happy.' More pertinently, perhaps, she added that no date for a wedding had been fixed because they had so much to do in their careers.

The worst thing about celebrity relationships is the absences. Actors, actresses and rock stars meet each other at celebrity parties, enjoy a 'whirlwind romance' and then say cheerio for a week or a month or six months while they go off on tour or start filming in the Peruvian jungle. It is very hard to deal with. Kylie Minogue's great love affair with Michael Hutchence went up in smoke when they were at opposite ends of the globe, pursuing their careers. Rob's friend Patsy Kensit once described how even something as trivial as your partner saying hello in the wrong tone of voice could send you into agonies of doubt if you were thousands of miles apart.

Rob and Nic were apart a great deal in the summer of 1998 as All Saints flew all over the world promoting their first album and Rob started work on his second in London. He was also struggling to come to terms with a traumatic event in his life – the death of his beloved nan.

Nic and Rob split up for the first time by telephone, after she had been away for a week. He was at home in Notting Hill and she was in a hotel room in Rio de Janeiro. There was a message from Rob waiting for her when she checked in. He simply told her to call but, proving the veracity of Patsy Kensit's observation, she knew something was not right. In her version of the conversation, he told her they should end their relationship, claiming they were apart too much. Reading between the lines, it was Rob the small boy wanting some attention and affection. He hates being by himself and probably wanted her to say she was dropping everything to return home and give him a cuddle. Celebrity life is just not like that.

The newspapers claimed that it was Nic who had called things off and that Rob was distraught. He certainly looked very down when he was pictured leaving the Groucho Club in Soho at 2.30a.m., after earlier attending the reopening of the

Heaven nightclub and then a party at the Café de Paris. He told reporters that he hoped he could sort things out with Nicole, who meant the world to him.

Jan Williams appeared just as disappointed as her son: 'I can't believe they have split. It was a match made in heaven and I pray they make up.' Rob promptly flew off to the Spanish resort of Puerto Banús to drown his sorrows with wine and women – at least that is how the newspapers saw it. Jan was again quoted at her supportive best, saying that he was upset because of the Nicole situation: 'He's looking on the positive side and wouldn't jeopardize his music career. He always tells me if he has got any problems.'

There is no reason to disbelieve Nicole Appleton's recollection of their first break-up, something she said she never understood. There is a curiously repetitive theme in the early press coverage of Rob's relationships, in that he is almost always the one who is dumped. A relationship of this intensity was completely new to him and he undoubtedly acted impetuously, his constant craving for attention and approval getting the better of him. His addiction to drugs had left him with a predilection to loiter in the darker recesses of his mind. In his relationship with Nic, he could really have done with lightening up.

Within days of her returning to the UK, they went out for dinner, got completely drunk and were seen stumbling around, with Rob, wearing a football shirt, giving Nic a piggyback. He proposed again at the end of August and she accepted.

Their respective careers, at first glance, couldn't have been going better. 'Bootie Call' was the third All Saints number one of the year when it topped the charts on 12 September. One week later it was replaced by Robbie Williams' first number one, 'Millennium', from the *I've Been Expecting You* album.

They both, however, had ongoing problems. Rob was doing his best with his addiction treatment and Nic would go along to AA meetings to support him. She, meanwhile, continued to be unhappy in the band, feeling that she and Nat were the poorer relations of Shaznay and Melanie. It also did not help when Melanie had a baby girl, Lilyella. Nic recorded a song she had written with the help of Rob and Guy Chambers called 'Love Is Where I'm From' but it failed to obtain a release, much to her disappointment.

They broke up again just after All Saints had switched on the Christmas lights in Regent Street. Once again, Rob seemed to suggest it out of the blue, with no rhyme or reason. And, once again, he regretted it almost immediately. The old romantic in him took over and he bought her 1,000 red roses.

Their final reconciliation lasted a mere two weeks, when a wild Christmas drinking session by Rob spelled the end. In a theatrical confrontation, Nic says she told Rob that if he walked out the door, he needn't come back. He left and that was basically that. His bender went from bad to worse and he passed out in the lobby of a hotel, where a cruel passer-by covered him in shaving foam and toothpaste and then called the papers to witness his humiliation. It was the end of a dreadfully sad, torturous year for both of them. It would not be completely accurate to describe Rob and Nic as star-crossed lovers because most of their bad luck they brought on themselves.

Once again, the ups and more frequently the downs of their relationship were public property. At the Brit Awards in February 1999, they found themselves the centre of attention simply because they were not sitting with one another. He went with his family and she was escorted by Huey Morgan of the Fun Lovin' Criminals.

Nic was subsequently quoted in a Sunday paper as saying that Rob was a mess in his personal life. She drew attention to his inability to forget he was Robbie Williams when he was out of the spotlight. That was a bit unfair because Rob did try to be ordinary and natural but hardly anyone would let him. When he took Nicole out for a Chinese meal in Stoke-on-Trent, he was continually hassled by people who recognized him. They could hardly be blamed for being excited at seeing a star ordering sweet and sour but it forced him to retreat into a shrinking world.

On one occasion, when he went to the airport to meet Nic, a man wanted Rob to speak to his girlfriend on his mobile phone. When he declined – this was private time – the man told his girlfriend, 'Wanker won't speak to you!' One can imagine that the chump in question has dined out ever since on the story and still, in his opinion, Robbie Williams is a wanker.

The distinction between the public and the private Rob continued to blur when he started talking about Nic to his audience at a concert in Newcastle upon Tyne, saying how much he missed her. Usually superstars do not share their private lives with their fans the way Rob does.

The Brits ceremony was not the last time they saw each other or went out together but the Christmas break-up was, for Nic at least, a form of closure. She still telephoned him for advice and a sympathetic ear. Then, at the Cannes Film Festival in March, she met Liam Gallagher. Intriguingly, her relationship with Liam developed along similar lines to the one she had just had with Rob. They, too, spent much of their spare time drinking, he gave her support in her ongoing strife within All Saints and they also had to deal with an early pregnancy. Crucially, this time she was determined to keep the baby and was strong enough to do so. Looking at the two relationships, there are so many similarities it does beg the question of what would have happened if she had become involved with Liam first and then met Rob. Her relationship with Liam has become so homely. Rob, it would be easy to imagine, dreamt of a similar lifestyle for himself where he watched television with his kids, ate roast dinners, had his mates round and enjoyed the love of the woman in his life.

After All Saints finally split and the lawyers moved in, Nic and Nat wrote their autobiography, which came out at the same time as their solo record career was launched in the summer of 2002. Most shockingly, Nic revealed all the deeply personal details about her relationship with Rob and their aborted child. It was a brave decision to be so open about what, in celebrity terms, is a very negative experience. Many women in show business have abortions in order to protect their careers but very few admit it, let alone talk it through from beginning to end. Perhaps Nic needed to cleanse herself of the details in order to put All Saints and Rob behind her and move forward with a new career and family.

Many were amazed that she could be so insensitive to Rob's personal feelings although he, too, has never been slow to air his dirty linen in public. He can always be relied upon to give an opinion about anything – if he is in character. It all depends on whether he considers Nic to be part of the story of Rob or of Robbie. It was an eye-opener for the public that Robbie Williams, the cheeky chappie, had been through such an ordeal. Although brutally frank, Nicole Appleton was nice about Rob; she wasn't bitter.

Rob's second album, *I've Been Expecting You*, is almost unbearably poignant if viewed as a memorial to his love affair with Nicole Appleton. From the title itself to tracks including 'No Regrets' and 'Phoenix From The Flames', it is a heartbreaking journey through the most difficult time of Rob's life. Nic even contributes a single line on the album at the start and end of 'Win Some Lose Some'. We simply hear her telephone voice declaring, 'Love you, Baby.' And then there is 'Grace', a song about the baby, Rob's child, that Nic aborted. They were going to call the baby Grace if it had been a girl.

14

Give Back Sum

After his break-up with Nic, Rob's love affair with all things Oasis rapidly went cold. Perhaps it was inevitable when she began a relationship with Liam Gallagher or perhaps he had just moved on in his life. It probably started off as nothing more than a spot of professional jealousy. Rob insisted he had not fallen out with the Gallagher brothers, although he did boast that people were leaving his concerts saying they had a better time than at Oasis.

The shambolic, unthreatening character of the latter days of Take That bore no relation to the multiple Brit-winning, number one machine that Rob was becoming – probably the only serious British rival to Oasis. The catalyst for the public falling-out was the Gallagher brothers punching below the belt as far as Rob was concerned by making less than flattering references to his weight – a topic that Rob has always been particularly sensitive about.

Liam referred to Rob in 1999 as 'Robbie tubby-arsed Williams' and declared that his music was 'rubbish'. Liam is a charismatic rock star but he is never going to win a war of words with someone as razor-sharp in that department as Rob. Liam is a name-caller, an unsubtle insulter. Rob bounced back with a classic: 'I knew I could write poetry but I also knew I only knew three chords. And those three chords can't last for ever . . . unless you're Oasis.'

Rob finds it impossible to let things lie. He could, for instance, never shrug off his animosity towards Gary Barlow or Nigel Martin-Smith even though his success was leaving them both well behind. The Gallagher brothers really got under his skin because they were picking on him as if he were the fat boy in class whom nobody liked. It was time for Noel Gallagher to join the fun. When Radio 1 listeners asked Oasis to record Rob's classic 'Angels' for a special session, Noel refused point-blank, adding that Liam would have to 'sing it with fifty meat pies in his mouth'. He followed that up in an interview in *heat* magazine in which he called Robbie 'the fat dancer from Take That'.

Rob couldn't believe it and reacted to it all, in his own words, like a thirteen year old. He sent round a wreath of white roses and lilies to the showbiz desk of the *Sun* with a note that read: 'To Noel Gallagher, RIP. Heard your latest album, with deepest sympathy, Robbie Williams.'

Liam responded by threatening that if he ever saw Rob in a club in London, 'I'm going to break his fucking nose.' He also maintained that the new Oasis record was 'the best fucking album out this year, better than anything Fatty will ever do'. Rob was determined to give as good as he got. He dusted off his talent for impersonation by mimicking Liam's monkey walk and facial expressions before telling reporters, 'So he's going to beat me up, is he? I'm just not angry enough to hit him. It's not my career going down the drain. But if he hits me, I suppose I'll have to defend myself.'

At this stage, the public slanging match became silly with the suggestion from Rob at the Brit Awards that he and Liam should settle their differences in a boxing match. William Hill offered odds (Robbie Williams 1–2, Liam Gallagher 6–4), while Lloyd Honeyghan, the former world boxing champion, said he would add the feuding pair to a bill at the Elephant and Castle Leisure Centre in South London. The idea was that the bout could raise £200,000 for charity. Rob entered into the spirit by saying he was definitely up for it and that it was nice to see Liam so angry. It was great knockabout fun and generated some free publicity for the boxing and bookmaking fraternity. It was called off by Liam, who said it would be childish and pathetic and, in future, he would let the music do the talking.

The war of words between Liam and Rob could be treated with a degree of caution if it were not for the Appleton factor. This sort of thing is meat and drink to pop columns with pages to fill, while record companies love the exposure it gives to new releases.

Liam overstepped the bounds of celebrity etiquette when he publicly stated that Robbie was queer at a *Q* Awards party. It was an odd, playground thing to say, especially considering Liam's partner, Nicole Appleton, had once been pregnant with Rob's child and the couple would soon make an announcement that she was expecting Liam's baby. Perhaps it had more to do with that than anything else but Rob was not amused. He left the ceremony abruptly and declared that Liam was 'fucking out of order'. A week later Rob took a somewhat puerile revenge by taunting the Oasis singer about his sex life with Nicole. He told his audience at the London Arena: 'Nic is my old bird. I have had her as well, mate. I bet you go to bed every night scratching your head, thinking, "Is he better than me?"'

Rob came to his senses after the baby, Gene, was born and was conciliatory on a Radio 1 interview. He said, 'At the beginning of it all, it was quite a laugh and then it just became too destructive. I wish them both the best of luck and I hope Nicky keeps safe and the baby does fine.' When Gene arrived, Nic expected Rob to call or send some message but she heard nothing from him. In her autobiography, *Together*, she concedes that the thought of Gene must hurt Rob and that she wished she could speak to him but they had no contact.

When Rob was at school, the girls would flit between the boys. Everyone was young and it was not the end of the world if Joanna Melvin preferred Lee Hancock to Robert Williams; Lee and Rob could still be best mates. This was different. This was adult, with life-changing consequences. How could he be friendly with a man who had everything he wanted for himself?

The personal trials and torments of Rob make the persona of Robbie Williams stronger. 'Robbie Williams' may be the creation to perform his songs but it is Rob who writes the words. He explained, 'If I feel terrible, I have even more things to write about. That's the tragic thing with me.'

By the time *I've Been Expecting You* had been digested, a clearer picture had emerged of where Robbie Williams would fit in the musical marketplace. The music sounded like a magpie had been let loose on the Radio 2 playlist. 'Let Me Entertain You' tipped its hat at mid-seventies Elton John camp rock – 'Pinball Wizard', 'Saturday Night's Alright (For Fighting)' – with a nod to Alice Cooper's 'School's Out'. 'No Regrets' was unashamedly Pet Shop Boys to the extent that Neil Tennant was persuaded to provide backing vocals; Rob brazenly phoned him up and said he had written a new Pet Shop Boys tune. 'Millennium' sampled the famous James Bond theme from *You Only Live Twice*. 'She's The One' was actually an old track by World Party, the group with which Guy Chambers had cut his musical teeth in the early nineties.

Rob's lyrics raised this musical pot-pourri above the ordinary. 'Millennium' may have conjured up an initial image of Sean Connery in a tuxedo but on second listening the lyrics include references to liposuction, detox and overdose at Christmas – hardly topics for the British Secret Service. They were very personal, self-aware and, best of all, ironic. There is nothing bland in his self-portrait, 'Strong', which opens the second album. It leads off with a jangly guitar melody that would make Noel Gallagher proud and then launches into a wonderful mixture of self-awareness and mockery – of breath that smells of a thousand fags and dancing like his dad when he's drunk. Rob is revealed as a natural poet. He must have died from embarrassment in Take That when he sang lead vocals on 'I Found Heaven' ('on the wings of love'); the new Robbie Williams would have found heaven in a pint.

I've Been Expecting You had a much slicker feel to it than *Life Thru a Lens*. The album jacket has Rob looking like 007 while inside he is pictured in a series of stills as if from a James Bond movie, complete with exotic women and locations. Guy Chambers was now rejoicing in the grandiose position of 'musical director', which sounded the sort of title you might give yourself if you were involved in the production of *Oliver!* at the Queen's Theatre, Burslem.

Unintentionally, that gave the game away about the 'new' Robbie Williams: he was putting on a show, the whole thing was a big entertainment, a musical entitled *West Stoke Story*, in which a working-class lad with a comic for a dad, who loves his mum, achieves fame and fortune, only to throw it all away when he gets led astray by a bad lot, rediscovers himself as a star and becomes 'a better man'. What's Andrew Lloyd Webber's number?

Guy Chambers is refreshingly frank about his songwriting with Rob. He admits that they 'plunder' the best bits of modern popular music. Sometimes that proved a little unwise, as when they had to pay a six-figure sum to a New York publishing firm. They had taken a verse without permission from an obscure 1973 song, 'I Am The Way (New York Town)', by the quirky American folk singer Loudon Wainwright III – father of Martha and Rufus Wainwright. They inserted it, more or less intact, into the lyric of 'Jesus In A Camper Van', which was on the *I've Been Expecting You* album and the US release, *The Ego Has Landed*. It was the seventh track on Rob's second album but if you order the CD today it has disappeared into the Bermuda Triangle of recordings. Instead, a completely different song entitled 'It's Only Us' occupies the seventh position.

Guy has observed that, while Rob would not claim to be the most original artist in the world, there is a strong argument that he is the most entertaining. He is also one of the most professional. For the second album it helped that Rob was more sober than before and, instead of hauling himself out from underneath the mixing desk, was making a contribution from a vertical position. His voice had also grown stronger since the anaemic warbling of 'Everything Changes'. It was an attractive blend of Elton John and Liam Gallagher with a soupçon of his dad thrown in for good measure.

The critics were impressed. The *New Musical Express* gave the album an encouraging review and summed up the image of Robbie Williams: 'a bovine sex god, rehab fuck-up, cabaret clown and UNICEF ambassador'. The record was so difficult to dislike. Robbie Williams was proving to be a pop star whom it was hard to fault. He was still hung up on the desire to be Oasis, and Liam in particular, but he would soon move on from that. The *Daily Telegraph* thought: 'Robbie and his showbiz mates the Gallagher brothers have one thing in common; all their songs are naggingly reminiscent of classic tracks that you can't quite put your finger on.'

Seeking the influences of Robbie Williams in the songs of The Beatles, Elton John and Oasis is fun but his heart is strictly Cole Porter sung by Frank Sinatra – witty lyrics that roll around on the tongue for a bit before merging into a catchy popular song. The public lapped it up. In 1998, his first two albums sold a combined total in the UK alone of 2.32 million copies, making Robbie Williams the biggest selling artist of the year.

Now was the time to dangle a foot in US waters. Unusually, the first two albums were packaged together for the American market under the title *The Ego Has Landed*. The reviews in

America, where it reached number 63 on the *Billboard* chart, were encouraging and not at all disparaging of the music as too British or idiosyncratic – the two excuses that would in future be offered to explain Rob's relative lack of success across the Atlantic.

One reviewer observed: 'This kid is a seventies variety show looking for a place to happen.' Another commented that the tracks were brimming with cleverness and raffish charm. The most ironic observation was that Robbie Williams was the drinking man's George Michael; up until then it was always Gary Barlow's name that was mentioned in the same breath as George's. One reviewer in San Francisco wrote: 'Like many great pop singers Robbie Williams knows how to uncover the beauty in sadness.'

A year after going home empty-handed from the Brits, Rob collected three. He was nominated for six but won Best British Single ('Angels'), Best British Video ('Millennium') and Best British Male Solo Artist. Even better was to come in March, when he collected two Ivor Novello Awards. The first was for 'Angels' (Most Performed Song) and the second was for Songwriter of the Year (with Guy Chambers). It may have been five years after Gary Barlow collected his first Novello but it was a sweet achievement.

Rob celebrated his success by buying his mum a new £1 million house in the pretty village of Batley, near Newcastle under Lyme. The mansion was set in twenty-four acres of grounds, which gave Rob, who did not have a driving licence, plenty of space in which to drive his vivid red Ferrari. Rob has never particularly enjoyed splashing his money around publicly. He doesn't, for instance, wear a lot of 'bling'. When he took delivery of the car, he sent it straight back to the showroom because he felt guilty about owning such a status symbol. He then changed his mind and made them bring it back. Rob enjoys the thrill of speed and loves racing go-karts but one suspects that if he had a licence he would never take the car out.

Instead he preferred to make his way around London on a Honda Shadow motorcycle.

Living in such a grand house did not seem to change Jan. Her new home had five bedrooms, three bathrooms and its own lake with an island in the middle, which was ideal for boating and picnics. She would still shop in Tesco or sit quietly reading in a Newcastle café but her purpose in life had radically altered. Instead of working all hours to provide for her family, she was able to put something back into the community through her counselling and setting up Rob's own charity, Give It Sum.

Rob had always loved Comic Relief. He was particularly impressed that every penny raised went towards deserving projects and also that the public were kept informed of where the money was going. With Jan's help, he arranged for his own charity to be administered by Comic Relief; their experts, who have a proven track record, make up the majority of the London-based committee. Jan became chairwoman and took her role very seriously. This was not, in any way, the idle plaything of a celebrity mother with too much time on her hands. She became an accomplished and authoritative speaker on two subjects close to her heart – her son and drugs and Robert and his charity.

The idea for Give It Sum was that it would allow Rob to put money back into his home town for deserving projects. The charity was funded entirely by Rob's own money and over the next ten years would award nearly £5 million to more than 400 deserving causes. The charity has flourished whatever Rob's own personal problems, his state of mind or the continent he is in. One of the first to benefit was his old school, St Margaret Ward, to which he gave £50,000. The idea was to promote the school as a centre for performing arts in the area. It would be a far cry from the days when Rob was there and, according to his mate Giuseppe Romano, the recorder was the only musical instrument taught. Significantly, the school has changed its name and is now the St Margaret Ward Catholic School and Arts College.

Jan, quite the politician, told *The Sentinel*: 'Robert has a very strong affection for his school and for Mr Bannon, his head-master. He has a vast admiration for him and for his other teachers.' She also explained her own feelings about the charity: 'The charity isn't something I am doing as Robbie Williams' mum. This is me. It's very much in my heart and I'm doing it because I want to do it. It's a vehicle for me to be able to chan-nel my own thoughts and feeling and desires into something. Robert isn't here and I can oversee things and feed them back to him and the committee.'

Her influence was also vital in his acceptance of a role as patron of the Donna Louise Trust, which raises funds for a chil-dren's hospice. Donna Louise Hackney was a local girl who had died of cystic fibrosis when she was sixteen. One of the Trust's committee members, a policeman called Keith Harrison, lived close to Jan and asked her one day if Rob might be interested in helping. It turned out he was. He visited the Trust's Treetops Hospice, which cared for up to eight dying children. Keith recalls that Rob showed a genuine interest and was quite obvi-ously moved by what he saw. One eyewitness reported he was 'almost overwhelmed' by the courage of the sick children. From the age of sixteen, when he joined Take That, Rob became progressively cocooned from real life. When con-fronted by reality, he reacts with compassion.

He makes a real effort to keep abreast of both the Trust and his own charity. He explained, 'When I was growing up in Burslem and Tunstall, it was instilled in me that Stoke-on-Trent people are the best – the most giving, welcoming and generous and the most capable of getting through hard times. And I've got to be honest, I've travelled around the world and you're right – we are!'

Rob's success obviously changed the lives of many people around him, his mother's perhaps the most. Ironically, she seemed to be liberated and was able to travel the world while the boundaries of her son's life gradually grew smaller. Some things did not change, however. When the then headmaster of St Margaret Ward, Conrad Bannon, introduced Jan to the school when she was presenting a cheque on behalf of Give It Sum, he asked, 'Do you know who this is?'

'Yes', shouted a chorus of young voices. 'It's Robbie Williams' mum.'

15

The Occasional Shag

Rob was busy recording his third album when Gary Barlow was dropped by his record label, BMG, in March 2000. He had recently married his long-time girlfriend, a dancer called Dawn Andrews, and the couple were looking forward to the birth of their first child, Daniel, later in the year. Gary was imagining all sorts of cheering at his demise down in 'Robbie-land'. He had won four Ivor Novello Awards for songwriting but it all came to a shuddering halt with one phone call. He sounded optimistic, 'I'm looking forward to having a family, living in the house I've bought and driving the cars I've bought.' The tortoise may, for the moment, have overtaken the hare in the music world but Rob was still behind in the most important of those three particular goals.

Rob had spent much of the previous two years touring and falling off the wagon. His favourite analogy to illustrate his drink and drugs excess is the book of tokens. He believes you are born with a book relating to all the important things in life, such as drink, drugs, sex and love. He 'went off far too early' on the first two, handing over his tokens recklessly until all he had left was a bunch of stubs. He wished he were like Keith Richards of The Rolling Stones, who had 'nicked somebody else's book'. What Rob probably needed was a book with more love tokens.

The glory he received while touring did not help. A record company insider, who has witnessed some of Rob's excesses over the years, believes the adulation is at the root of the cocaine problem. 'When you are live on stage, singing in front of thousands of people who literally "love" you, it is an incredible high. How can you match that feeling? Where do you go? The whole sex, drugs and rock 'n' roll cliché is actually real. The drugs blurred the edges so you feel invincible. I have seen girls at his concerts going in and out of his dressing room to give him blow jobs right up to when he is due to go out on stage. Robbie always wants to push everything as far as he can. He loves himself but he just goes too far.'

For someone who had done rehab, Rob seemed incredibly prone to temptation. He went too far during one utterly debauched night in Dublin, which demonstrated his need to go to excess. At an after-show party he was, according to an eye-witness, 'off his nut' and 'absolutely crazed'. He woke everybody up by banging on the doors of the hotel rooms looking for drugs. At the same time he had various 'good-time girls' in his room keeping the 'pop star' company. One fellow party-goer recalled, 'He ended up crawling around on the floor of the hotel lobby, dribbling from the mouth. There were these two girls, rough as anything, trying to get him up so they could get him back to his room.' Rob did not seem to appreciate that, for him, one drink was all it took.

Rob had nobody special to share his life. After he split from Nic, he was briefly taken with Andrea Corr, the elfin singer with the Irish harmony group The Corrs. They went on a shopping trip to Dublin and hung around a few bars. Rob fuelled interest by losing his temper with a photographer who trailed them to a pub outside Dublin one afternoon. Pressure of work and the rebound factor meant it was pretty much a non-starter. Rob did send her a massive bunch of red roses, but they failed to do the trick.

He was seen out with Billie Piper, then a very pretty teenage pop star. They were introduced to one another by Jonathan Wilkes, at the time Rob's flatmate, and went to a few pubs around Notting Hill, where Rob lived. The *News of the World* quoted a 'friend' who claimed the couple had great sex together – something neither of them commented on. They saw each other only a few times before Billie started a romance with multimillionaire broadcaster Chris Evans, who wooed her with a Ferrari filled with red roses and whom she subsequently married. Rob evidently had the wrong approach: he sent the roses but forgot the Ferrari.

While Rob played the field, one young woman meant a little more in the early part of 2000. Her name was Tania Strecker, presenter of *Naked Elvis*, a late-night, offbeat quiz show on Channel 4. She was a well-connected girl in the same mould as Jacqui Hamilton-Smith. She was absolutely stunning: six feet tall with legs that Rob described as 'going on and on . . . and on'. She was also the first of his real girlfriends to have a child, a three-year-old daughter, Mia. Rob does not find children a problem at all – in fact, quite the opposite. They spent Millennium night in St Moritz and a month later she accompanied him to the Brits.

Tania, who had dated Guy Ritchie before he married Madonna, is the stepdaughter of Rob's manager David Enthoven and had known Rob since the mid-nineties. She had seen for herself the private Rob before she began a closer friendship with him. She is the only woman to receive a glowing mention in *Somebody Someday*, Mark McCrum's evocative account of Robbie Williams on tour in 2000. Rob admitted that he had not had a proper relationship since Nic Appleton but did say that Tania was the last person he 'walked out' with. He complimented her for being a 'nice person'.

The whole world would have liked Rob to conduct a real romance with Kylie Minogue. They first met in the early nineties when he was in Take That and she was the jewel in the crown of Stock, Aitken and Waterman. They were showbiz mates. Rob thought she was tiny and wanted to wrap her in cotton wool. He hoped she would say hello if she saw him walking down the street. Kylie, in return, nominated Rob as her favourite member of Take That and shrewdly thought he would be a star on his own.

In 2000, someone at EMI had the bright idea of putting Kylie and Robbie Williams together. She was on the verge of one of the great comebacks in pop, while Rob was their biggest artist. She had been in independent label wilderness but was now with Parlophone, which, like Chrysalis, was a subsidiary of EMI. The important thing was to reposition her in the marketplace as a mainstream artist; an alliance with Robbie Williams would give her timely credibility. It was not yet cool or chic to admit to liking Kylie Minogue.

Rob readily agreed to write three songs for her comeback album, *Light Years*. He and Guy Chambers came up with the highly camp 'Your Disco Needs You', a smooth, mellow track called 'Loveboat' – because Kylie asked him for a track with that title – and 'Kids', which became their joint single release. Rob also included the track on his new album, *Sing When You're Winning*. The lyrics to 'Kids' are typical Robbie Williams: mischievous and tongue in cheek. Only Rob could come up with a rap rhyming sodomy and Billy Connolly. 'Kids' was a superb bass-driven dance track, although Rob seemed to be struggling with a high-pitched falsetto for most of the song. Surprisingly, it made only number two on release in October, perhaps suffering from not being the first single from the album and from the fact that *Sing When You're Winning* was already a huge-selling record.

The first single was, in fact, one of Rob's most famous. 'Rock DJ' was like Marmite – you either loved it or hated it. More than 600,000 in the UK liked it enough to buy it, making it Rob's third number one and the fifth biggest selling single of the year. The video was more interesting than the song. He is trying to get the attention of a female DJ but fails even when he strips off. So he continues to remove his skin and his flesh and his organs until he is just bones. The special effects won a prize at the MTV Europe Video Awards.

Sing When You're Winning built on the success of the first two albums and brings the curtain down on the first part of Robbie's solo career. He again grafted self-healing, self-revealing lyrics on to decent melodies. There is a hint that Robbie Williams was getting too pleased with himself – from the sleeve's pictures of him celebrating in a football shirt, being carried shoulder-high by other players, all of whom are Rob, to the hidden track at the end of the album. On *Life Thru a Lens* there was one hidden track, on *I've Been Expecting You* there were two, but on this third offering we waited twenty-two minutes and twenty-five seconds to be told, 'No, I'm not doing one.'

Reviews were mainly excellent. *Mojo* magazine described it as his best album yet. *Rolling Stone* noticed the 'melodic wit and stylistic valour'. Even across the Atlantic the signs were promising, with both *Entertainment Weekly* and *Billboard* magazine offering praise. One respected critic, John Aizlewood, suggested that a more apt title, however, would have been *Sing When You're Whining*.

The album contains one of Rob's finest hours, the lyrical lament 'Better Man'. *Q* magazine commented that the track 'made the wondrous "Angels" sound shite.' *Sing When You're Winning* was the bestselling album in the UK in 2000, with about 2.5 million copies sold.

Rob embarked on a gruelling tour to promote the album. Nobody realized yet how much pressure he put on himself touring. At Wembley Arena, he galloped through a mammoth set of seventeen songs, including eight from the new album. The album was relatively new but already songs like 'Supreme' and 'Knutsford City Limits' sounded so familiar. All the Robbie trademarks were on show: the cheeky grin, the heartfelt look that can melt a female heart at thirty paces, the football shirt that declares he's just a lad. There was a feeling that at any carefree moment he might take off all his clothes. There was no set, just a video backdrop, proving that Rob needs no props or diversions to hold centre stage. The encore was masterful: 'My Way' (the Sinatra version, cigarette in hand, just like his dad), 'Millennium', 'Angels' (sung by the crowd naturally, cigarette lighters in the air) and the very silly 'Rock DJ'. Before he left the stage, Rob shouted, 'Are you going to go home happy tonight?' The irony is that the audience probably went home a great deal happier than the performer they had queued for many hours to see.

Superficially, Rob seemed in good form in public. When Kylie joined him on stage in Manchester to perform 'Kids', he had no idea what she was going to wear when she came on. It turned out to be a tiny slip of a costume that left very little to the imagination. Kylie recalls, 'For a second he completely lost it. He was sweating and I loved it.' These sparks were reserved for their professional life, although Rob did enjoy Kylie's company. A record company insider recalls, 'He would follow her around and she was like "Robbie, you stink" but I think she ended up quite liking him really.' Any romance would have been a show business fairy tale but Kylie had a steady boyfriend at the time, James Golding, and there was never anything between her and Rob. That did not stop him enquiring publicly, 'Do you reckon she'd shag me?'

At the time Rob was seeing a lot of Geri Halliwell, the former Spice Girl. They had met when she was still in the group and he was briefly dating Mel C. Geri fulfilled the number one function for any important woman in Rob's life: she mothered him. She had a metaphoric arm around him, giving him security. Jonathan Wilkes described Geri, revealingly, as their big sister. Nobody had suspected there was anything to their friendship until she was spotted leaving Rob's home in Notting Hill in the small hours.

Their first holiday together in St Tropez in August 2000 was paparazzi paradise. It did not escape the notice of cynics that *Sing When You're Winning* was about to be released and Geri's autobiography, *If Only*, had just been published in paperback. The front page of the *Sun* declared: 'Robbie and Geri. It's love.' It was certainly good business, as 'Rock DJ' topped the charts.

They took different flights to Nice but rendezvoused at a villa down the coast that Geri had rented for a couple of weeks. There were plenty of opportunities for the photographers, who fortunately were in prime position right from the start. Soon after arriving, Rob joined Geri at the pool, she in a toned body-revealing bikini, him wearing checked Bermuda shorts. They chatted, swam and dived and played with Geri's beloved shih-tzu, Harry. Then they were off on a scooter tour of the area. Much was made of Geri wrapping her arms around his chest as a gesture of love but it was more likely fear at being his pillion passenger. Geri's red bikini photographed beautifully when she went jet-skiing. The whole jaunt made an excellent photo spread in *OK!* magazine, although her other guests at the villa stayed well away from the photographer's lens.

The couple had time to have a row in a local restaurant, when Geri allegedly was upset at Rob apparently paying too much attention to Clare Staples, the fiancée of hypnotist Paul McKenna. Rob left early after he and Geri exchanged some witty repartee, which involved liberal use of the f-word. Geri was reported as ending the night throwing up in the ladies' loo. It was, perhaps, an early indication that Geri could be just as much of a handful as Rob.

The 'romance' between Geri and Rob has divided opinion between those who think it was a promotional stunt dreamt up by their record company – they were both with EMI – and those who think it was real love. The truth is probably somewhere between the two. The hysterical media coverage of their year-long friendship did raise their profile at useful moments but it was a real relationship. After all, they did not *have* to go on holiday together on several occasions during the year. Geri has constantly denied that she and Rob slept together, although not everyone believes that. A record company insider reveals, 'Geri and Robbie were brought together by the label. They are both following a path but they were shagging. But Geri can be a bit demonic. In fact she is as mad as a fucking hatter.'

Unlike Geri's whirlwind 'romance' with Chris Evans, which lasted about a week at the time of the release of her number one record 'Lift Me Up', an unexpected and genuine affection sprang up between Geri and Rob. In her later book, *Just for the Record*, Geri writes that they were perfect playmates for each other. They also offered mutual support. He was particularly supportive when she admitted to being at her lowest ebb with her eating disorder. Nearly ten years later she revealed on *Piers Morgan's Life Stories* that Robbie had understood her problem and had encouraged her to get proper help. That, she said, had probably saved her life. It was a 'very poignant friendship'.

Unfortunately, Geri was not with Rob to return the favour on two nights when he could have used her friendship and support. They were two of the lowest points in Rob's history of substance snakes and ladders.

The first was in September 2000, when he rolled up to the premiere of the Sex Pistols documentary *The Filth and the Fury* at the Screen on the Green in Islington. It was the start of a night to remember (or forget). Rob was in his best, comic humour when he arrived. A journalist barged up to him to find out why such a poppy person was at a punk premiere. Rob, ever the actor, looked confused: 'I've come to see *Toy Story 2*, me,' he said. The reporter then asked if there would ever be a Take That movie. 'There is one in production,' said Rob, deadpan. 'It will be a bit like *Absolute Beginners*. We're thinking of calling it *Absolute Shit.*' After the film he had a pee up against a wall before hooking up with actor Nick Moran for a trip to the fashionable West End drinking club Soho House. Rob only popped in for one but ended the night the worse for wear in Stringfellows, minus his clothes. Until then he had been clean for more than six months.

The second, almost cataclysmic, night of shame occurred in Stockholm at the EMI party following the 2000 MTV Awards in November. Rumours were already rife that he was on a downward spiral at the time, after shooting for the video of his single 'Supreme' had to be cut short because Robbie was, as a spokesman said, 'suffering from severe exhaustion and gastroenteritis'. Exhaustion in celebrity circles invariably signals that drink or drugs have got the better of a particular star. Rob travelled to Sweden, perhaps against the best advice, and performed his duet with Kylie Minogue at the awards ceremony. At the subsequent party he got into a row with Nellee Hooper.

The millionaire record producer is very much his own man and does not suffer fools. He has his own inner circle, a tight-knit 'crew' of which Robbie Williams was most definitely not a part. A friend explained, 'Nellee has a class and elegance and likes to surround himself with beautiful girls and rich friends from the upper echelons of society. He also likes to be the centre of attention and would not appreciate Robbie if he was in over-the-top mode and behaving like a twat.' Their antipathy towards one another would not have been helped by Nellee's friendship with Jacqui Hamilton-Smith.

On seeing Rob at the party, Nellee allegedly told him a few home truths. Rob ended up punching him in the face. Nellee, who is a fair bit smaller than Rob, responded by kicking him in the goolies. They then started rolling around on the floor and Rob ripped Nellee's shirt before being hauled off by his bodyguard. Like a good lad who believes a fight is an excellent start to an evening, Rob then proceeded to get hammered on sambuca before being helped to his bed. It was even suggested that he ended the night foaming at the mouth but this was denied the next day by a spokesman for his record company, who claimed he was 'exhausted' and that the whole Nellee incident was a 'simple misunderstanding'. Rob was whisked off to a hotel in Barbados for a good rest. He later admitted that he had been drunk but also said he had flu.

When he returned, Geri was there to fuss over him. They spent a low-key New Year, at Rob's suggestion, in the Swiss ski resort of Gstaad, having a laugh together. They went ice skating, with Rob gallantly preventing Geri from falling over. He was pretty nifty on skates, having had tuition from former Olympic champion Robin Cousins, now a judge on *Dancing on Ice*, when he was filming the video for his number one 'She's The One', which was set in an ice rink.

Geri flew to LA with Rob after the New Year 2001 and all seemed well. She went with him to AA meetings, waiting patiently outside to see him safely home. She would spend hours chatting to the wives and girlfriends of the addicts inside. Friends thought Geri saw herself as a guardian angel to Rob. Somewhere along the line, however, Rob and Geri fell out, which is a shame considering how close they were for a time.

The change in their relationship seems to have coincided with Rob revealing, with deliberate indiscretion, that they were friends who enjoyed 'the occasional shag'. At a charity auction held at Sotheby's in April 2001, he auctioned off his pants, with a picture of a tiger on the crotch and announced, 'These are the pants I shagged Geri in.' Geri thought it a typical lad's silly boast, and, as part of a robust denial, let him know she found it upsetting. After this incident, Rob is barely mentioned in her autobiography. He did not feature when she talked about her life in LA even though, by then, he was living in the same city. Confrontation between the two had probably been inevitable – they are both strong-willed, used to getting their own way and liable to fluctuate between euphoric highs and dismal lows.

The world got the message that Rob and Geri were no longer best mates when she ended up on the cutting-room floor of the documentary *Nobody Someday*, the film of the best-selling book of his life on tour. He famously described her to journalist and friend Adrian Deevoy, as a 'demonic little girl playing with dolls and a tea set.'

16

Me and My Shadow

One of the more surprising songs on the soundtrack of the hit film *Bridget Jones's Diary* was Robbie Williams singing the Frank Sinatra classic 'Have You Met Miss Jones?'. You could almost hear people wondering, 'Is that Robbie?' The film was a big hit worldwide, including in the US, where he was asked to perform the song on the *Tonight Show with Jay Leno*.

The performance went down really well and Rob began to wonder if he could record a swing album dedicated to Frank, Dean Martin and Sammy Davis, Jr – the famous Rat Pack. On hearing of the plan, Guy Chambers was impressed enough to observe that it was as if he was born to do it. They began to work in earnest selecting the songs for the album that would become *Swing When Your Winning*.

Few outside the pubs and bars of Stoke-on-Trent would have been aware of Rob's lifetime devotion to Sinatra and his great contemporaries. In *Somebody Someday*, Mark McCrum describes how, before going on stage, Rob kisses photographs of Frank, Dean, Sammy and Muhammad Ali in turn. The first three knew how to swing and the great boxer knew how to win.

Practically everybody in his home town had heard him sing 'Mack the Knife'. While not associated with Frank, the song, from *The Threepenny Opera*, is one of the most evocative tunes of the big band era and invariably features on *The X Factor*'s big band week. For years it has been Rob's favourite song to perform at karaoke or at parties.

He had first heard his father sing it at a holiday camp – a typical space filler between jokes for a crooning comedian. Eric Tams, who heard father and son perform together when Rob was a lad, recalls, 'Pete used to sing a lot of the songs on the *Swing* album. He used to stand there and he would get a fag out and sing them all while he smoked. When Rob did them, I heard Pete singing as well. Pete's got more of an American drawl. He listened to the records and Rob listened to his dad.'

Coco Colclough recalls Rob singing 'Mack the Knife': 'He used to love that. One of the things about Rob was that you would be in a pub and you would say, "Rob, get up on the table and sing" and he would do it. The rest of us would have needed to have had twelve pints to get up on a table and then we would have fallen off.' Lee Hancock remembers a fortieth birthday party for Eileen Wilkes at The Place in Hanley, when someone shouted out, 'Sing this one here, Rob, "Mack the Knife".' Lee had never heard it before but recalls, 'It was absolutely fantastic.' It was the first time he realized that Rob really could sing.

Even when he was in Take That and was supposed to rest his voice when not working, Rob could not resist getting up. Eric Tams heard him perform at the open mic night at the Sneyd Arms in Tunstall after he'd had one too many: 'He came off and said, "Don't you dare ask me to get up there again!" He was a bit over the top with drink.'

'Mack the Knife' and the songs of Sinatra were ideal for young Rob because he could use his theatrical talents to interpret the songs. Zoë Hammond observes, 'It suited him to do something where he could really play up and act.' She also recalls that he already loved Frank's music when they were acting together as children: 'That wasn't just a thing that happened as he grew up. He loved him even when he was a little lad. I knew he grew up on that sort of thing. If we were rehearsing, he would stand at the piano and lean across like they did in those old black and white films. He would move about as though he was taking that era off. When I saw him do the concert of *Swing When You're Winning* on the telly, I said to my mum, "God, it's dead freaky", because it just took me back to watching him when he was podgy and little. He was brilliant.'

Frank Sinatra was peerless in his ability to interpret a song. He had no equal in finding fresh nuances in rhymes as hackneyed as moon and June or love and marriage going together like a horse and carriage. The sneering killjoys in the music criticism business took great delight in denouncing Rob's musical tribute as impoverished fare, which was mean-spirited and totally missed the point. *Swing When You're Winning* was not meant to be a copy of Sinatra or Dean Martin or Sammy Davis. It was a celebration of their style, which brought their music to several million younger listeners who had probably never heard of these greats.

Rob and Guy wrote an introductory number, 'I Will Talk and Hollywood Will Listen', which set the tone and also ensured some publishing royalties for them from sales. 'Mack the Knife' naturally followed, as well as – thanks to technology – a duet with Frank on 'It Was A Very Good Year'. Rob was thrilled that Sinatra's estate gave him permission and described it as a dream come true. He added wistfully, 'I hope Frank likes it.'

For many, however, the highlight was Rob's interpretation of 'Mr Bojangles'. The song tells the story of legendary tap dancer Bill Robinson and became famous as a show-stopper for Sammy Davis, Jr. Even Rob admitted to getting overcome with emotion when it came to singing the climactic line 'Oh Lord, when he shook his head'.

The fans loved it. *Swing When Your Winning* went straight to the top of the charts in November 2001 and stayed there for six weeks. It went on to sell more than two million copies in the UK and seven million worldwide. Rob had the Christmas number one in both the album and singles charts.

The only single release from *Swing* was 'Somethin' Stupid', a duet with Nicole Kidman. The song had first been a hit for Frank Sinatra and his daughter Nancy in 1967. After her enormous success with the film *Moulin Rouge*, in which she sang, Rob met Nicole in Los Angeles and persuaded her to record the duet. Their version breathed fresh life into the classic song. The video was even better. Shot in a bedroom, it was sensual and sexy, with Rob and Nicole entwined in steamy embraces.

The pair were very complimentary about each other. Rob said he was worried when they met that he would behave like an idiot or try to lick her face. Instead they had chatted and he'd had a 'real blast' with her. Nicole agreed that it was fun, that Robbie was very talented and that she was seriously thinking of getting a tattoo on her ankle. One of Rob's endearing characteristics is that he can be a little starstruck at times. He was mesmerized by the Kidman scent – three parts vanilla and one part musk. For her part, Nicole was nervous recording a song with a famous pop star. In the end, the recording took little more than an hour. They spent far longer promoting it.

Nicole flew into London in early October for a cosy chat with Michael Parkinson for his show *Parkinson*, and Rob courteously acted as her host for a day before the recording. He took her go-karting and bought her an expensive dinner before a visit to the blackjack tables, where she had to lend him £100.

The gossip frenzy began the following night. Nicole, wearing a smart black suit, white shirt and tie, went straight from filming *Parkinson* back to the Dorchester Hotel at 9.30p.m.; five minutes later, Rob arrived. He was wearing tracksuit bottoms and a cricket jumper and went straight up to her suite. It was apparently the second night in a row he had visited her. He was clocked by the *News of the World* leaving at 2.55a.m. precisely. They had enjoyed room service together, bottled beer for her and soft drinks for him. When he left, he was smiling and chatting on a mobile phone. A spokeswoman for Robbie reportedly confirmed that he spent the night in Nicole's room. He hardly 'spent the night', which in pop star terms had only just begun. The spokeswoman added, 'They are friends and they were hanging out', which was a lot nearer the truth.

The device of putting two stars together romantically to promote a film or a record is becoming such a cliché. PRs love it. Bookmakers offered odds of 16–1 that Rob and Nicole would wed in the new year, 2002. There was a better chance of Rob flying to the moon. The whole thing degenerated into farce when two blonde, ex-lap dancers from the London club Spearmint Rhino claimed they had enjoyed a threesome with Rob just hours before his first visit to the Dorchester and that he was an 'astonishing' lover. They had apparently met Rob when they delivered junk mail to his house. Nicole Kidman? The romping ex-lap dancers? Where does the truth lie? The truth is that it really doesn't matter because it was just a bit of fun and nobody got hurt. Rob has not been spotted any time since in Nicole Kidman's hotel room. They did have a laugh together, though. Rob may be arrogant at times but he is not a no-conversation, self-preening bore.

Unreported but far more relevant to the real Rob was his encounter with an attractive girl he picked up one night after spotting her in a London club. She was thrilled to be getting off with a star like Robbie Williams and was expecting to tell her friends the next day of her fantastic night of passion. But when they arrived at his house, instead of sweeping her up in his arms, he just wanted to talk.

Rob had his own Rat Pack but they were not a group of impressively famous people falling over their egos. Rob was at the centre, of course, but by his side was his best friend, Jonathan

Wilkes. After the devastation of his split from Nic Appleton it was Jonty, as friends and family call him, who helped him pick up the pieces. Their relationship is a vitally important one in Rob's life. Jonty is the footballing, drinking, singing, acting, golfing, pinball-playing mate who understands what it is like to be a lad who grew up in Stoke-on-Trent. Far from being a chancer hanging on to the coat tails of a famous friend, Jonathan was the rock offering Rob support when he was down and nearly out.

They are not related, although many people believe them to be. They were never neighbours nor did they go to the same school, belong to the same golf club or 'grow up together'. Their mothers, Jan Williams and Eileen Wilkes, met by chance on holiday in Majorca and hit it off immediately. Little Jonty was four and Robert, as he was always introduced, was nearly five years older. Both boys had elder sisters – Kay Wilkes, whom they were always a little frightened of, was Rob's age – as well as lively mums who liked getting out and having a laugh together and dads who were larger-than-life characters who could light up any room they were in. Graham Wilkes, Jonty's father, who died in 2008, was a well-known face in the world of entertainment and sport in the Potteries through his role as a professional toastmaster. His signed photograph hangs on the wall of a Tunstall curry house – a sure sign of local celebrity.

When Jan and Eileen returned home from Majorca they decided to keep in touch. They shared an enthusiasm for musicals and the theatre – an interest that would bring their sons together. Rob and Jonty were members of the chorus of children in *Hans Christian Andersen* not long after they met. For once, Rob did not have to worry about being accepted. Jonty was his young acolyte who hung on his every word. So much so that during a performance at the Theatre Royal in Hanley, Rob persuaded his young chum that there was a change in the script that night and they should lift up their nightshirts and reveal their bottoms to the audience. The cheeky ingredient, so important to the Robbie Williams image, is a quality he was born with. He has never been slow to flash his bum – or any other part of his anatomy – if he thinks it will get a reaction.

Zoë Hammond remembers Jonty as a little 'lard-arse', which means 'cry baby' in the local slang: 'He couldn't take anything as a kid. You'd only have to say to Jonathan, "Why have you come in then?" and he'd be squealing. And he'd make it quite clear to everybody around him that he didn't like what you had said. He was a bit of a creep at times but he was very small.'

Rachael Gilson, who was at school with Jonty's sister, Kay, would see him when she went round to the Wilkes's house. Her mother, Margaret Heath, recalls, 'Rachael said he was always a flipping nuisance. They were forever having to throw him out of the bedroom. I remember him being in the local shop. He was a gorgeous little boy with blond hair and he would go straight to the front of the queue and you would always forgive him because he was so cute.'

Even Eileen Wilkes admits her son could 'always cry easily and turn the taps on'. That is why one of the boys' favourite childhood turns was doing a Laurel and Hardy double act for their families. Rob, bigger and chubbier, would be fat Ollie, while Jonty, small and skinny, would be Stan, contorting his face into the comedian's famous blubbing expression.

Rob, such a brilliant mimic and a genuinely funny boy, gave Jonty the confidence to perform himself, even if in those days he was very young and not much good. Jonathan admits that, when he was a little kid, Rob was like his big brother. He was also a role model, the boy Jonathan aspired to be. They did not, however, live in each other's pockets as children. While Rob lived in Tunstall and went to St Margaret Ward High School, Jonathan was five miles away in Endon and attended the Hillside Primary School and Endon High School. Like all good friends, they could always pick up where they left off. 'They had a natural rapport,' observes Eileen Wilkes. 'They used to laugh all the time, even if they hadn't seen each other for weeks or months at a time.'

The Williams and Wilkes families cemented their friendship by joining up in the school holidays to go caravanning or, sometimes, skiing. 'If there was a talent competition where we were, then the boys were always the first up,' recalls Eileen. 'They both had great confidence to play to a crowd.' There was no doubt who was the more talented. Rob was an accomplished entertainer as a boy, while Jonty had a voice like a foghorn.

'You couldn't compare the two. I'm not being horrible but Jonathan wasn't a patch on Rob,' says Zoë Hammond. 'But there was an age gap and I do remember that Jonathan really loved the theatre.' The difference in their ages never seemed to affect their friendship: 'They were definitely mates even though Jonathan was younger.'

When he was with Jonathan, Rob was less likely to get up to mischief, preferring a game of Monopoly to causing trouble in Tunstall Park. Eileen Wilkes's explanation for a friendship that was unaffected by the difference in their ages is that her son has always been 'more grown up for his age and Robert not so grown up'. That view would be reinforced when the friends started living together in London a few years later. In the meantime, they joined their mothers in Olde Time Music Hall and Jonathan had a very small role in *Oliver!*, which proved to be such an important production in the development of Robbie Williams the performer.

Jonathan shared Rob's aversion to school work, preferring to play football and support Port Vale. He lived and breathed football. He was even Vale's mascot for one game. There is no greater honour for a young fan than to walk out on to his team's pitch dressed in the squad colours, surrounded by his heroes.

For a while, it looked as if the course of the two friends' lives would diverge irrevocably. While Rob's ambitions for stardom were taking shape in Take That, Jonathan was on the threshold of a career as a professional footballer. He was captain of Stoke-on-Trent Schoolboys and, at one time, was on the books of their beloved Vale. More promisingly, Jonathan was taken on by Everton as an adolescent defender when he was spotted by a scout while playing alongside his father Graham in a local lads and dads team. Twice a week, he would make the journey to Merseyside to rub shoulders with other young hopefuls.

The highlight of Jonathan's footballing life was when he played against Liverpool, who featured a certain Michael Owen in their boys' team. Sadly, the Everton lads were trounced 4–0, with the England striker of the future scoring all four. Guess who was meant to be marking Owen? Despite that setback, Jonathan was absolutely certain that his future revolved around the 'beautiful game'. 'Football was my life,' he admitted. 'It was all I knew.' Alas, his hopes were dashed by his lack of size. One of the chief Everton backroom boys told him when he was fifteen: 'You're not going to be good enough for Everton, son, you're too small.'

Jonathan was devastated and quickly became disillusioned with the football scene. He tried a week at lowly Chester FC but was totally disinterested. A couple of other offers from Wrexham and Crewe came in but barely raised a shrug of the shoulders. After being so close to a career with a top club, nothing else seemed worth getting out of bed for. While Rob's career was at its Take That zenith, his old pal from Stoke-on-Trent felt at rock bottom: he'd just turned sixteen with no academic qualifications to speak of, no prospects and no idea what to do.

He did exactly what Rob would have done under the circumstances: he went on a six-month spree of drinking bitter, putting on loads of weight and feeling rebellious. The one bright point in this teenage torment came when he had his tonsils out. His mother, Eileen, recalls, 'Miraculously he could sing afterwards. He really got into the singing lark.' Jonty discovered that when he went up to do karaoke, it no longer cleared the pub. He also tried his hand at a few jokes and a bit of banter and discovered he liked being an entertainer. He even produced a demo of a song cheerily entitled 'You Are Always Going To Be Alone'. He pulled himself together, confident that he could 'sing and make people laugh'. He also, according to Eileen, started 'sleeping in a grobag', which resulted in his height spurting upwards to over six feet. His present height of 6ft 3in makes the Everton rejection seem slightly comical now.

It was his father, Graham, who managed to kick-start Jonathan's show business career by using his contacts to help secure him a Blackpool season. Jonathan became the youngest headliner in the resort, doing an exhausting twenty-nine songs a night, seven days a week. His show business break had absolutely nothing to do with Robbie Williams, although Rob would take every opportunity to visit his pal so that he could spend the day on the famous Blackpool rides. Jonathan was seventeen when he started in Blackpool and only twenty when his three-year contract came to an end. It was the making of him. *Jonathan Wilkes and the Space Girls* became one of the most popular shows in town and, for the teenager, surrounded by girl dancers and with good money in his pocket, it was as if he had died and gone to heaven.

Blackpool is a quintessential English institution, cheesier than a pound of Stilton. It was a million miles away from the cool youth culture of mid-nineties Britain. While Rob aspired to a legitimate Glastonbury music scene, his mate was appearing in charity shows alongside the Grumbleweeds, Schnorbitz, Frank Carson and Joe Longthorne. Jonathan was a prizewinner in the Cameron Mackintosh Young Entertainer of the Year competition when he impressed the judges with his Tom Jones-style rendition of the Prince song 'Kiss'. The irony is that Jonathan was living the sort of career that was Rob's heritage – the mainstream cabaret of Pete Conway. He was fast becoming an accomplished performer: 'I had to sing the same bloody songs every night and try and make them believable to an audience that was the toughest in the world.' He may not have been breaking into the consciousness of Take That fans but Jonathan Wilkes was a huge favourite among the Lancashire granny set.

Jonathan's ambitions stretched further than Blackpool Tower, so he jumped at the opportunity to present a television programme called *The Hype* for the former digital channel BBC Choice. It would mean moving down to London. When he mentioned it to Rob, his friend did not hesitate to invite him to live with him in Notting Hill in what Graham Wilkes described as a lads' paradise: 'They had pinball, table football and the biggest television you have ever seen.' Pride of place was a platinum pool table that Rob had bought in a swanky shop in New York. He had popped in wearing jeans and the shop assistant assumed incorrectly that it was well out of his price bracket at a quarter of a million dollars. 'I'll take it,' said Rob casually, handing over his credit card, much to everyone's amazement.

The roles of the two friends were subtly changing. Jonathan was no longer the snotty kid described by Robbie as a 'little twat'. Instead, he became the big brother and protector. 'There may be an age gap but it would always be Jonathan, looking out for Robert, who would say at the end of the evening, "Let's go, mate,"' observes Eileen Wilkes. It was Jonathan, at the time of Rob's worst drink and drugs excesses, who would be desperately trying to stop hangers-on providing his friend with supplies.

They shared a special bond. Jonathan was the only person – apart, perhaps, from Jan Williams – who could say to Rob, 'Oi, you're being a bit of a prick here.' When Jonathan had a bad car accident while he was doing a pantomime in Scotland, Rob rang him up on the hour, every hour, to cheer him up, telling jokes and dusting off his Frank Spencer voice. In the eyes of the army of Robbie Williams fans, Jonathan Wilkes was officially the 'best friend'.

Inevitably, thoughts turned to a career in pop music for Jonathan. His father had found him new management and a deal soon followed with Innocent Records, an imprint of Virgin and label of Billie Piper and Martine McCutcheon. Rob was delighted at the thought of sharing his world with his buddy. He declared, 'It will be like Popstar Towers at our house.'

They already used to have songwriting competitions in which they would give themselves five minutes to cobble together a smash hit. During one such game at a villa in the south of France, Rob wrote a truly awful song called 'Where's Your Saviour Now'. Frustrated, he closed his eyes and prayed, 'John Lennon, if you're there, send us a song.' He then proceeded to write the sublime 'Better Man' in half an hour. Jonathan wrote one called 'Dave's House', which was pencilled in for his first album. It all seemed a little too easy.

The general public, not realizing that Jonathan had already served a tough apprenticeship, could be forgiven for thinking he was a young man enjoying the privilege of success thanks to his friendship with the nation's favourite pop star. Jonathan could hardly complain when Robbie Williams was the number one topic of any interview he gave on the release of his first single, 'Just Another Day', a song he wrote himself when he was 'having a really bad day'. It was released amid a blaze of serious media interest – seventy-five interviews in two weeks – but entered the charts at a profoundly disappointing number twenty-four which, considering how the charts work these days, is absolutely nowhere.

Perhaps there was a built-in resentment factor against Jonathan because of his connection to Robbie. The howls of derision began. This was very problematic, as an album, *Borrowed Wings*, was finished and a second single, co-written with Canadian rock star Bryan Adams, was ready to go. The single reached number one in Dubai, Sweden and Germany but that was not enough to prevent Innocent, who had spent £1 million trying to muscle the song into the UK top three, from putting the album 'on hold'. A five-album deal bit the dust and Jonathan was officially dropped by the record company.

Jonathan was very proud of the album. He had written and recorded it while still presenting on television. Rob contributed two songs, one unintentionally. Jonathan won 'Sexed Up' from him as a side bet during a game of pool. Rob would eventually take it back for a future album, claiming that he would write him another one. He did, however, do Jonathan an enormous favour by persuading him to perform the duet 'Me and My Shadow' and, just as importantly, to go on stage at the Royal Albert Hall and sing it before a live audience. It revealed that Jonathan could genuinely sing and was an accomplished performer in his own right. He also showed he was the master of the cheesy showbiz remark when he declared, '"Me and My Shadow" is the perfect best-mate song.' The one-off concert of the *Swing* album was a fantastic success and the sales of both video – one of the most successful ever – and album provided Jonathan with a tidy nest egg and helped him to finance a new £600,000 house in Chiswick, round the corner from his friends Ant and Dec.

The performance at the Albert Hall was not the first time they had appeared on stage together to sing a duet. When Jonathan was performing the Robbie Williams' song 'She's The One' during a concert in Brighton, the man himself unexpectedly came on stage and casually asked, 'Do you want a hand, mate?' Jonathan, who was as surprised as the audience, replied, 'I could do with one, mate.' On another occasion, when Jonathan was in panto, Rob hijacked the event by coming on stage in the middle of a song. He was dressed as a gorilla.

Jonathan and Rob's friendship is unlikely to be broken by events or geography. Rob has 1023 tattooed on the topside of his wrist. 10 stands for the letter J and 23 for the letter W. Jonathan, who has never gone in for tattoos, has 1823 etched on his wrist, representing the letters RW for Rob.

Jonathan's is the voice of normality, the good guy part of his friend's conscience. He is very middle of the road and an ordinary bloke. His favourite album is *James Taylor's Greatest Hits* and he prefers Ribena to Guinness. He shares Rob's affection for Stoke-on-Trent; when they shared a flat, the pair of them would order oatcakes from the High Lane Oatcake Shop to be sent to them in London. If Jonathan took Rob round to his parents' house, Eileen would tell him, 'Put the kettle on, Robert.' It was a valuable dose of normality for a superstar surrounded, inevitably, by superficial yes-men.

PART THREE

ESCAPE TO LA

17

Mulholland Drive

Rob was at a crossroads in his life. At the end of 2001 he badly needed to change things. He could not settle in London, where he was feeling increasingly imprisoned and generally down. He would open his bedroom curtains to be greeted by a telephoto lens and a group of pointing girl fans, usually Italian. As far as he was concerned, his life had become like *Groundhog Day*, a ghastly repetition of the worst day of your life. He could no longer go out to the pub or local café without so much hassle that all he wanted to do was rush back home, slump on a sofa and watch the History Channel on his giant TV. His fame had become out of control and the days of going out with his mates to have a laugh, tell jokes and play football were long gone.

Jonathan Wilkes was moving on with his life, so he couldn't offer as much support as in the previous few years. He had moved out of the flat, setting up home in Chiswick with his girlfriend, a dancer called Nikki Wheeler.

Since Tania Strecker, Rob had not had a proper girlfriend and there seemed little chance of him finding one in the goldfish bowl his life had become. His every move was forensically examined and it created a climate of mistrust. There would always be available lap dancers but he was unlikely to find the first Mrs Williams hiding behind a thong in a strip joint. Rob could always have one-night stands.

A record company executive recalls when Rob was in a Holborn club one evening. He was chatting and laughing with a group of friends and appeared not to have noticed the attractive blonde in high heels and figure-hugging dress, who was perched on a bar stool. Eventually he got up, went over to where she was sitting, whispered a few words in her ear and went back to his table.

'What did he say?' asked the woman sitting next to her.

'He just said, "Come home with me", but I've got a boyfriend.'

The woman exclaimed, 'But it's Robbie!'

A minute or two passed before Rob got up, said his goodbyes and, without glancing over, strode out the door. Five seconds later the blonde picked up her bag and tottered after him. That was the reality of life in London but, as he graciously once put it, a one-night stand was having a wank in someone else's body.

Rob recorded most of *Swing When You're Winning* in Los Angeles. He liked the place. Nobody bothered him because hardly anyone knew who he was. Just as importantly, he felt safer. He doesn't advertise the fact too much but Rob worries about his personal safety. He had been able to cope with being given a tough time by Stoke City fans but the prospect of 'deranged' fans of Robbie Williams was a different matter.

Rob had bodyguards around as part of his daily life and he'd become used to it. But nothing can prepare you for the element of surprise, as Leona Lewis found out in October 2009, when she was punched in the face at a harmless book signing in Piccadilly. Rob's 'Leona' moment came at a concert at the Hanns-Martin-Schleyer-Halle in Stuttgart on 21 February 2001. A crazed fan dashed on stage while he was singing 'Supreme' and pushed him off because he believed he was not the real Robbie Williams but an impostor. Apparently he thought the real Robbie was elsewhere. Rob fell five feet into the area normally occupied by a photographer or two taking pictures. Security came to his rescue and hauled his attacker off him.

Rob was much shaken but, to everyone's surprise, he did not storm off and play the wounded martyr. Instead, he got back on to the stage and asked the audience if they were OK. When they shouted, 'Yeah!' he responded, 'Well, so am I. And I'm not going to let any fucker get on stage and stop you having a good time.' He powered his way through the rest of the concert before deciding that he wanted to get out of Stuttgart immediately.

Although everybody was impressed by Rob's mature reaction on the night, the unspoken question that hung in the air was: 'What if the attacker had been brandishing a knife?' Fans have run on to stages before and usually the artist can deal with it – Keith Richards used to whack fans with his guitar if they came too close – but Rob, who is not a little fellow, had no chance to react. Jonathan Wilkes said he spoke to Rob straight after it happened: 'It shook me up and it shook him up. He was shocked and scared.'

As a result, Rob could no longer feel comfortable about someone rushing up to him with an autograph book or hearing the doorbell ring in the middle of the night. He had survived his 'surprise' moment. John Lennon, famously, did not.

Security and anonymity were two of the three main reasons why Rob decided to move to LA. The third reason, little realized at the time, was his struggle with confidence. As Robbie Williams he had been able to conceal his insecurity behind swagger and bravado. It had always been there, however – the feeling that he was not worthy of the applause. During the last tour it had got so bad that he wouldn't go on stage in Ireland without Jonathan in the wings to support him. Eileen Wilkes says, 'It was a low time. Robert was on such a downer. He lost his confidence and just felt he wasn't good enough.'

Unsurprisingly, David Enthoven gave Rob his full support when he suggested that he might spend six months in the California sunshine. It was agreed that he needed to recharge his batteries after a punishing schedule. Mark McCrum reported that Rob was keen to dispense with the pressures of being Robbie Williams for a while. Rob said he was looking forward to living a more normal existence. LA may have seemed an odd destination for anyone seeking a dose of normality but the city has so many celebrities that it is used to them and there is no novelty factor. There's always somebody you recognize at the next table in a coffee shop. If Rob had decided to get away from it all at a mountain retreat in Peru, you could guarantee that he would have become a one-man tourist destination. In the decaf society of Hollywood and beyond, however, he could be seen standing in line to buy a latte at the Malibu branch of Starbucks and nobody would raise an eyebrow.

Rob still made sure he had adequate personal protection when he moved into the Sunset Marquis Hotel in West Hollywood to begin his exile. He stayed there for several months before renting, for $15,000 a month, a Tudor-style house in Beverly Hills, complete with compulsory swimming pool, which belonged to the actor and comedian Dan Ackroyd. He could have bought a small house in Tunstall for the price of a short let but there was no point yet in buying a house if he really was going to stay just six months.

Rob had made one or two friends in LA before his move. He met Ashley Hamilton at an AA meeting and the two hung out together. Ashley was the stepson of Rod Stewart, who had been married to his mother, Alana Hamilton, while he was growing up. He had married the actress Shannon Doherty, star of *Beverly Hills 90210*, after knowing her for just two weeks. He was very Hollywood but enjoyed Rob's company, 'He is so cool. We have a lot in common.'

One of the things they had in common was a love of tattoos and Ashley introduced Rob to the Shamrock Tattoo Parlor on West Sunset Boulevard. Rob was happy to help Ashley with his ambition to break into the music business. They even worked on some songs together and one of them, 'Wimmin', a typically raucous Robbie track, was released in the UK in May 2003 but failed to make much impact. Ashley was one of the co-writers on the track 'Come Undone', which Rob saved for his next album. They were never best friends but they enjoyed each other's company for a while.

Rob's closest new friend was the actor Max Beesley. The two enjoyed the same sense of humour. Max was already well known on British TV screens but not many realized he was also an accomplished musician. His father was a jazz drummer and his mother a singer, and as a young man it looked as if he would follow in their footsteps. He studied percussion at the Guildhall School of Music in London before finding work as a keyboard player and drummer on tour with the group Brand New Heavies. He met Rob when he was drumming with Take That on tour in the early days of the group. He chose acting over music, however, and was looking to break into Hollywood when he hooked up with Rob again. That ambition was thwarted, at least temporarily, when he co-starred with Mariah Carey in *Glitter*, widely thought to be one of the worst films of all time.

Max would join Rob for jam sessions at his house and then the two would go to gigs together in some of the least public venues in the city. He was almost as paranoid as Rob about the paparazzi, having been pursued relentlessly during a three-year relationship with Mel B (Scary Spice), which had just ended. He had also had a number of other celebrity girlfriends, although he maintained that he enjoyed the quiet life when he stayed with Rob. One girl, who spoke to the newspapers, suggested, however, that the pair referred to Rob's house as Pants-Down Palace.

In these early LA days, Rob was keen to watch as many gigs as he could. One of the first concerts he went to was Aerosmith at the Forum. Aerosmith are huge in the US and provided Rob with an early indication that in LA he would not be the centre of attention every minute of the day. Photographer Fraser Harrison, who was at the gig, recalls, 'He was walking around backstage very aimlessly. He hadn't been drinking at all and was just sipping from a can of Coke. He was in a good and relaxed mood. I think he was getting used to being seen out in public over here, although nobody really recognized who he was.'

Routine is very important to Rob, perhaps because of his addictions. In London, that routine consisted of staying in bed until lunchtime but nobody does that in LA. Rob soon found himself getting up early, grabbing a coffee and chatting to new friends before heading off to the Crunch gym on Sunset. This is not a gym for the man or woman with a fuller figure but one where the bodies beautiful of this world tone and preen themselves. A frosted glass panel separates the men's showers from the lobby, so many a masculine silhouette can be admired from reception.

One of the first things Rob had done in LA was to check out the AA and NA meetings. He does it in every new city. He started attending the Red Hut on Sunset where, on any given day, he might bump into Matt Perry or Robert Downey, Jr. Not everyone at these meetings is an addict; some are just there to make connections and others are journalists hunting some juicy gossip. Rob, however, stood a better chance of making real friends at a meeting than in a singles bar on Sunset.

An enormous bonus for Rob was the presence of his right-hand woman, Josie Cliff. Josie, who is about the same age as Rob, was described by Mark McCrum as 'scarily switched on'. That may be so but she seems to know how to handle Rob and he trusts her implicitly. As a thank you and a gesture of their ongoing friendship, Rob sang at her Malibu wedding to Lee

Lodge, the producer of his live shows. A wonderful exchange, observed by the writer Chris Heath when he was staying with Rob to gather material for the riveting portrait *Feel*, brilliantly sums up the relationship between the two. Josie asks Rob if he needs anything and he replies that he needs the love of a good woman. Josie says that can be arranged but Rob insists that he wants a *good* woman. Josie, without hesitation, responds, 'Coffee in the meantime?'

The British community in Los Angeles, rather like in other major cities around the world, still has the feel of the colonies about it. Everyone may wear shorts and swimsuits instead of tuxedos and cocktail dresses but the principle of (non-alcoholic) drinks before dinner is basically the same. When Rob joined them, the king and queen of the British community were Sharon and Ozzy Osbourne. They welcomed Rob into their world with great warmth and friendship. One of the highlights of Rob's week was Sunday lunch at the Osbournes'.

When Ozzie received a star on the Hollywood Walk of Fame, Robbie Williams went along to support him. Journalist Cliff Renfrew, who was there, recalls, 'Robbie was roundly booed by the crowd when he was introduced. It was really because they didn't have a clue who he was.' Ozzy and Rob can relate because of their mutual problems with drink and drugs over the years. And, despite his rock 'n' roll history, Ozzy is quite a family man, which Rob admires.

Sharon Osbourne remains hugely popular with the British community in LA. She is down to earth, pragmatic and cares deeply about her family – just like Jan Williams. Cliff Renfrew observes, 'Sharon is like a second mother to Rob over here.' As a gesture of family friendship Rob invited Kelly Osbourne, Sharon and Ozzy's daughter, to be his support act for the 21-date European tour he was planning in the summer of 2003.

Rob was also able to relate to the problems of Jack Osbourne, the teenage son who ended up in rehab in the spring of 2003. Jack's is a classic case of too much too young, rather like Rob in Take That. Jack's bad behaviour, however, seems very tame compared to Rob's debauched excess. One friend explained, 'Jack is only seventeen and he is just trying to find himself.' Sharon Osbourne was in tears after she visited Jack at the clinic in Pasadena. The best person to give her advice, of course, is Jan, drugs counsellor and mother to errant pop star.

Tom Jones was another icon who lived not far away and the two had got on well since the Brits in 1998. Rob had been to see Tom's show in Las Vegas and Tom had taken the trouble to give him a mention so that Rob could stand up and take a bow. On another occasion, Rob went round to Tom's Bel Air mansion and was surprised not to see his long-suffering wife, Maureen, who has shunned the limelight for forty years. Apparently, she was nervous about meeting a star of Rob's magnitude and had to be coaxed downstairs for an introduction.

Through his friendship with Ashley Hamilton, Rob met Rod Stewart's daughter, Kimberly Stewart, Ashley's half-sister. They were thought at one time to be enjoying a romance but, basically, they were part of the same circle of friends and would go out to dinner and socialize with Ashley and his girlfriend, Sara Foster, a model.

Poor Rod must have thought Rob was the Stewart family stalker, especially after he met the veteran rock star's estranged wife, Rachel Hunter. Rachel provided Rob with something he badly wanted, an instant family. Rachel was very nearly the perfect woman for Rob in that she embodied the two most important elements he looked for in a member of the opposite sex: she was a loving mother and she was a lad's goddess who regularly appeared in that masculine bible, the *Sports Illustrated* annual swimsuit issue.

Rachel was a middle-class girl from Auckland in New Zealand and, like Rob, her parents split up while she was still a child. Her blonde good looks and long legs led almost inevitably to a modelling career, which she began when she was seventeen. Although she was becoming a well-known face in magazines, her celebrity was assured when she married Rod Stewart in 1990. She was twenty-one and he was forty-five. The age gap did not seem to matter, as the couple became a fixture of the Hollywood A-list and had two children – Renee, named after the Four Tops' classic, 'Don't Walk Away Renée', and Liam. The age difference seemed to matter a great deal more at the beginning of 1999, when the couple split just as Rachel hit the watershed age of thirty. It seemed she wanted to achieve more in her life than simply being Mrs Rod Stewart. Rod was said to be devastated by the break-up but moved on to a new blonde partner. Rachel, however, has drifted; she's been linked with various Hollywood names, including Bruce Willis. She has also made no secret of seeking therapy to help her cope with being a single parent.

The romance between Rachel and Rob came out of nowhere and has prompted a great deal of speculation about its authenticity. They started becoming friendly in the spring of 2002. Just how 'hot and heavy' this friendship actually became is open to question. At first, there were the usual denials that anything was going on, but the pair were trailed by a photographer to a bowling alley in an unfashionable area of Studio City. The Los Angeles picture agency Fame had been following the couple for a month in the hope of getting the right set of pictures. They showed the couple happy, relaxed and affectionate, and were sold all around the world for a rumoured $250,000.

The genuineness of their intimacy was questioned when a series of raunchy shots of the couple appeared in the *News of the World*. They were pictured romping, semi-naked, next to a secluded hotel swimming pool. According to an eyewitness, 'They were pretty steamed up.' Rachel took her bikini top off and, at one stage, Rob let his towel slip to the ground so that he was naked (again). The moment the pictures appeared, everybody started shouting foul and claiming that it was all a set-up. It was alleged that the location was, in fact, the back garden of the house where Rob was staying, a place where no photographer would have had access without permission. Rob was accused of selling photographs of a 'fake sex romp'. Renowned PR Max Clifford commented, 'If you're not very careful, you end up like Geri Halliwell or Anthea Turner'.

These pictures may well have been a set-up – certainly Los Angeles observers believed them to be – but celebrities stunt things up for the cameras all the time. It didn't prove they were not having a relationship. Cliff Renfrew observes, 'They did hang out together as friends. I think some kind of relationship did occur but there was definitely a big publicity element as well.'

The problem for Rob, in this instance, was one of credibility. He went to LA to get away from it all, claiming he wanted to be anonymous. That ambition looked threadbare if he was setting things up to keep his name in the spotlight. The Rachel affair did keep Rob in the newspapers during his quiet year. Neither of them, however, were big enough names in America to garner much publicity there. Really, Rob needed to pull a girl-friend like Britney Spears out of the hat, although he was briefly linked with Christina Aguilera, who was potentially more interesting to the newspapers than the bland Miss Hunter.

Reports as early as the summer of 2002 were suggesting all was not well with the couple. It was Rachel, however, who was with him when he went to watch the first night of Jonathan Wilkes in *The Rocky Horror Show* in Bromley, Kent. Rob was in his best Robbie form when Jonathan, in drag, performed the show-stopper 'Sweet Transvestite'. He barracked, 'Don't think you're coming round my house looking like that!' and informed the press that it was not the first time he had seen Jonathan in suspender belt and mask. He was also asked how Rachel was enjoying things and replied deadpan, 'Rachel who?' They left quietly together via an underground car park.

Rachel's mother, Janeen, met Rob on a visit to LA from her

home in New Zealand and thought he was lovely and they made a happy couple. Even Rod Stewart was quoted as giving his approval to the relationship: 'He's a good guy and I like him because he's a good footballer too.' Rod had an album to promote and there were whispers that privately he was not jumping for joy over the affair. For his part, Rob admitted that he was commitment-phobic, which did not bode quite so well.

Rob and Rachel were not seen much at the renowned celebrity haunts around Beverly Hills, preferring a quieter friendship revolving around coffee shops, nights in watching a movie with Rachel's children or the odd trip to support the LA Lakers basketball team, which is a sport Rob quite likes if there is no football.

This homely, comfortable existence was soon to be disrupted by the classic celebrity problem – separation. Rachel was left behind while Rob was promoting a new album, *Escapology*. She was seen spending a weekend partying in Las Vegas amid speculation that she was involved with someone else, a musician called Wes Scantlin. Rob and Rachel did spend a family Christmas together though and he bought her a Mini Cooper car. He had previously bought her a scooter when the two had visited London.

The rumours persisted that all was not well and, two days before Valentine's Day 2003 and the day before Rob's birthday, he and Rachel officially split up, a decision they reached over dinner. The press had a field day with stories of Rachel dumping Rob. He was strangely silent about it all, allowing Rachel and her spokesman to speak to the press about it. Based on past experiences, his reaction suggests Rob liked Rachel, she hadn't done or said anything to upset him and chances are they will remain on reasonable terms in the future. She graciously gave a world exclusive to *Hello!* magazine where, over nine pages of photographs, she confirmed the split: 'We are, and always will remain, the greatest of friends. I will always absolutely adore him. He is a very special guy to me. There is no one else involved.' A spokeswoman for Rachel added that it was difficult to maintain a relationship when they were both so busy and often in different countries – absolutely true. Tellingly, the break-up with Rachel caused little disruption in Rob's life. They spent an enjoyable summer in each other's company and she had been good for Rob while he settled in to LA.

A few days after the break, he seemed on good terms with himself at the Brits when he accepted his fourteenth award (Best British Male). He recited a joke Lonely Hearts ad: '29-year-old Aquarian, slightly chubby, seeks boy or girl for nights of poker and AA meetings.'

On a trip back to the UK, he popped in with Jonathan to see his pal's family in Stoke-on-Trent. Eileen was pleased at how well Rob was looking. She told him, 'You look great.'

He smiled and answered, 'I have never felt so well. I am looking after myself.'

Rob had been drink- and drug-free for a year when he went to LA. During that time he hadn't spoken to his father. A 2002 television documentary entitled *Robbie Williams Is My Son* followed Pete Conway as he found himself out of a job when his long-standing gig as an entertainer in a stately home turned luxury holiday camp in Nottingham came to an end. He was shown packing up his belongings, in preparation for his move back to Stoke-on-Trent, musing on the fact that he had not spoken to his son for over a year. Rob's new lifestyle, aimed at overcoming his well-chronicled problems with drink, drugs and personal demons, did not include his father, who appeared, in Rob's mind, to be part of the problem rather than part of the solution.

Eventually, after eighteen months, Pete was travelling on a train from London to Stoke when he bumped into Jonathan Wilkes at the buffet counter. Pete asked, 'How's that son of mine doing?'

Smiling, Jonathan replied, 'Why don't you speak to him?' and promptly fished out his mobile phone and dialled Rob's private number. 'Hello, mate,' he said when Rob answered. 'I've got your dad here' and passed the phone.

After a couple of minutes of being slightly guarded with one another, father and son were soon cracking jokes just like in the old days. As a result, Rob invited his dad to visit him in Los Angeles, where he had recently bought his first home in the US. They played table tennis in the garage and resumed the comic banter that had always existed between them. Intriguingly, after originally being frank and honest with the camera crew, Pete had clearly been told by 'Robbie's people' to watch what he said in the future – and not to talk about Rob. Although privately he might think this is a bit 'precious', he is happy to go along with it if it means regular contact with his son. Pete has hardly spoken about Rob in public since.

Rob's new home was a beautiful $5 million mansion – with a lift between floors – in a secure estate off Mulholland Drive. In the States this is known as a 'gated community', which means people cannot wander into the area. Instead, they have to pass security at the entrance. Guards also undertake regular patrols around the estate. It was all designed to make Rob feel a lot safer than he ever did in London. The houses are linked by a network of private roads, which meant Rob could drive as much as he wanted without the worry of passing his test. His pride and joy was a black E-type Jaguar convertible that cost £75,000. He also had a cream-coloured Cadillac. Rob was seen having driving lessons from his chauffeur, who lives at Rob's mansion and is a permanent bodyguard as well as a driver. Occasionally, Rachel Hunter was seen driving Rob around but most of the time it was the chauffeur behind the wheel.

The house was the perfect setting for a wedding and Jonathan Wilkes and his girlfriend, Nikki, fell in love with it when they went out to visit. They asked Rob if they could get married there and he readily agreed. Outside there is a meditation garden, which you reach by crossing a little bridge. They decorated it with flowers and candles for their marriage ceremony in 2004. Jonathan described it as a 'fairy-tale setting'. Rob was best man and gave a moving speech in honour of his best friend.

To the watching world, Rob's new life seemed idyllic. David Enthoven made the observation not long after the move that Rob was still in the early stages of recovery from his drink and drugs problems. The security was better in LA, he wasn't bothered much, he had good friends and was working well on a new album, yet he wasn't happy. It soon became apparent that the problem was more than having the odd bad day thousands of miles away from home and family. Rob finally revealed what ailed him: he suffered from depression and it was an illness. Thanks to the honesty and openness of well-known sufferers, such as Stephen Fry and Alastair Campbell, the public are a little more understanding now than they were in 2002. This was not a joke or a pampered celebrity being dramatic. Rob had been on antidepressants for six months.

18

Beyond My Wildest Dreams

While Rob was in LA, his management team was negotiating a new contract with EMI. Rather like a famous footballer, there was much talk of Robbie Williams going to another label but that only served to bump up the asking price to stay. EMI knew they had to keep him at all costs. An insider reports, 'He paid the salaries of everyone at EMI for years. He could afford to be a bit arrogant because he knew how important he was.' When the new deal was announced at EMI's West London offices on 2 October 2002, Robbie Williams was worth £80 million. It was the biggest deal in British recording history.

The £80 million figure seemed a little random and the full details will never be made public. The wisdom in the record industry was that there was a signing fee (perhaps £20 million) and the rest was a projected figure of what the deal would be worth over the next four albums. The *Financial Times* thought EMI had a 25 per cent stake in a new company that Rob was setting up. The deal was an investment in all things Robbie – not just records and publishing but also tours and merchandise – very much reflecting an industry that would be changing rapidly in the years ahead. Rob had insisted on certain clauses that would improve the Robbie Williams brand over the next few years, paying particular attention to promoting DVD and Internet sales. He also wanted a bigger commitment from EMI for a big promotional push in the USA.

Rob, wearing a Motley Crue singlet that showed off his many tattoos, exclaimed, 'My mum told me it would be really uncouth of me to talk about money . . . But I'm rich beyond my wildest dreams.' As a result of his staggering new deal, the *Sunday Times* 'Rich List' of 2003 estimated Rob's personal fortune at £68 million, which may not have given Sir Paul McCartney (£760 million) any sleepless nights but was still an awful lot of money for someone who liked playing football and walking the dogs.

The timing of the new deal was perfect. After a relatively quiet time in Los Angeles, Rob was back centre-stage of the whole music industry one month before his fifth studio album, *Escapology*, was released. The strategy worked brilliantly. Despite being released in November, *Escapology* racked up sales of two million in just two months and, again, Rob had the bestselling album of the year. Suddenly the £80 million looked like a particularly shrewd investment. EMI chief executive Tony Wadsworth observed, 'Signing an artist like Robbie is a lot less risky than most of our business. In the last five years he has sold 20 million albums around the world.'

Escapology seemed like a long-awaited album even if it was only a year since *Swing When You're Winning* had topped the charts. Rob was now living in Los Angeles, an exiled superstar. On this album would he be a new Robbie Williams, a mellow man from Hollywood? Or would he be the old cheeky lad from Stoke-on-Trent, full of witty one-liners and dark humour? Or would he have become so introspective and miserably self-aware that Morrissey would have told him to cheer up? The answer, unsurprisingly, is that he was all of these and none of them. Rob was quite fortunate in that anything was going to be completely different from *Swing*, which was a one-off. Rob's progress, or lack of it, with *Escapology* should be analysed with respect to his third solo album, *Sing When You're Winning*, which was such a perfect embodiment of the Robbie Williams brand.

Rob says he thought of the title for the new album when he was out driving in the Hollywood Hills one day and he started thinking about Houdini, the most famous escapologist of all time. Tiresomely, it was suggested it was a thinly veiled reference to his escape from Take That. If you want to go down that road, it is far more likely that it was an escape from his life in Britain. The album cover is a breathtaking homage to Houdini, with Rob suspended by his feet above the Los Angeles skyline as if in mid-bungee jump. Rob had originally favoured calling the album *Bum Gravy*, so at least *Escapology* was an escape from that notion.

Musically, the critics identified only one track, 'Monsoon', as sounding like Oasis. While it may be fun to spot the influences on the sound of Robbie Williams, it does devalue the musical content a little. The lyrics to *Escapology*, however, did not disappoint. The very first track, 'How Peculiar', was almost an elongated ad lib, with no formal lyrics written down before recording, so it became a stream of consciousness, with Rob allowing a train of thought about a crush he once had on someone to prompt the song. 'How Peculiar' sounds very much like the old Robbie Williams and would not have been out of place on *Sing When You're Winning*. It is, however, a false impression of what is to come.

The very next track, 'Feel', was the most talked-of song on the album, not just because it was the first single. It is a mature, silky production of a gentle song, with a universal sentiment of someone searching for love. Rob is very proud of 'Feel' and called it a 'beautiful' song. Dominic Mohan of the *Sun* described it as sheer genius. Surprisingly, it failed to reach number one in the UK, peaking at number four. The December chart scene was changing, thanks to the growing influence of television talent shows and all the hype that brought. Just a year after he topped the Christmas charts, Robbie could not get close to the sales of Girls Aloud, the winners of *Popstars: The Rivals,* and their first single, 'Sound of the Underground'.

The most successful songs on *Escapology* are infused with melancholy with a twist: none more so than 'Come Undone', the second UK single from the album, and a retrospective look at the drugs and alcohol troubles that have beset him. To some extent he is blaming his environment, the England he has now left behind. When he sings of being a son, it is of England, not of long-suffering Jan Williams.

The reviewers singled out two tracks above the rest. The first was 'Revolution', which featured a duet with gospel singer Rosa Stone, and was another song about loss of hope and love. The second was 'Nan's Song', the simple, acoustic ballad that is a tribute to Betty Williams and closes the album. It was the first song Rob had written completely by himself and revealed his gentler, more harmonic side. One critic wrote: 'It is from the heart and he wears it on his sleeve.'

Rob took a greater responsibility on *Escapology,* perhaps because of fewer distractions in the California sunshine. He recorded the vocals naked, claiming it was very liberating. He was very involved in the video for the album as well as the design for a new logo for the Robbie Williams brand. He drew it on the back of a cigarette packet. It was very simple: a circle with RW across the middle, and a star at the top of the R instead of the hole. The effect looked like a brand of cigarettes, which was perhaps what gave him the idea – cigarettes and Rob are very much an item.

Rob played the guitar live for the first time at a BBC showcase for the album in London. He announced, 'There's been a redundancy at our place and I've had to start playing this thing.' The redundancy in question was Guy Chambers who, to the astonishment of the music world, had been dismissed from Rob's inner sanctum in the same month as he signed the £80 million deal. Apparently relations between the two men had not been all sweetness and light during the making of *Escapology* and tensions had risen since the time Rob had called Guy 'a musical genius' he was lucky to have in his life. Only two years previously the dedication of the *Sing When You're Winning* album read: 'To Guy Chambers who is as much Robbie as I am.'

Although the reasons for the split and subsequent ill feeling between the two men are complex, the dedication does actually go some way to explaining it. Rob went through waves of hating everything about Robbie Williams the artist. He told Chris Heath, who spent a month with him in Los Angeles, that he wanted to kill off Robbie. If that was the case, even partially, then Guy's position was undermined. Then there was the constant whispering that Guy was, in fact, totally responsible for the sound of Robbie Williams and that the man himself had little to do with it. Rob would have been outraged at the idea. Guy co-wrote the songs, co-produced the albums and directed the tour band. He was in danger of becoming a bit like Gary Barlow, which would not go down well with Rob. There was also the suggestion that Guy was less than enamoured of some of the product on *Escapology*, particularly 'Come Undone', which Rob wrote with others.

The media reported the falling-out was over Guy's unwillingness to sign an exclusivity agreement with Rob. Guy, it was said, wanted improved terms. The huge deal with EMI had turned Robbie Williams almost into a corporation and no business would tolerate a director working for the opposition. Imagine the boss of BT helping Orange on the side – it's a nonstarter.

Guy was thought to want to concentrate on new projects, in particular a girl band called The Licks, managed by his brother, Dylan Chambers. He co-wrote their first single, '69', which he released on his own Orgasmatron label the same month he was fired. Guy explained, 'I've simply said I cannot work with Robbie any more. I don't understand what all the fuss is about.'

Rob's spokesman issued a terse statement: 'Robbie Williams wishes Guy Chambers the best of luck with his band, The Licks.'

Guy and Rob were two very different people who gelled perfectly for a while under the umbrella of Robbie Williams. Guy Chambers was not Lee Hancock, Max Beesley or Jonathan Wilkes. He was never really a member of Rob's Rat Pack. When he and Rob were together, they usually worked on songs: that was their relationship. Guy was a family man who lived quietly in London with his wife and young family. Rob had sung 'Angels' at his wedding in 1999, so there was a degree of friendship there too.

Songwriting partnerships that seem made for life do end. Tim Rice and Andrew Lloyd Webber are synonymous with musicals but they wrote only three together. Elton John and Bernie Taupin were joined at the hip but even they split for several years as a songwriting team. Nothing was set in stone that Rob and Guy would be a team forever.

The problem for Guy was that while he may have seen it as just a tiff, Rob doesn't really do tiffs – he does feuds. His bad blood lasts for years. The fallings-out with Nigel Martin-Smith, the Gallagher brothers, Nellee Hooper and others were not resolved overnight with a cup of tea and a handshake. Rob gets angry and he gets even. Usually this is non-violent, but not always, as the Hooper skirmish illustrates. Usually it is a witty war of words, as when Rob bought the Oasis album *Standing on the Shoulders of Giants* in Camden Market and took it back the next day, declaring, 'Noel Gallagher has run out of other people's ideas.' Sometimes Rob is too annoyed for banter though. When he heard that the guitarist Bernard Butler had called him the bastard offspring of Bob Monkhouse, he went up to him at a recording studio and asked, 'Are you Bernard Butler?'

'Yeah,' said Bernard.

'You are a fucking c**t,' said Rob.

Eileen Wilkes observes, 'If people attack Robert, he will get back at them.'

The chances of Guy Chambers coming back into the fold any time soon were slim to nil. Instead, Rob started preparing for a new tour without his former collaborator.

The fans seemed unconcerned. The 121,000 tickets for the first of his two nights at Knebworth in the summer of 2003 sold out in thirty minutes on the morning they went on sale. The second night was sold out by mid-afternoon, so a third show was added to accommodate the ticket frenzy. Rob could gain some satisfaction from selling out the two nights two hours faster than the previous record, which was held by Oasis. The 'fat dancer from Take That', as Noel had once called him, shifted 650,000 tickets across Europe in a day, bringing in an estimated £23 million in receipts. Tours were massive business and EMI would be reaping the benefits of Rob's popularity.

The concerts themselves, at the beginning of August 2003, were a triumph, although the papers chose to concentrate on the problems fans had reaching the site, forcing some to miss the event completely, or the five and a half hours it took others to get out of the car park. Robbie Williams appeared suspended upside down from a rope, just as he was pictured on the front cover of *Escapology*. When, with dexterous technology, he was set the right way up, his face filled a huge video screen. He looked completely and utterly astonished, scarcely able to believe what he was seeing. All those people! Rob was like a rabbit caught in car headlights for at least three numbers – 'Let Me Entertain You', 'Let Love Be Your Energy' and 'We Will Rock You' – as he absorbed the enormity of gazing out at a sea of people using every blade of grass of the Hertfordshire site. He shouted, 'You look fucking amazing.' He was reduced to tears by the sheer scale and the warmth of the response to him.

The first night coincided with Jonathan Wilkes's birthday and he was brought on stage to mark the occasion. He was introduced to the crowd as Rob's 'best friend' and enjoyed a rousing chorus of 'Happy Birthday'. Rob also brought his mother on stage to take a bow. She was dressed casually in trousers and a comfy top and gave the impression that some-one had given her a sharp shove from the wings. The next night she seemed to have glammed up for the film cameras and looked more prepared and ready for a cocktail party. These were the biggest concerts of Rob's career to date and he wanted to share them with his mate and his mum. On the last night the highlight for many was a duet with Mark Owen. Everybody loves a good reunion and the former band mates performed 'Back For Good'.

The duet with Mark was not included on the *Live at Knebworth* album, which was released the following month, in September 2003. The first track seemed to consist of five min-utes of loud applause. Surprisingly, it reached only number two in the album charts in the UK but had the consolation of being the fastest selling live album to date. Eventually it sold more than 3.5 million copies worldwide. Even more impressive were the sales of the accompanying DVD, *What We Did Last Summer*, which was out in time for the Christmas market and became the fastest selling music DVD of all time up to that point, eclips-ing his previous record holder, *Live at the Albert Hall*. Robbie Williams, it seemed, was on a conveyor belt going faster and faster.

19

Tin Tin and the Radio Adventure

Stephen Duffy had not had an easy life in music. In an issue of *Mojo* magazine he was listed as the thirteenth most unlucky person in rock. It was almost a badge of honour: not only was he in the unlucky list but he was also number thirteen. The basis for his inclusion was a 'one that got away' story.

When he was at Birmingham Polytechnic in 1978 – School of Foundation Studies and Experimental Workshop – he was friendly with a student called Nigel Taylor. They would put the world to rights in the café at Rackhams department store in Corporation Street and together, with another local lad, Nick Bates, who could play keyboards, they decided to form a band. Nigel changed his name to John, Nick changed his to Nick Rhodes and they set about deciding on a name for their new venture, eventually settling on Duran Duran after a character in the sixties film *Barbarella*. Stephen, at this point, wrote lyrics, played bass and sang lead vocals. There was no Simon Le Bon.

The fledgling group found regular work at a local club, The Rum Runner in Broad Street. Within the group things didn't gel and, after eight months, Stephen moved on to other things. It was 1979, one year before Duran Duran signed with EMI and started on a path that would see them become one of the biggest eighties groups. He explained, 'We were making such a row. I thought, "We'll only need to clean this up a bit and we could be famous", and I wasn't sure at the time I wanted to do that. I mean, I was nineteen.' Instead Stephen did what he has continued to do throughout his career – the unexpected. He spent six months on the dole and wrote a novel about growing up in Birmingham.

Stephen then formed an unremembered group, the Subterranean Hawks, before he had better fortune with a band called Tin Tin, who released a couple of singles on WEA records, including a song he wrote, 'Kiss Me', which has stuck to him like glue for nearly twenty years. The song is a melodic, catchy love song. When *Sounds* asked Stephen what it was about, he gave a reply of which Robbie Williams would have been proud: 'It's about oral sex. Or it might not be . . .'

Even in these early days of his career, Stephen displayed some of the qualities that would fit well with the lad from Tunstall, who was still in short pants and coming out of his Showaddywaddy phase. Stephen admits to being bemused by the money on offer from record companies. He describes himself as provincial, talks about his mum and, on one occasion, went round the house and destroyed all the pictures of himself. He released a new version of 'Kiss Me' in February 1985 and it reached number four in the charts, ensuring its inclusion in many eighties compilations over the years. His first solo incarnation was as Stephen 'Tin Tin' Duffy, which some radio DJs enjoyed changing to Stephen 'Duff Duff' Tinny.

Stephen has had to get used to answering the same old questions about Duran Duran. He even asked his record company to delete the association from his biography but it mysteriously reappeared. Obviously he would have become very wealthy if he had stayed. He would answer that he was not envious. It was certainly true that he has had a rich and varied career in music and the arts, which he may not have experienced within one of the most popular bands of the last thirty years. Besides the novel, he opened a club, designed his own line of clothing and started a band with his brother Nick, a talented artist. They called it The Lilac Time and over the years their melodic, folk-oriented music attracted a cult following throughout the world.

After releasing four albums, they split up in 1991 and Stephen pursued a solo career as Duffy before they reformed in 1999. At the time there was an important addition to the line-up: a blonde keyboard player and singer called Claire Worrall. She also happened to be a member of Rob's touring band. One day in the tour bus she played Rob some tracks from their album, *Looking For A Day In The Night*, which was going to be released under the name Stephen Duffy & The Lilac Time. Rob liked them.

While Stephen was no longer involved in an eighties world of big-haired electro pop, there was something about that era that intrigued Rob. He had always enjoyed the music of The Human League and the Pet Shop Boys. Stephen had once said in an interview that when he was with Duran Duran, they sounded partly like The Human League. When Rob joined forces with Guy Chambers, he had been obsessed with Brit Pop. Perhaps it was time to explore other avenues.

Over the coming weeks Claire would play Rob some ideas for new songs from Stephen until it was arranged that the pair would get together at Air Studios in Hampstead, London. They gelled in Stephen's small attic studio, where there was just enough room for the two of them and a small dog. They both plucked at acoustic guitars, with Rob suggesting an eighties feel to some of the melodies Stephen was picking out. At the first session they wrote a song together that would end up on Rob's next album as 'Sin Sin Sin'. At their next meeting they came up with a song called 'Radio', which begins 'He's chosen my attic'.

Rob abandoned his usual mid-Atlantic twang in favour of a vocal that had a very eighties quality. It sounded like nothing Rob had done before. It was soon decided that Stephen would fly out to Los Angeles and take up residence at Rob's house while they worked on a new album. He had to get used to Rob's homely if eccentric life. One night the lift doors opened at 4a.m. and out stepped Rob, who asked Stephen, 'Do you want to watch *Celebrity Wife Swap* with me?' It was all slightly surreal.

Mind you, Stephen's life was slightly surreal. He spent a winter watching bears in Alaska, where the only road in town led to Canada. He flew into New York the day before 9/11 and recalls being covered in dust, holding hands with strangers and singing 'All You Need Is Love'. Rob, it's easy to imagine, might have done the same thing.

Rob had time for once. He celebrated his thirtieth birthday with a party at his home, which proved memorable because his sister Sally and boyfriend Paul decided to get married. Rob paid for them to do it in style in Las Vegas.

He could take it easy because the next Robbie Williams album would be a greatest hits package. Rob followed the norm with these sorts of compilations and included a couple of new numbers, which always bolsters royalties. The first was 'Radio', which was released as a single in October 2004 and became his sixth UK number one. Stephen commented, 'I've only had a number one in Iceland before.'

The *Greatest Hits* album was out two weeks later in time for Christmas. This had become the Robbie Williams tradition – a powerful sales and marketing drive to cash in on the lucrative Christmas market. Again, it worked, and Robbie had the best-selling album of 2004 despite it being on sale for only ten weeks of the year. It was also the fastest selling greatest hits album of all time in the UK.

On the back of the CD booklet was a Latin phrase: '*si quid habet mammas vel rotas, res habebis difficiles aliquando.*' Robbie, it seemed, had become more cultured until someone translated it: 'If it has tits or wheels, it will cause you trouble.' He managed to squeeze in another single before the end of the year – a complete contrast to 'Radio'. The track was from the hit film *Bridget Jones: The Edge of Reason.* 'Misunderstood' was a lilting ballad, much more identifiable as latter day Stephen Duffy and a track that raised anticipation for what their collaboration might produce.

Rob and Stephen were able to write the new album in the relative peace of California. They wrote far too many songs and the hardest part was cutting back the tracks. They shared the production credit on *Intensive Care,* suggesting that Rob really wanted to re-emphasize that he had moved on from Guy Chambers.

Rob took a break from the album to fly back to London for the Live 8 concert in Hyde Park. He performed a triumphant set beginning with 'We Will Rock You' as a tribute to the late Freddie Mercury. He described it as one of the proudest days of his career. In many ways *Intensive Care* is the most interesting album of Robbie Williams' career. How would he manage in the big world without Guy and Steve Power, who was also missing from the new Team Robbie? He would have enjoyed the comments of Alex Petridis in the *Guardian* who wrote: 'He [Robbie] and Duffy have crafted a beautifully-turned pop-rock album that pricks the myth about Guy Chambers' dominant role in Williams' success.' He observed that Stephen was a fantastic songwriter whose career was not one of relentless commercial success. *Intensive Care* seemed to take Stephen's haunting melodies, put them in the Robbie washing machine and, hey presto, they became big songs. Lucy Davies in *BBC Music* online wrote: 'Gloriously imperfect, the personality makes the album, and it's his best yet: almost worth the 80 million.' The *NME* was not so overwhelmed, stating: '*Intensive Care* is OK in a sort of karaoke way.'

The release formula was the same as before. 'Tripping', the

first single, came out at the beginning of October and reached number two in the UK chart. It barely sounded like Robbie, especially when he employed a falsetto voice for the chorus. The album went to number one, selling 373,000 copies in the first week alone, but was only the third bestselling album of the year.

The *Guardian* review is more interesting than the usual run-of-the-mill critique. Alex Petridis tells the story of the press launch, when Rob arrived with old reviews; he had chosen bits that he thought were wrong or misinterpreted and marked them with a highlighter pen. He thought it confirmed two things about Robbie Williams: first, no one was able or willing to tell him what to do; and secondly, he really cared what people thought of him, to the point of seeming 'slightly crackers'.

Intensive Care, in retrospect at least, doesn't seem as memorable as some of Rob's other albums, perhaps because it lacks a big song like 'Angels', 'Rock DJ' or 'Millennium' – the ones that Robbie's fans like to sing along with. The lad himself would have been delighted to learn that worldwide the album was his most successful, selling more than eight million copies. While the album was high in the charts, Rob announced his biggest ever world tour, which would start in April 2006. Stephen was given Guy's old position as tour director.

Surprisingly, they did not continue as a songwriting partnership. Rob had other plans for his next album. Perhaps the two men are both restless spirits who don't like to stay in the same place very long. After his association with Rob, Stephen Duffy would no longer feature in any list of unluckiest men. There appears to be no ill feelings between him and Rob and that says it all, considering the latter's track record of rifts and feuds. When the tour ended, Stephen proposed to Claire Worrell, who was singing backing vocals. They are now married and live away from it all in rural Cornwall.

Intensive Care was not released in the US – although Americans could buy it on iTunes – revealing the stop–start relationship Rob has had with his adopted country. Everybody has analysed his failure to break into the US and one of the reasons given is that he couldn't be bothered to try. That's not true. When *The Ego Has Landed* was released, he played a number of small gigs at all manner of venues as if he were just starting out in Take That. His old golfing buddy, Tim Peers, recalls being in New York in 1999 when he heard that Rob was performing at a small hall in Chinatown called the Bang Bang Room. He was disappointed to find it was sold out but went along anyway on the off-chance. He was standing outside the back when a huge limousine pulled up and out stepped Rob: 'I shouted to him, "Rob" and he turned round, came running over and gave me a hug. He took me into the VIP area and his mum and sister were both there.' The breakthrough never happened. Rob failed to have an American 'Angels' moment.

Rob's journalist friend Adrian Deevoy reported that Rob blamed Capitol Records, the American partner of EMI, for treating him with indifference. The suggestion was that Rob was too English at a time when there was no wave of British success in the American charts. In the first three years of the millennium just four British singles made the US top ten. A record company executive observed, 'The States does not get irony. Not being big in the States really got under Rob's skin.' Take That biographer Rick Sky confirms, 'It has always been very important for him to crack the States.'

The problem for Rob was that it did not get any easier. The same year he played before a small crowd in the Bang Bang Room, he sang in front of 80,000 people at Slane Castle in Ireland, where every person there seemed to be chanting 'Angels' back at him. How could he go from being the biggest artist in the rest of the world to topping the bill at a venue that could fit into a stadium's toilets? Rob was not alone in facing this problem – it is one that also beset his former friends Oasis, who have also made little impact in America.

His fantastic new deal with EMI promised to herald a new impetus in the US and the front cover of *Escapology* featured on a huge billboard on Sunset Boulevard. Rob excelled on talk shows but still the album managed only number 43 on the *Billboard* chart. The single 'Feel' was a massive success worldwide but failed to make the top 100 in the singles chart. It was popular in Canada but sales refused to cross the border.

20

Acting Gay

Rob finally lost his sense of humour over gay rumours and innuendo after allegations that he had sex with a man in a toilet at a Manchester club when he was in Take That. The story appeared in *The People* newspaper under the banner 'Robbie's secret love' and also said that he had tried to have sex with the same man again the following year. Rob might have ignored this claim if the article had not also charged that he was about to deceive the public by hiding his true nature in the autobiographical book *Feel* by pretending his only sexual relations had been with women. The claims were also published in the magazines *Star* and *Hot Stars*.

The suggestion that he was lying about his sexuality was a step too far for Rob and he sued the publications for libel. Specifically, he was not taking legal action over allegations of homosexuality but over the suggestion that he lied about his sexuality. Rob won the case and in December 2005 agreed to an out-of-court settlement, including costs of more than £200,000. His counsel, Tom Shields QC, told the High Court in London that the publications had agreed to the settlement after admitting they were wrong. Mr Shields said, 'Mr Williams is not, and has never been, homosexual.' He added that the book *Feel* did not lie about the singer's sexuality.

How on earth did Rob's sexual status end up in the High Court? For years, it was just a bit of a laugh, wasn't it? That's true up to a point but there was a suggestion, if you looked, that there was a limit to how far Rob found it funny. Liam Gallagher overstepped that boundary when he taunted Rob at the 2000 *Q* Awards that the 'Q' in his Best Songwriting *Q* Award stood for queer.

For years Rob has made a joke about gay rumours, teasing his audience in an 'Oo, you are awful' sort of manner. In the lyrics of his 1997 hit single 'Old Before I Die', he posed the question, 'Am I straight or gay?' It's practically the first thing anybody ever wants to know about Robbie Williams. He has had to answer it in almost every interview since the very beginnings of Take That. They were such a camp band that the whispers about their individual sexuality took hold early on. There is absolutely no evidence to suggest Rob or any of the others in Take That are gay. The rumours where Rob was concerned always involved him and Mark. They were room-mates and best friends within the group. One of the funniest schoolboy interpretations of the song 'Back for Good' goes 'I've got your lipstick, Mark, still on your coffee cup.'

Rob continues to tease when the gay question is asked, both in interviews and in the lyrics of his songs. His attitude, since the first time the sexuality question was raised, was: 'If everyone thinks we're gay, let them think it. We're not bothered.' He did, however, understand that boy bands are inevitably camp – all hand gestures and flamboyance. Take That's extrovert good-time image was a million miles away from the introspection of indie bands.

Leafing back through the Take That photo album, there are an awful lot of camp beefcake shots of glistening shaved chests. Pride of place goes to a publicity still in which they wore brightly coloured boxer shorts, boxing gloves and butch stares.

Gary, who worked hard on his physique at that time, resembled Vanilla Ice's kid brother with a bleached blond spiky haircut. Almost as provocative was a picture of Gary and Mark smiling sweetly, bare-chested, enjoying a Jacuzzi together. When appealing to the teenage girl market there is always a fine line between masculinity and femininity, a subtle balance between sexual promise and unthreatening, cheeky grins.

Rob's friends back in Tunstall were not entirely comfortable with the gay association. They knew Rob was playing a lot of gay venues. These were tough lads who liked a pint. Coco Colclough recalls one time in the pub when Rob said to him, '"You'll never guess who'd come in the toilets with me." I thought, "Hold on a minute, gay club, what are you telling me here?" And he said, "Jimmy Somerville came over to me and said, 'Ooh, I thought you were ever so good.'"'

Rob, ever an actor, can be quite theatrical and luvvie when the mood takes him. Coco observes, 'You had to get your foot in the door somehow and he didn't mind doing it. It didn't mean he was going to be gay by doing that kind of thing.' Lee Hancock remembers Rob telling him that he had a 'load of gay following'. He observes, 'People who don't know him always ask, "Is he gay?" I have never seen him with any blokes. I know he's been with girls and I could never see Rob as being on the camp side.' Rick Sky believes Rob is just a good actor in these matters: 'There is a lot of mystery to him. He is all things to all people, rather like plasticine. He likes to fuel the gay rumours.' He would almost dare the rumour by openly going to the gay club Queer Nation in London.

His friendship with Jonathan Wilkes is another element of his life that has prompted many a nudge and a wink. They have always reacted to unfounded whispers that there is more to their relationship than just being mates with knockabout good humour, a total lack of outrage and a fierce loyalty to each other. Their duet on *Swing When You're Winning* encapsulated their public personae. They punctuated their routine for 'Me and My Shadow' with cheeky ad libs about Stoke-on-Trent and being gay. The sleeve notes for the album jokingly suggested they like to sing the song together in the shower at home. Jonathan admitted that they played up to it 'because it's such a joke'.

A year after he left Take That, Rob gave an interview to the gay magazine *Attitude* and was specifically asked by the interviewer, Ben Marshall, if he had slept with men during his time in Take That. He replied no 'without the usual sniggers that often make this question so depressing to ask'. That was a serious no but he might as well not have bothered because the rumours refused to go away.

Mel B once answered a question on children's television about Robbie's relationship with the Spice Girls by declaring, 'Neither Emma, nor Victoria, nor I have gone out with him. Anyway he prefers men.' Then there was Liam and his remark at the *Q* Awards. It didn't stop there, however. In a television documentary in 2004, entitled *The Truth About Take That*, his former manager, Kevin Kinsella, stated, 'I don't think he is bisexual. I think he is totally gay.' Even Howard Donald chipped into the debate, 'Robbie just doesn't know what he is. It wouldn't surprise me if he is gay.'

Rob is certainly an attractive and appealing figure to men. He admits to having been propositioned by hundreds of men and takes it as a compliment if a good-looking woman *or* man tries to chat him up. He has also said many times that he is not turned on by blokes and that they do not 'float my boat'. Somehow that quote only lasts until the next interview.

It may be that at some point in the future Robbie Williams may be arrested in a Los Angeles toilet for improper behaviour and the 'I told you so' brigade will be able to feel very pleased with themselves but at this stage there is no evidence that Rob is gay. There is every indication, however, that he has had sexual encounters with more than his fair share of the opposite sex: 'I've shagged for Great Britain.' His problem has always

Robbie's family mean the world to him. They have stood by him through all his problems. Above left, kissing his mother Jan after a charity football match. Above right, outside the Heaven nightclub in London with his sister Sally. Bottom, on *Top of the Pops* with his father, Pete Conway, who is always proud of his son.

With Kylie. The fans wanted a romance but it was strictly business.

With Nicole Appleton. Their volatile relationship proved to be one of the saddest episodes of Robbie's life.

With Tania Strecker, the step-daughter of Robbie's manager, David Enthoven. Robbie described her legs as going on and on . . . and on.

Me and My Shadow: Robbie and Jonathan Wilkes relaxing in Edinburgh in March 2002.

Robbie made a spectacular entrance at his first Knebworth concert in August 2003.

The right way up, he salutes the crowd of 125,000 people.

He has never been shy about his bits. Above, Rachel Hunter, his first LA girlfriend, gets an eyeful. Below, an unphased Max Beasley just carries on strumming.

Only Bobby Moore knew what this was like. Robbie lifts the trophy after his England team defeat the Rest of the World at Old Trafford to win the Soccer Aid match in 2006.

Four years on and Robbie is struggling to keep up with actor Mike Myers. Robbie missed a penalty as England slumped to defeat.

When a picture paints a thousand words. Robbie and Gary at Old Trafford in June 2010.

Ayda Field has been by Robbie's side for more than four years. She was unmoved by his impersonation of Grizzly Adams in Amsterdam in 2007.

Robbie treated Ayda to a Valentine's Day afternoon spent watching Brentford defeat his beloved Port Vale.

As Mr and Mrs Williams, they looked much happier on a trip to see Jonathan Wilkes's show *Pantos On Strike* at the Manchester Opera House.

Ayda gives Robbie a touch of glamour when they arrive at the O2 Arena for the Brit Awards in February 2011.

Robbie Williams: the ultimate performer – at the 2010 Brits when he received the Outstanding Contribution to Music award.

In typical pose, listening to the audience as they sing along.

Reunited with Take That at the 2011 Brits where they won Best British Group.

been that while he can prove a positive – obviously sleeping with sexy girls – he can't prove a negative. He affirmed that he is not gay many times and just cannot win. He wryly observes, 'I must be the only gay man in history that doesn't fancy men and has never had sex with them.'

The decision to take legal action over anything involving gay allegations is a risky one in that it may turn away the important gay fan base. Many of the biggest names in music have carried a huge gay fan base along with them to help sustain their popularity: Madonna, Kylie and Abba are three of the biggest; Robbie Williams is another. Often one of the biggest mistakes an artist can make is to deny being gay robustly. Jason Donovan famously made the cardinal error of suing *The Face* magazine for alleging he was and, though he won the case, it badly damaged his career.

Inevitably Robbie Williams faced the wrath of gay rights campaigners. Peter Tatchell, of the human rights group OutRage!, said, 'Whatever Robbie's intention, his legal action has created the impression he thinks it is shameful to be gay. If he sees nothing wrong with being gay, why did he sue for libel? He has previously teased his gay fans with comments appearing to confirm that he has had gay relationships. In the light of his legal action, were these teasing remarks a cynical attempt to exploit the gay market?' Mr Tatchell's interpretation of the events may or may not be the right one but Rob ran the risk of alienating his fan base of both sexes if they thought all along he was a liar.

Robbie Williams has not changed his image over the years. He was always the cheeky chap with a touch of the music hall about him. Typically, on the same day that he won the High Court case, Robbie was his usual self on *The Today Show* in Australia. He announced, 'There is plenty of time to settle down with the right girl – that's, of course, if I'm not gay. That's what they keep suggesting but I'm not gay in Australia. I'm gay in a lot of places but not there for some reason.' It was good, old-fashioned, knockabout Robbie. The man, Rob, however, is much more complex and nothing like as flippant.

Rob doesn't appear to have suffered lasting damage from any gay backlash after his legal action. Newspapers, however, hate losing and tend, collectively, to regard victors as the enemy. It would be interesting to see how the next Robbie Williams album was received.

21

Rude Awakening

In the television documentary *Take That – For the Record* in late 2005, Rob had some nice things to say about his former band mates. He said Jason was a 'lovely man', Howard was 'never anything but nice', Mark was 'a genius' and Gary was 'an amazing songwriter with an amazing voice. I apologize for saying you weren't. I had my head up my arse.' He also said that he would rather have Gary's family life and children than the fourteen Brits he had collected to that date. He didn't actually put it like that. What he said was: 'Fourteen Brits! Fuck off! But, in all seriousness, I would swap everything I have for that.'

Rob came across well in the documentary but so did the others. How quickly we had forgotten what they looked like and how good it was to catch up. Howard had become a DJ, Jason had been acting and Mark's solo career had failed to take off but he had won *Celebrity Big Brother*, which revealed the affection the British public still had for him. Gary was making lots of money as one of the best songwriters of his generation. Rob was Robbie Williams, the most successful British male star of the previous decade.

At the end of the programme, the four he left behind are filmed in a stately home, Cliveden in Buckinghamshire, sitting around a crackling log fire, waiting for Rob. He doesn't show. They don't take the opportunity to tell the camera a few home truths about Rob. Instead the scene is moving and low key. Take That biographer Martin Roach believes that perhaps this 'moment of genuine humility' on behalf of the four was when the public's allegiance shifted from Robbie to Take That.

The fans, though, had never left Take That. They were still there; they were just ten years older. In 2003, during the wilderness years, they were voted by readers of *Smash Hits* the biggest and best boy band ever, ahead of both Westlife and Boyzone – and New Kids on the Block. Now more than seven million viewers had watched a documentary about them.

At the time of filming, a greatest hits package was scheduled for release but there had been no talk of the band reforming. That changed rapidly and just nine days later they announced that they would reunite for *The Ultimate Tour*, starting in April 2006. When the tickets went on sale at the beginning of December 2005, twenty-six dates were quickly sold out. The album, *Never Forget: The Ultimate Collection*, sold just about a million copies, coincidentally almost exactly the same number as the *Greatest Hits* had managed when it was released ten years earlier.

At this stage, it is worth assessing where Rob and Take That were in their respective careers. The band had reformed and was just starting out on the comeback trail. In November, the same month as the documentary was screened, Rob broke the record for the most number of concert tickets sold by an artist in a single day, 1.6 million. The figure went straight into *Guinness World Records*.

One of the things Take That did before they went on tour was to part company with Nigel Martin-Smith, who had been instrumental in setting up both the TV documentary and the album. Apparently Jason had said that he would not do the tour if Nigel were involved. It would have been music to Rob's ears.

Rob sent an enormous bunch of flowers to the boys at their hotel when they arrived in London to play Wembley Arena on 8 May. Coincidentally, they were staying at the Conrad in Chelsea Harbour, just across the road from Rob's penthouse flat and another one he had bought for his mother. He had bought a place there because of the greater privacy it gave him compared to his old haunt in Notting Hill. On the night of the concert Rob waited at the hotel bar to greet them and they all sat up talking into the small hours. Gary, in his book *My Take*, describes how nervous Rob seemed to be, with all sorts of twitching mannerisms, constantly eating or drinking and on the move the whole time. He also revealed the true extent of his feelings about Robbie Williams. He said that whenever he thought of Rob, he thought, 'you absolute fucking c**t'. The outburst seemed so unlike Gary Barlow – perhaps refreshingly so.

One crucial difference between the two camps emerged during that first meeting after so many years: Rob hated touring whereas his former band mates loved it. He had to play fifty-nine dates from South Africa to Australia, from Santiago, Chile, to Milton Keynes. He began in Durban on 10 April and ended in Melbourne on 18 December. By that time he was not in the best of health and he had to deal with the fallout from his new album. *Rudebox* had taken everybody by surprise.

Rudebox was an album that Rob really wanted to do. He wanted to go back to his musical roots, not Take That's 'Do What U Like' but the rapping, electro sounds of his teenage years before he became a pop star. He had loved the eighties music, not just The Human League and the Pet Shop Boys but also the early days of rap and house music, Public Enemy and Happy Mondays. On this album he decided not to have one collaborator in the manner of Guy Chambers or Stephen Duffy; instead he moved towards cutting-edge producers and friends.

Many column inches would be written about *Rudebox* but

often ignored is the contribution of some of the most popular people in music today – people who don't make bad albums. The acclaimed producer Mark Ronson produced four tracks, including 'Lovelight', on which Rob had to dust off his best falsetto again. Ronson describes it as one of his favourites of any song he has worked on. He also produced the hypnotic 'Bongo Bong' on which Lily Allen, who was not a household name then, sang backing vocals. She also sang on the catchy retro track 'Keep On'. The rap on the track is so complicated that Rob once said he could never do it live because he would never be able to remember all the words. Ronson also produced 'Good Doctor', in which Rob raps a long list of prescription drugs, including Hydroanoxycodeine and Menocrabedene. It was not an easy rhyme. Rob has never said if he was looking in his own bathroom cabinet to gain inspiration.

Another top producer, William Orbit, oversaw Rob's version of The Human League's 'Louise'. Orbit had been acclaimed for his work with Madonna on the *Ray Of Light* album, as well as for many of the early hits of Nic Appleton's old band, All Saints. Rob had always wanted to work with him. Orbit also produced the track 'Summertime', which was a nod to Rob's 'lost year'. He had written it when he shared drug-fuelled times with Ant Genn. Rob explained that while the song was upbeat, at the time he could not have been more depressed and lost.

As well as 'Louise', he managed to persuade Stephen Duffy to let him include his eighties classic 'Kiss Me' because he wanted to show him what a good track it was. The Pet Shop Boys worked with Rob on 'We're the Pet Shop Boys' and the better song, 'She's Madonna', one of the strongest on the album. Rob has always been a little coy about his inspiration for the song, although it's not hard to imagine it being about the relationship between Tania Strecker and Guy Ritchie, whose next girlfriend was Madonna.

Lyrically, the most interesting tracks are the ones entitled 'The 80s' and, following that, 'The 90s'. They are the most obviously autobiographical, as he canters through his life in those two decades. In the first he mentions losing his virginity and the death of his Auntie Jo. In the second he tells the story of getting in to Take That, complete with spending the afternoon on the bowling green with Tate (Lee Hancock) before going home to hear the news. The track became controversial after it was revealed that Nigel Martin-Smith had objected to some nasty lyrics about him. After some legal shenanigans, they were withdrawn.

Rob had wanted this album to seem less like work and use his friends and football buddies as much as possible. One of his new mates in LA was a fellow Brit called Brandon Christy. Brandon was an aspiring stand-up comedian and had a deadpan delivery that Rob loved. Brandon also had an impressive musical pedigree as a composer and engineer as well as playing keyboards both in the studio as a session player and on tour. He was closely associated with the renowned songwriting and production team The Matrix, which was not surprising because one third of that trio, Lauren Christy, is his sister. Brandon and Rob joined together to write 'The Actor' with another LA-based musician, Craig Russo. Brandon recalls that when he and Craig were producing the track, they soon realized that they would get only two or three takes from Rob because of his hectic schedule. They were happy to let Rob do what he does best, bring 'character and performance' to a track: 'It allowed us to capture a real moment – a great pop singer, brimming with energy and enthusiasm just minutes after having written a song, giving an outrageous and creative performance.' 'The Actor' was a song reflecting Rob's poor opinion of that profession since he'd moved to LA.

An old friend of Max Beesley, Jerry Meehan, wrote the music for several tracks, including 'The 80s' and 'The 90s'. These two songs were voted the favourite tracks by members of the popular Robbie fan site *purerobbie.com*. Jerry went to music school in Manchester with Max and later studied composition at the Guildhall School of Music in London, which was also, coincidentally, attended by Guy Chambers. He had worked with Stevie Wonder and Beth Orton as well as several leading classical artists. He had also joined up with Max to compose an award-winning film score for *The Emperor's Wife* in which Max starred. Jerry joined Robbie's touring band in 2003 to play bass alongside Max on keyboards and percussion and he and Rob became firm friends.

In retrospect, one of the major headaches for the album, full of wit and verve, was that it is judged almost entirely by the title track. Rob was sent the basic music by Kelvin Andrews and Danny Spencer, who hail from Stoke-on-Trent and were influential on the Manchester club scene when Rob joined Take That. Then they called themselves Candy Flip, a slang term for taking ecstasy and LSD at the same time. Their biggest hit was a house version of The Beatles' classic 'Strawberry Fields Forever', which reached number three in the charts. They turned up in LA some years later as dance producers Soul Mekanik. Even though he did not know them in his Tunstall days, Rob was delighted to be working with two lads from the Potteries. He observed, 'It's like finding two Pharrell Williams in Stoke-on-Trent.' They practically moved in to Robbie's house while they worked together on four songs, wrote many more and fashioned 'Rudebox' into an electro music classic.

The single was released in July 2006 and only reached number four in the UK although it was a big number one around Europe. The *Sun* newspaper described it as 'the worst song in history' and bashing Robbie Williams was well on its way to becoming a national pastime.

The album, which came out in October, went to number one on its week of release, selling nearly 150,000 copies. While the album reached number one in fourteen countries, sales of more than two million were below expectations for a Robbie Williams album. Perversely, many of the reviews were outstanding. The *New Musical Express*, who had described Robbie as 'your least favourite pop star', loved it. Priya Elan described it as an 'amazing pop album' and the 'best thing he had ever put his name to', advising listeners to leave their preconceptions at the door, as she had clearly done. She added insightfully, 'It remains to be seen if it will be his undoing with the mainstream and those tabloids.'

The mainstream hated it: the *Guardian's* Alex Petridis, who had been so positive about *Intensive Care*, wondered what Robbie's core audience of 'mums, *heat* readers and couples who buy two CDs a year from Tesco' would make of it. He added that it was 'packed with half-baked ideas, bad jokes and music that any other star of Williams' stature would be terrified of the general public hearing.' Paul Flynn in *The Observer* described it as an 'absolute howler'. Mark Ronson was not surprised by the reaction and told *purerobbie.com*, 'I guess any time someone does something vastly different, they're bound to get some flak for it. I've never played "Lovelight" or "Bongo" for anyone and not got a positive reaction.'

'Those tabloids' were not at all positive. The *Daily Mirror* described him as a 'porky karaoke singer' and suggested he could have a new career as a roadie for Take That. Priya Elan had already voiced concern that Rob's Take That past was coming back to haunt him.

While he had been touring throughout the world, Gary Barlow had been writing new material for the first original Take That album for ten years. This was an astute move because nostalgia can get you only so far. When *Beautiful World* was released in November 2006, it wasted no time in going to the top of the charts. Take That were taking a leaf out of Rob's book by releasing a record so close to Christmas. The strategy paid off for them as well because they outsold all of Rob's solo albums.

Eventually *Beautiful World* sold more than 2.6 million copies. It was a triumph for Gary, whose songwriting had matured over the years. Although he sang on the majority of tracks, the other three all had solos and a songwriting credit on each track. The first two single releases, 'Patience' and 'Shine', were Take That classics and both went to number one.

'Patience' would win the Brit Award for Best British Single, which was seen as a further humiliation for Rob, who had no nominations. While *Beautiful World* was an astonishing success, it's worth pointing out that *Rudebox* was a far bigger album outside the UK, selling a million more copies. *Beautiful World* was number one in just one other country, Ireland. The problem for Rob was that his former band's fantastic success gave the media a stick with which they could beat him.

With hindsight it could be argued that Rob could have done things differently with *Rudebox*. There was nothing wrong with an artist producing an album out of left field. The Beatles surprised everyone when they released *The White Album* – but they were The Beatles and the greatest band of all time. From a commercial point of view, 'Rudebox' was probably the wrong single to release because the reaction totally set the tone for the reception afforded the album, especially as that, too, was entitled *Rudebox* – the first time Rob had named an album after one of the tracks. 'Rudebox' was probably no more radical than 'Radio' but somehow it seemed so. Much would be made of Rob being snubbed at the Brits but the song was nominated for an Ivor Novello Award, which was some consolation.

One track, 'Summertime', would have been a well-received single but it was an old Robbie song and did not properly reflect the rest of the album. Perhaps 'Lovelight' should have been the lead single. It was the second release but only reached number eight in the charts a week before Take That stormed back. *Rudebox* is not a dull album but somehow it seems a little hasty, with five cover versions and a schedule that had to be worked round Rob's world tour. He was, it appeared, stretching himself too thin.

Nowadays Rob can shrug off *Rudebox* as a project with which he had a lot of fun but at the time he was devastated by its reception and, in typically dejected mood, believed he was finished. Three years later he would admit that he thought, 'That's it. I'm not a pop star any more.' Contrary to media hints, he was not jealous of Take That's success because he loved their music and told *heat* magazine that he would have happily toured with them if he had not had his own album and tour taking up his entire time. He also said, 'There was a time when I thought I was fucking Superman. But I'm not.'

Rob cancelled a raft of concerts on the Asian leg of his tour in November, suffering from 'stress and exhaustion', amid rumours he was losing his ongoing battle with depression. The same month, he told Stephen Fry in a ground-breaking BBC documentary about depression: 'I could get up in front of 35,000 or 40,000 people and go, "Look at me, I'm ace!" Then as soon as I got off stage I'd get in the tour coach and go back to my bedroom and pull the duvet over my eyes.'

He did manage to perform his Australian concerts, when he did six stadium shows in front of nearly half a million people in December. After his concert at the Subiaco Oval in Perth, the biggest concert ever held in the capital of Western Australia, *PerthNow* online observed, 'Williams often looked manic and demented, but as quickly turned earnest and endearing, showing an uncanny knack to mesmerize a stadium full of people.' Rob seemed tired but managed to joke with his audience when he introduced the song 'Lovelight': 'Don't worry, it's not "Rudebox".' He still sang the controversial track but as part of an encore that included 'Let Me Entertain You' and 'Angels', so nobody minded.

Exhausted, Rob went back to Bel Air. On the day Take That were receiving their Brit Award, on 15 February 2007, he was in the Meadows Clinic in the Arizona desert receiving treatment for addiction to prescription drugs. In their acceptance speech, Take That didn't mention Rob but there was no reason why they should. He had nothing to do with their latest success. The host, Russell Brand, threw in a few barbed comments at Rob's expense, saying he was in rehab while Take That were the 'kings of showbiz'. Brand was just trying to get a laugh – that's why he was there – but he did make the interesting point that the Rob and Take That relationship was like a Shakespearean epic.

Rob had admitted himself to the clinic the day before his thirty-third birthday. He was in a sorry state and, fearing for his immediate well-being, David Enthoven and Tim Clark had taken steps to ensure he was looked after. They had a plane standing by to take him from Los Angeles to the clinic in Arizona.

His team issued a statement: 'Robbie Williams has today been admitted into a treatment centre in America for his dependency on prescription drugs. There will be no further comment on this matter.' That, of course, was a green light for the media to comment in any way they wanted. Rob, it was claimed, was addicted to a daily cocktail of thirty-six espressos, twenty cans of Red Bull and smoked sixty cigarettes a day – although it was never made clear who carried out the daily inventory of his excess. Others suggested that he was addicted to vicodin and seroxat. Dr Miriam Stoppard, the *Daily Mirror* agony aunt, wrote: 'Robbie Williams needs a good shaking, if not a good slapping, to bring him to his senses.'

Nigel Martin-Smith chipped in: 'If I was a Robbie fan, I wouldn't be worried. He'll go to his rehab, have a lie down and a couple of Anadins and be fine.' A model called Lisa D'Amato, who had dated Rob briefly a few months before, appeared in the *News of the World* confirming that he needed antidepressants to help him get through the day. She said, worryingly, that he would shake in his sleep.

His mother Jan provided another viewpoint. She said she

would be going over to visit him as soon as he finished his treatment and added, 'Going into rehab is the best birthday gift he could have given himself.'

The clinic, where Whitney Houston, Kate Moss and Tara Palmer-Tomkinson had also received help, may have resembled a beautiful retreat where one would love to spend a summer holiday but the reality was very different. Rob shared a dorm with four others and slept in a single bed with lights out at 10p.m. He would have to face each new day at 6a.m. The focus was on calm introspection and sorting one's head out without the distractions and potential buzz from television, newspapers, magazines, caffeine and sugar. He also needed to be gradually weaned off the drugs he was taking – a process that had to be carefully monitored to avoid any health complications. Tara Palmer-Tomkinson observed after her treatment, 'It was one of the hardest things I have ever done. There are no comforts.'

Certain antidepressants are feared to cause suicidal thoughts if abused. The distressing fact is that Rob, aged thirty-three, living the height of luxury in Los Angeles, was probably in a worse state than he was all those years ago when he first rolled up to Clouds clutching bottles of champagne. In a candid interview with Chris Heath, who has become a good friend to him over the years, Rob quietly admitted that if he had not gone into the clinic when he did, he would have died from an overdose.

22

Just One Night With Robbie

The girl with the fabulous tanned physique and the long blonde hair recognized Rob as he table-hopped around the bars of the Chateau Marmont in Hollywood. Suzanne Coppin expected to see famous people in the exclusive venue, always telling her friends, 'You need an Oscar to get in here.' She didn't have an Academy Award herself but, like many attractive young women in Hollywood, she was an aspiring actress and model.

Suzanne enjoyed listening to British artists, in particular Bryan Ferry and Roxy Music. More important to this occasion, she loved the song 'Rock DJ' and so was able to tell the three girls she was out with who the man 'ricocheting off the tables' was. All four could see that Robbie Williams was 'on the prowl'. He was wearing a striking blue and white waistcoat and, with his hair newly trimmed, looked in good shape. Suzanne observes, 'I thought he was adorable.'

It was a Friday night so the bar was 'booming', but she managed to make eye contact with Rob from across the room. Eventually he made his way towards them. Suzanne says, 'When he passed by our table, my friend Sydney offered him a bite of her sandwich and he stopped.' Sydney wouldn't have known it but this particular chat-up line was bound to get Rob's attention – he's a man who has loved his sandwiches ever since he used to raid Rachael Gilson's fridge when he was a teenager.

Suzanne recalls that they invited Rob to sit down: 'He sort of wedged himself in between us. It was obvious he loves the ladies, enjoying the attention of four girls. We were sitting so close that our hips and arms were touching. I remember that he noticed that none of us were drinking and that we were all sober. He said it was a coincidence that we had met tonight and then he confided that he had been in rehab recently. He seemed very pleased that we weren't drinking.

'As we were talking, Sydney suddenly leaned forward and interrupted and said, "Wow, you are really good looking." He was so genuinely pleased and surprised and so humble and seemed so flattered. He sort of put his hand on his chest and he was, like, "Thank you". He was so earnest; it was really cute. Later on he interrupted her to pay her a compliment and he said, "You look just like Wonder Woman" because she has big black hair and looks like Lynda Carter.

'He had a nice rapport going with the four of us so I guess he stayed twenty or twenty-five minutes. He noticed there was an atmosphere at the table. Two of the girls were mad with each other over a boyfriend. He said, "You guys are having a fight. I can tell." And then he played referee as they explained what it was about. So everybody made nice and we resumed a more general conversation. And then he said, "I can tell you are still mad with each other." It was funny.'

Rob got 'very buoyant' when the conversation turned to football, or soccer as they call it in the US. He invited them all to watch his team, LA Vale, practise the following day – always a prospect to quicken a girl's pulse. He told them he had formed the team for friends who used to join him for five a side games but they were now a serious team and played in a league. They all nodded enthusiastically and took down Rob's mobile number. Although Suzanne had told her friends Rob was a British singer, none of the four had any idea just how big a star the man passing over his phone number was. After he left, the girls decided that Suzanne could follow up on the meeting: 'It was kind of understood that I would go in for the kill. We didn't want a cat fight. So after a while I texted him, "Hold me." Then he wrote back, "Which lovely is this then?" And I said, "It's the blonde one." And he said, "Oh, fantastic." Then he texted, "May I make a suggestion – go home, feed the dog, put on your pyjamas and come back to mine and I promise not to make any sexual advances unless you want me to."'

Suzanne turned him down. She doesn't like sleeping over at other people's houses and she was playing hard to get. 'So I declined the invitation for the night, so then he said, "Oh ok, so why don't you come to soccer with me instead? And then we can go and see a movie." And that's how we left it. The next day he texts to say, "I have just had pinkberry frozen yoghurt for the first time." I congratulated him but told him I had to work and couldn't make soccer. He said that then we would just go to the movies.

'Then he texted me at about eight o'clock and said, "Promise not to be mad at me." And I said, "Sure". And he said, "I forgot what your name is." I totally understood. I never remember what my name is either.'

Rob decided he didn't want to go to the movies after all in case the paparazzi were out. Suzanne recalls, 'He warned that it would be bedlam so he proposed going over to his house which, you know, I recognized as a complete demotion but I wasn't going to split hairs. So I went to his house. It was in a pretty exclusive neighbourhood in Bel Air. Britney Spears lived near and The Pointer Sisters. So I drove over from Hollywood in my beat-up red '92 Saab. I parked on the street because there were, like, you know, a dozen Bentleys and Aston Martins in the driveway. I parked at a discreet distance from them.'

Rob opened the front door as Suzanne walked up and was

very natural, called her Susan and decided that they would go and rent a DVD: 'So then he said, "Let's go, then" and I started heading towards the Bentley and he started heading towards the street. And it was kind of like, "What's happening?" And he said, "Oh, we are going in your car." And I was, like, in this wake of terror. We get to the car and he opened his side up and there was, like, this cascade of rubbish crushing under his feet. He squeezed in and said, "This is very telling, isn't it?"'

They drove over to a local video store in Bel Air plaza, a little strip mall amid all the luxury. From the outset, Rob was affectionate, giving Suzanne little pecks and putting his arm around her waist when they walked from the car to the store. Rob said he wanted to look for alien documentaries and explained that he was a conspiracy theorist and loved all the theories about aliens. 'We were just sitting on the floor looking at stuff when I saw the flashes from the paparazzi. I just panicked, covering my face because of the pictures and he was, like, "Oh, bloody hell!" And we both get up and he's looking out the window to see where they are coming from. He was irritated more than anything and kind of assumed a predatory attitude like he was going to get them, if you know what I mean. I think they would just pass by the stores because there were so many neighbourhood stars.'

Eventually they settled on a film called *Déjà Vu*, the Denzil Washington thriller with a dash of science fiction, and went back to Rob's house. Suzanne describes it as a 'run-of-the-mill Bel Air mansion' with a big marble foyer leading to a sweeping staircase and then a hallway with, to the right of that, a massive kitchen with a twelve-foot high ceiling. In the kitchen seemed to be most of the soccer team, drinking beers, chatting and joking around. They seemed to be oblivious of Suzanne. Rob showed her into a small room off the kitchen with a few couches dotted around and a huge big-screen TV. Rob brought in plates of take-out with piles of chicken, ribs, corn and coleslaw – 'kind of soul food'. Rob's mates kept on shouting things to him through the window, which was not exactly a romantic setting but Suzanne found it fun. 'It was just casual and natural', she thought.

It was, in any case, difficult to feel romantic with Sid the wolf holding court. There were lots of dogs but Suzanne quickly realized Sid was leader of the pack. She recalls, 'Sid was in our presence, especially when the food came out. He was sniffing the food and Robbie was gently shooing him away and I got up to get a glass of water or something and then when I came back Sid was eating my food. And then Rob said he was going to take plates and he asked, "You done?" Yeah, like I was going to eat it after Sid had eaten it.'

Rob didn't exactly jump on Suzanne but he was getting in the mood: 'He was really playful. He was really physical, kept pulling me on top of him and we were, like, rolling around. It was sexual but not predatory – more complimentary, as if to say, "You are so pretty and fun." Then we went back into the kitchen and he had this monolithic-sized refrigerator and the freezer section filled to the brim with ice lollies. He seemed to have one in his mouth all night, a real oral fixation with them. Then he rattled off the calorie count of everything in the fridge.'

Suzanne recalls that right from the start Rob was very open about everything. He told her that his dad was visiting him from England and that Pete was a comedian. Rob offered to give Suzanne a tour of the property. They didn't get past the hot tub, which Suzanne thought quite beautiful, with a waterfall cascading into it. 'I said, "Oh we have to go into the hot tub.' And then he just kind of dropped his trousers in front of me. I wasn't expecting it at all but all of a sudden there was, like, Robbie Williams' wiener. Oh God!' Rob has never been shy about his manhood, proud of its girth and by the description afforded it by a girl at Butlins – 'a baby's arm holding an orange.' Suzanne noted that Rob had good reason to be proud.

She stripped to her bra and pants while Rob slipped on some swimming trunks for their session in the hot tub, which was, perhaps surprisingly, not at all sexual. Instead they talked of weight problems and, more significantly, about depression. Suzanne had been in therapy for depression herself so was able to relate to some of Rob's problems: 'We were, like, comparing notes. We talked about antidepressants. I had the impression that he had been on and off them for years. I said I didn't like this one or that one and he did the same. We did have quite a lot in common to talk about. It was strange sitting there in the hot tub. There were so many themes to the day. It was, like, you know, we laughed and cried.

'Then we got out of the hot tub and he sort of led me to the bedroom, which I thought was kind of presumptuous but I didn't want to mouth off to him. It was a pretty small bedroom. The bathroom was very big but the bedroom not so much. It was like it belonged to the adolescent son of a studio head. There were lots of trophies and pictures of teams all around. It was, like, awfully neat as well but like somebody who didn't necessarily have a proclivity for cleaning had tried. He told me that he had made his own bed but it looked like he had used his left hand!'

They did not immediately get down to it. Rob wanted to talk about the pursuit of happiness first. Suzanne told him that she thought that the path to happiness was through helping others: 'He said, "That's not true. I've donated millions to charity and look at me – it's not true." And then we talked about how evil the media was. He hated the media like they were al-Qaeda. I was terrified that he thought I was going to be revealed the following day as a reporter. I was trying to breeze past it and I was, like, "I don't think they are that bad . . .' and I could tell he was annoyed. And he was, like, "You are just being contrary." And I said, "Oh, is it a deal breaker that I am defending the media?" And he said, "Yeah, I'm afraid it's a prerequisite that you have to hate the media if you are going to be with me." I thought it was funny how disastrously I handled it.

'He told me one of the reasons he left England was nobody was sympathetic. He would be at hotels and people would be throwing things at the window and screaming obscenities and climbing the walls to try to get to him but when he called the police to come and help they were, like, "You love them when they are buying tickets to your shows but when they want to hang out with you, you hate them." They were completely unsympathetic and were, like, mocking him.'

All the time they were talking, Rob had put *Shark Week* on the TV. 'That was strange,' recalls Suzanne. 'The mood was shifting between romantic and therapeutic and we had all this shark carnage in the background and, like, people's limbs being torn off and bloody water . . .'

Then Rob jumped up and started up *You Tube* on the computer: 'He showed me this clip where he was coming out all cockily, like, striding down the stage before this massive audience and then he started singing and he slipped. And he just continued singing from the ground, from his prone position. It was really endearing.

'Then he moved on to the nickname Blobby Williams. He was not happy about that. I sort of laughed, "Oh Blobby, it's so brilliant." I meant that blobby was just so big it was funny. I was trying to stifle a laugh but I was not entirely successful. I was fucking up left and right. The irony is that I was picked on as a kid so I could sympathize.'

The sex, when it happened, was spontaneous. One minute they were talking about how many women Rob had been with: 'He said he didn't have as much sex as people thought. He thought it might be because he was a pop star and not a rock star. I remember he was marvelling at the fact that he had never had a venereal disease and that he had just had a clean bill of health from his doctor.' The next minute Rob was all action.

Suzanne thought the sex was excellent considering it was their first time together and the circumstances leading up to it were 'somewhat awkward'. Rob was energetic and enterprising, although Suzanne daren't look up in case she saw a shark. She gave him ten out of ten, which he would have been pleased to hear.

Afterwards, Rob wanted her to stay over. When Suzanne said no, he suggested he go over to hers: 'I just sort of laughed because my tiny apartment was in the same state as my car. I thought it would be hilarious. He was really sleepy so I don't think he minded. He just walked me down the stairs. Everyone had gone and we said goodbye. I knew it was just one night. I slept with him way too soon. Shit!'

Suzanne vividly recalls her night of sex and therapy with Rob. She is quite clear what, among all the things they talked about, gave him the most anguish, and it wasn't the media or weight problems: it was depression. 'I think he just has a pre-disposition, a chemical disposition to depression that he can't seem to attack. Obviously fame, money and antidepressants can only eliminate it to whatever extent. It always kind of haunts him.'

23

Field of Dreams

Rob can be pretty funny about actresses. He thought they had a tendency to be bonkers. This was Hollywood so, inevitably, he would come across more actresses per square foot than in any other place in the world. He wasn't enjoying the Los Angeles dating scene much, mainly because he wasn't going on many dates. He tended to find it all superficial – perfect tans, perfect hair, perfect teeth. Everything always seemed so perfect, which, of course, it wasn't. When he first met a young actress called Ayda Field at the end of 2006 he was not in a good place and not ready for a relationship – certainly not with an actress.

They were introduced by the actor Callum Blue, star of *Dead Like Me* and another Brit living in LA, who told Rob in the best matchmaker fashion, 'I know someone who would be perfect for you.' Rob didn't know it then but he would eventually agree with Callum's prediction. Rob stood Ayda up on their first date, which was a good start. Eventually they went to a party together and spent the evening talking.

Rob doesn't really chat; he's usually talking about things that are more important to him than the weather forecast or traffic. Ayda lent a sympathetic ear because, at the time, Rob was in a very bad way, on a descent that would leave him no choice other than another visit to rehab. Rob was not ready to develop a relationship and told her so. They did go out on a couple of dates soon after meeting but it didn't lead anywhere. Ayda, who is half Turkish, did do something right, however, when she first went out with Rob – she didn't blab about it, although that may have been because she had absolutely no idea who he was. Rob explained, 'She certainly wasn't some kind of hysterical Robbie Williams groupie.'

Rob could have been forgiven for returning the compliment. Ayda Field was not a household name. She is the type of girl who those who meet her describe as 'nice'. She had been brought up in an exclusive environment in Los Angeles, a million miles away from Tunstall, but there were telling similarities between her family background and that of Robert Williams. Her father, Hal Evecan, split from her mother, Gwen Field, when she was two years old. She was also very fond of her grandmother, Marjorie Field, who died in 1997 at the age of eighty-three. Ayda said of her grandmother, 'She continues to inspire me every day of my life' – a sentiment close to Rob's heart.

Gwen became a successful independent film producer and Ayda was brought up close to the acting fraternity but, surprisingly, she showed little interest in that glamorous world when she was younger. The beautiful family house was in an exclusive stretch of Coldwater Canyon Drive where all the homes are worth seven figures. In front of the house was a tennis court, where young Ayda, who is five years younger than Rob, practised for hours with the family guard dog acting as a ball boy. Ayda definitely seemed more sporty than theatrical when she attended the exclusive Harvard-Westlake School a few miles along the road. Besides playing tennis, she was a keen runner and was in the school team. She was also a champion at hula hoop, always a skill with which to impress boyfriends.

Harvard-Westlake is a private school, where the privileged

students can enjoy their days studying on the huge number of seats outside. This is quintessentially Californian; it is a place that the average high school pupil in the UK can only dream of while watching television. The film star Jake Gyllenhaal was also at the school, although he was a year below Ayda. Jake was always going to follow his parents into the world of film, whereas Ayda was more interested in politics. She secured a place at the prestigious Duke University in North Carolina to read political science and economics.

When she returned to LA after graduating, Ayda needed a job. The very first week she was back at home, she went for an acting audition to play an Italian woman, Angela Moroni, on the famous US soap *Days of Our Lives*. Ayda told the producers that she was Italian and had just come to America. She secured the role after inventing a whole family back story for herself and even started using an Italian accent on her answering machine. Rob would have loved such bravado; it was just the sort of thing he would have done. She moved on to comedy roles in well-known American shows, such as *Studio 60 on the Sunset Strip* with Matthew Perry and *Making It Legal*. She also shone in a sketch show called *Blue Collar TV* where she could show off her ability to change accents and characters. She explained, 'I can go from being Anna Nicole Smith in the morning to a 400-pound woman in the afternoon to an alien in the evening.' The only time she would have made an impact in the UK was when she guest starred in an episode of *Will and Grace*.

Ayda didn't bring lots of emotional baggage to the table. She lived alone with a dog and three cats in the same block in Sherman Oaks as Jennifer Aniston's mother, Nancy. She was funny, bright and sporty, and still waiting for a script like *Friends* to fall into her lap. Of course, she is slim and pretty but her heritage has given her a touch of the exotic that made her stand out from the usual tits and teeth Hollywood wannabe. Ayda is several classes above arm candy. All these qualities Rob would have noticed when he bumped into her again at a party a few months later. This time they clicked.

Crucially for post-rehab Rob, he was able to build a relationship with Ayda with little media hassle. She was busy making a new sitcom called *Back to You* with Kelsey Grammar, in which this time she had to play a Spanish woman, Montana Diaz Herrera. Grammar's track record in *Frasier* and *Cheers* had raised hopes that this would be a big show but disappointingly it ran for only seventeen episodes. Rob, however, was impressed that she was working for a living. The pair started dating seriously.

In past relationships, or those that were just friendships, Rob has been pursued relentlessly by the paparazzi. That changed with Ayda. They were able to slip into the cinema, walk the dogs or stay at home and watch TV without the constant clicking of cameras. Rob is prone to watching the box in his underpants as if he were a member of the Royle family squeezed on the sofa between Dave and Denise.

The British press quoted a friend saying, 'He hasn't been this into a girl for a long time and they're doing all the couply things. He's smitten and the feeling's mutual.' Any quote from a 'friend' in the media should be looked upon with suspicion because Rob's friends don't talk about him at all. In fact, sometimes he sets people little tests to see if they will be admitted to his circle by telling them something outrageous and untrue and seeing if it appears in print. On this occasion, however, the 'friend' was right.

Rob was beset by insecurities about the new relationship. He was, he admitted, forever looking for signs that they weren't meant to be together. In the first year of their relationship, they broke up three times. The biggest crisis came when Rob decided it was time to think about recording again. He was still writing with Brandon and other friends but had yet to formulate a plan. One of the ideas he was toying with was returning to live in the UK. The problem for Rob was that he couldn't find an excuse to stay apart from Ayda. 'She just kept on being this wonderful person,' he said sweetly.

Ayda also received the nod of approval from his father, Pete, in a roundabout way. When he was leaving after meeting her, he turned to Rob and said, 'You're in trouble there, son', because there was absolutely no reason to ditch the relationship.

Ayda wasn't too delighted with his incessant playing of the game *Football Manager* on his computer but grew to tolerate it. She took an indulgent interest in his obsessions – football and, more recently, UFOs. As a child, Rob had seen an unidentified flying object in the skies above Tunstall and filed the experience away to explore later if he ever had the chance. Then, in Los Angeles, he saw an object the size of a football field whizzing over his house in Bel Air. While accepting that the explanation might have been a military one, Rob wanted to explore the possibilities. Rob's interest in UFOs and aliens was covered in the media with the suggestion that he was slightly loopy, which was not the case. He brought cynicism to it but that didn't mean he wasn't going to pursue the subject vigorously.

The writer Jon Ronson made a superb radio documentary about the trip he made with Rob, Ayda and Brandon Christie to attend a conference about alien abductees in the town of Laughlin in the Nevada desert. Brandon was the embodiment of Rob's cynical side. One of the key speakers was Ann Andrews, who believes her son has been the victim of an alien abduction and has written a number of books about it. She showed some blurry photographs of UFOs.

After her address, Brandon walked to the front of the hall and announced, 'I just wanted to ask: why don't you buy a better camera?' Rob was dying of embarrassment. Brandon, who has the timing of an accomplished comedian, never talks about Rob, but he did confide something to Jon about Rob's interest in the extraterrestrial. He thought he was torn:

'There's the side that wants to go along with it, but there's also a very sarcastic, sceptical side that I'd like to think is the real side.'

The whole trip had a touch of the surreal, especially when the keynote speaker said to Rob, 'You look very much like Robbie Williams.' Everyone started asking Rob for an autograph, including an American who had no idea who he was but thought his daughter might. Rob remembered to buy fifteen UFO DVDs before they left the conference and headed back to LA. The last scene Jon describes is of Robbie and Ayda sitting on the balcony of his mansion gazing up at the night sky.

Ayda liked to travel and Rob found he had time to see places without the worry of a concert to perform the next day. They were finally photographed together in Amsterdam. Rob looked barely recognizable – like Grizzly Adams on lifeguard duty. He sported a bushy, greying beard, a beanie hat, celebrity shades and a bright orange puffa jacket. Ayda wore sunglasses and a fur hat.

Despite romantic trips around Europe and to Mexico, Rob and Ayda still seemed to have an on–off relationship. In June 2008, everyone thought it was all over and the press announced it was the 'final split', which it wasn't. Most of the time Ayda may have been happy to live quietly with Rob and walk the dogs in the Hollywood hills but her career had become very static. It is a sad fact of life in the film capital that if you are not visible, you are quickly forgotten. Ayda would soon be thirty, when roles might not be so easy to come by. Her only role in the last couple of years was well down the cast list of a forgotten comedy film called *Play Dead*.

Ayda seemed to have accepted life as the girlfriend of a very famous pop star. She came over to the UK and took an interest in all things British. This included a trip to watch Port Vale lose two–nil away to Brentford on a freezing cold afternoon. Rob had become the biggest shareholder in his home town club when he bought a stake worth £260,000 in 2006. It was a gesture to

show that 'my heart is still there'. Ayda managed to look interested throughout the match, which was even more impressive
because it was Valentine's Day and a trip to the Griffin Park
ground might not be on every girl's list of romantic treats.

She seemed more at home back in Los Angeles, where they
were pictured hand in hand, with genuine smiles, strolling
down the street with Jonathan Wilkes, who was pushing his
baby son, Mickey, in a pushchair. His co-manager Tim Clark
flew in to LA and was reassured that Rob was happily writing
new material at home: 'He's in fine spirits and I think what he's
working on sounds wonderful. I would hope that a new album
will be coming out next year. There are never any guarantees
but that's what we would hope.'

Rob missed being part of music. He missed being able to turn
on the radio and hear one of his songs. The media was full
of stories about Robbie being on strike in protest at a regime
change at his record label. Tim Clark, apparently accused the
new boss of EMI, Guy Hands, of acting like a 'plantation owner'
over his plans for the company, which had been taken over
by financiers Terra Firma. Rob was contracted to provide one
more studio album and another greatest hits package as the
final part of his original £80 million deal.

This was really a battle for Rob's management to fight. They
were looking to improve Rob's future position by gaining more
control over his back catalogue and, in the future, being able
to release his music through his website – as Radiohead had
done for their album *In Rainbows*.

The reality of the situation was that Rob never stopped working on new songs. It's what he does and what he enjoys. While
negotiations continued, he was back at his home studio in Bel
Air, hanging out with Ayda and working on ideas with friends
Kevin Andrews and Danny Spencer.

It did not stop the media from stirring things up with some
amusing headlines: 'Let Me Not Entertain You says Robbie the

Striker' suggested the London *Evening Standard;* 'Sing When Your Whining' announced the *Daily Mirror*, which even chose to write an editorial on the matter: 'With the superstar on the picket line, burning lyrics in a brazier to keep warm and rattling a bucket for donations, we won't have to buy his next album.'

Rob was going to call the record in question *El Protagonista*, a reference to spaghetti westerns. Clint Eastwood was always that character, the man who comes into town to clear up the bad guys but you are not sure if he is a bad guy as well. His 'management' team thought it sounded 'pretentious' and was a bit of a mouthful for the average DJ and asked him to come up with something else. He recalled a song he had in his head called 'Reality Killed The Video Star', which was a headline he had seen once in a newspaper. It was a song inspired by Rachael Gilson but, in the end, was one of many ideas that never came to anything. The title, however, stuck and became more apt when Rob began working with the legendary British producer Trevor Horn, whose first famous record had been 'Video Killed The Radio Star' by the Buggles.

Horn was one of the most influential producers of the eighties, writing and producing many of the most famous songs of that era. His work was always very recognizable, in the same manner as Phil Spector's Wall of Sound was in the sixties. The song that best summed up the Horn style was the notorious 'Relax' by Frankie Goes To Hollywood. Horn had seen them perform it on television and thought it more of a jingle than a song. It wasn't a jingle when he had finished with it, after spending a reputed £70,000 in the studio. Horn liked to take unfinished work because he could 'fix it up'. The end product stayed in the charts for forty-two consecutive weeks.

Horn won a Brit Award for Best British Producer in 1985 and 1992, as well as a Grammy in 1995 for Record of the Year for producing 'Kiss From A Rose' by Seal. He produced the Pet Shop Boys' album *Fundamental* in 2006, an association that would lead to him working with Robbie Williams. Rob had been a guest star at the Pet Shop Boys concert at the Mermaid Theatre when Horn was acting as musical director. *Fundamental* was nominated for a Grammy as Best Dance Album. Sometimes pop can be a small world. Chris Heath, Rob's collaborator on *Feel*, had also worked with the Pet Shop Boys on a book called *Catalogue.*

Rob had about fifty songs ready for Horn to work on. He said, 'I've never felt as positive about any record I've done before. It's shaping up so fast. It sounds big. Very . . . We're fucking buzzing.' Rob loved working with Horn, whom he described on his website as a 'genius' and gushed, 'He is totally amazing.' Trevor Horn brings a huge orchestral sound to melodic pop songs. Rob knew he had to shape up, so he shaved off his beard.

Rob decided he would move back to the UK while the album was being finished at Horn's studios in West London. He bought himself an enormous rock star mansion in the middle of the Wiltshire countryside and would stay there for a few days each week before driving up the M4 to London to see how Trevor was developing his sound. Compton Bassett House was £8 million worth of unashamed grandeur. Originally built in the eighteenth century, it had been extensively restored, with eight bedrooms, a library, a luxury leisure complex, tennis court, a pavilion, two staff flats and a swimming pool in the basement, decorated with Greek-style Doric columns. Much was made of Rob buying it because it was in an area where crop circles frequently occur but it was more likely to be because Jonathan Wilkes had a less grand country retreat near Swindon.

Rob had been thinking about his home country. His sister Sally explained, 'Robert has missed Britain. He has wanted to come back for the past year or so. He has enjoyed his life in LA – he can move around freely and the sun always shines – but it's a pretty soulless place.' Rob was also concerned about his mother's health. She had undergone heart bypass surgery just before Christmas 2008 and Rob flew in to offer his support. Although described as being in a 'critical' condition after the operation at a private hospital in Cheshire, Jan made a good recovery.

Rob's own recovery, since the low point of rehab in Arizona in early 2007, had gone so well that he could now seriously plan his comeback. He was slightly irked that the world saw it as a comeback when he preferred to think of it as the next album after the last one.

24

The Return of
Robbie Williams

The music world had moved on since Rob was last promoting a new record. Now *The X Factor* has taken over the world of entertainment and the biggest in the business queue up to perform. Genuine A-list stars like Mariah Carey, Whitney Houston, Rihanna, Britney Spears, George Michael and Michael Bublé are now happy to appear on the show that might have been considered beneath them just a few years before. An appearance on the biggest TV show in the UK, however shambolic the performance, is guaranteed record sales. It is gold dust, especially when Simon Cowell and his fellow judges get up from their seats to lead the standing ovation, the studio lights sparkling merrily off their flashing teeth.

Robbie could not have picked a better place on 11 October 2009 to remind the British public he was back, a week before his new single, 'Bodies', was released. He was seen mentoring the contestants, giving them all a hug and making helpful comments of encouragement like 'You're a better singer than I am.' And then came the moment to perform on the results show. Host Dermot O'Leary called it the 'return of Robbie Williams'.

Rehearsals had gone well and Rob was ready for, if very nervous about, his big entrance when the doors to the stage would open and he would triumphantly spring on. The opening bars of the song began but the doors refused to open as planned. Rob, the supreme performer, was not expecting that to happen and was thrown into a panic. Farcically, he had to force them open himself. The audience were not aware of the drama as Rob battled his way through the song, playing catch up and looking slightly stunned and sweating.

Afterwards Rob revealed what had happened on an online blog: 'I don't know if you've ever had 10 million plus people ready to judge you on your first performance back in three years. But let me tell you, if the door between you and them isn't opening, that's enough to throw you off your stride. I had to wedge it open myself. That was brute strength, shifting something I probably wouldn't be able to move in the cold light of day. So there's a bad start.' Rob, however, thought it had gone well and was pleased to be back performing.

The following day the newspapers carried pictures of him on stage, looking wide eyed and spaced out. The *Daily Mirror* called it his '*X Factor* Shambles.' Columnist Polly Hudson could not understand 'why the hell' Rob bothered coming back. She observed, 'He might profess to enjoy performing, but life in the spotlight and all the judgement that goes hand in hand with it blatantly makes him totally unhappy.' Polly ended, helpfully, 'So – for the good of us all – naff off Rob.' Tony Parsons was more amusing: '*X Factor* is blighted by pitiful karaoke singing, arthritic dancing and sweaty mediocrity – and that was just Robbie Williams.' Rob even had to deny suggestions in the media that he was high on something. He said simply, 'I can only say I wasn't – because I wasn't.'

Clearly it was a difficult night for Rob. He could have come on and done his famous Frank Spencer impersonation, which would have taken everyone by surprise. 'Bodies' is an interesting song and one that grows on you but perhaps was not the right choice for our first glimpse of Rob in a while. The anthemic, arm-waving, singalong, lighter tune 'You Know Me', a plusher Trevor Horn production, might have been a safer choice.

'Bodies' was released the day after *X Factor* and was in direct competition with Alexandra Burke, the winner of the previous year's show. She had also performed the night before and her single 'Bad Boys' easily outsold Rob's – but then it always would because *X Factor* merchandise is almost impossible to beat. 'Bodies' finished up at number two but sold 89,000 copies in the first week, his best opening seven-day sale since 'Rock DJ'. Singles do not matter very much any more and sales of the album would be a far more important barometer of Robbie Williams' current position.

What a difference a week makes! A changed Robbie Williams took to the stage to perform at the opening night of *BBC Electric Proms* at the Roundhouse in Camden Town, his first proper concert for three years. He managed to perform a huge concert in a small venue. Trevor Horn was there with a backing orchestra, as well as Rob's own band. He performed songs with all the old bravura and banter, seemingly much happier in front of this live crowd than the television audience of *The X Factor.* He told them, 'You nearly made me cry – then I realized it's not *X Factor.*'

Rob had not lost any of his ability to engage the audience. Introducing 'Feel', he announced, 'I'm a bit sad because it was my auntie's favourite song and I am sure she's looking down on me . . . she's not dead, she's just really condescending.' He sang 'No Regrets' and dedicated it movingly to Gary Barlow, whose father, Colin, had died a few days earlier: 'I've a new best mate and his name is Gary Barlow. I'm sending all my love to you.'

He sang 'Bodies', 'Morning Sun', 'Blasphemy', 'Deceptacon' and 'You Know Me' from the new album. As Andy Gill, in *The Independent* noted, he sent everyone home 'with a hum in their heart' by ending with 'Angels', 'Millennium' and a version of 'Video Killed the Radio Star'. Gill wrote, 'Despite my own deep-seated antipathy, even I was impressed by the easy assurance with which Williams made light work of a risky gamble.' Even the *Daily Mirror* liked it – the 3a.m. girls said his performance was 'fab'.

Quietly, and without the glare of cameras, Rob and Gary had seen something of each other since that meeting at the Conrad Hotel. Nobody knew yet what had gone on but as a result Rob was seen arriving at the recording studio Take That were using in New York. The conspiracy theorists believed they were recording new material. Everone hoped it meant good news, buoyed by the fact that Rob had TT tattooed on his wrist. It would be some time before all the facts came out but, in the meantime, there was a very brief and low key appearance together.

It only took less than a minute – 57 seconds to be precise. Gary had organized a special concert in aid of *BBC Children In Need* at the Royal Albert Hall on 16 October, so the 'reunion' with Robbie was not the point of the night nor, for many, the most interesting thing. They did not sing a nostalgic chorus of 'Do What U Like'. Instead, Take That performed their 2008 number one 'Greatest Day' before Gary took the microphone and announced, 'Tonight, for the first time, I want to introduce an old friend. Please welcome Robbie Williams.' There were hugs and bows and that was it. Rob sang 'Bodies' and later slipped on stage and stood next to Gary when everybody joined Paul McCartney to sing 'Hey Jude'. For the moment, a fleeting hello between Robbie Williams and Take That seemed secondary to Cheryl Cole singing with Snow Patrol or, best of all, the surreal duet between Dame Shirley Bassey and Dizzee Rascal.

Reality Killed The Video Star had been released just a few days earlier and was engaged in one of the closest chart battles for years with JLS, who had come second in *The X Factor* in 2008. Both albums sold more than 200,000 copies and Rob lost out by little more than a thousand copies. While that was disappointing, the suggestion that the album was a flop is not a fair one. Rob's album was the third fastest selling of the year after Susan Boyle's and JLS's – both television creations – and the tenth biggest seller of the year. Even more significantly, and it is something that is never taken into consideration by the media, on the week of release Rob's album was the biggest selling in the world. In the US it limped to number 160 on the *Billboard* chart, so some things never change.

The reviews were mixed but the *Guardian*'s Alex Petridis, who has been an excellent judge of Robbie Williams' music, was impressed: 'Anyone can hire Trevor Horn and some crack writers and knock out an album of polished pop-rock, but perhaps only Robbie Williams would release an album of polished pop-rock consumed with angst, self-doubt and songs justifying his interest in extraterrestrial life forms.' The key word perhaps is polished. The album did not have any rough edges – nothing to make you sit up and say 'wow' for good or bad reasons.

Michael Deacon in the *Daily Telegraph* enjoyed the 'exultant and lovely' 'You Know Me' but thought 'Bodies' a 'clumsy' song. He made the observation that there are three types of Robbie song: the needy but uplifting piano ballad ('Angels'), the synthy Pet Shop Boys impression ('Supreme') and the winking novelty song ('Let Me Entertain You'). *Reality Killed The Video Star* had all three styles: 'It is the work of a man who has remembered what he is good at.' The *Daily Mirror* didn't like it. Gavin Martin called the tunes mediocre and the vocalizing 'very weak'.

One of the most discussed songs was 'Blasphemy', which belonged in the piano category and was co-written by Rob and Guy Chambers, which many took to be a sign of impending reconciliation. The song had been written some six years before on a lazy afternoon in Los Angeles when the pair were working on *Escapology*. It's a very pretty song and did leave one hoping that, at some point, they might work together again. In his latest autobiographic book *You Know Me*, again with Chris

Heath, Rob reveals his regard for Guy. He describes him as a 'brilliant eccentric' and adds, 'I love Guy. I still love Guy.'

More of the songs on the new album seemed melodic ballads than on previous albums, perhaps reflecting that Rob was now in his mid-thirties and couldn't 'entertain' on every track. Rob can't help being older and producing a less exuberant record, one that better reflects his age and experience; he has had a lot of experience.

Rob went back to *The X Factor* for finals night and sang 'Angels' with the eventual runner-up, the likeable Olly Murs, who seemed the sort of bloke who might genuinely have been mates with Rob at a different time. Even Simon Cowell said of Olly, 'He's like a new Robbie.' Rob's return to the show was almost as big a letdown as the first. He managed to come in a fraction early at the start of the song. The *News of the World* called it 'a second shambolic appearance'. For Rob, it seems, *The X Factor* needs to come with a government health warning.

Simon Cowell did not appear to mind and clearly holds Rob, who lives not far from him in Los Angeles, in some regard. There was even talk of Rob becoming a judge on the show. He said, 'I'd love to have him there because I think he would be a good judge. Full stop.' Rob could replace Louis Walsh, who once described him as 'a jumped-up karaoke singer', which did not go down well. As Cheryl Cole would agree, being a judge on *The X Factor* is a career lottery win. Perhaps a stint as the judge on the American version would be just the boost to ignite Robbie's US career finally.

The most notable change in Robbie Williams that was presented to the world in late 2009 was that he seemed to be joined at the hip to his girlfriend Ayda Field. She featured in the video for 'Bodies' and was in the wings at his appearances, giving him a kiss for luck. She wasn't a drinking buddy, someone he could go out with and drink twenty-four points of Guinness. She was a sobering, calming influence. He quietly took her to Tunstall, to see his old home in Greenbank Park.

He was just in time, because the Ancient Briton pub, scene of so many earlier hijinks, has since been knocked down for redevelopment.

Ayda joined Rob in the studio when he popped into Jackie Henderson's radio show in Sydney, Australia, to promote the new album. It was just another interview until Henderson asked, 'Sydney has a bit of a reputation for proposals with celebrities – is there any news you want to share?'

Rob turned to Ayda and said, 'Is there anyone you want to get married to?' before asking, 'Will you marry me?'

Ayda quickly answered, 'Yes.'

Rob went on, 'I love you so much. Would you be my betrothed until the end of time?'

Ayda did not hesitate, 'I would love to be your betrothed until the end of time.'

Rob then sealed the deal by placing a novelty ring, which Henderson provided for the occasion, on her finger.

At first nobody knew quite what to make of this extraordinary scenario. Could it be true? Did Robbie Williams really propose on air? Many fans seemed to believe it but that was probably just wishful thinking. For the rest of the day, the Net was buzzing with messages of congratulations. That's the thing about Rob's fans – they genuinely want him to be happy. The obvious observation to make is that Rob would not share such a private thing with a radio station. It was a classic case of confusing the man with the star. As Robbie Williams, he might do anything, but the real man has a track record of keeping anything important secret. He might have played out this scene if they were already engaged. Ayda, too, is a very private person and would not want to share such an intimate thing in her life.

Rob's spokesman was quick to quash the speculation, saying it was all a joke. 'He did say it but he did it in a jocular manner. They are not engaged.' The only problem was nobody told his mum. Jan went on BBC Radio 5 to confide that they were engaged and she was sending them a card. She explained, 'He wanted to do something different. I'm really pleased for them. I've got a lovely daughter-in-law. I've always wanted a daughter-in-law. It was no surprise, no surprise at all.' She thought they would be marrying 'in the not too distant future'.

So the whole episode was a prank but he forgot to tell his mother. While the radio interview was clearly a set-up, Jan's quick and positive reaction does suggest she had expected something to be made public and perhaps had assumed this was it. Rob had to spend the next few weeks denying it all. He said, 'I'm probably going to get married but I didn't get engaged last week. It was just part of the interview. Then my mum went, "Oh yes, oh yes, I've bought the hat, I've bought a card." She just wants grandkids and wants to speed up the process.'

The chaos over the proposal that never was did have the fall-out effect of half convincing the world they were engaged. That opinion was strengthened when Ayda started to hide her left hand. When photographers eventually caught a glimpse of her third finger, she was sporting not a cracker ring but a huge diamond. It was hard to ignore that sort of evidence. It was enough for *Hello!* magazine to feature them on the front cover: *Robbie and Ayda, Ready to Marry* – Planning a 'fun ceremony full of love'. The new rumour was that they would have the 'fun ceremony' on Valentine's Day. Nobody bothered to work out that Rob would be rehearsing hard that day for his appearance at the Brits just two days later, when he would be collecting his award for Outstanding Contribution to Music.

It was very much the end of an era: the most successful artist in the history of the award would be closing the final ceremony on 16 February 2010 at the famous Earls Court venue before it moved across London to the O2. He followed some of the most famous stars of the past twenty years, many of whom had touched both his life and career. Geri Halliwell was there with Mel B, picking up an award for the most memorable Brit moment for their performance in 1997 when Geri wore her famous Union Jack dress. She had presented Rob with Best

British Male in 2001 when they were close. She said then, 'The winner is healthy, talented and, according to press reports, giving me one. So it's about time I returned the favour and gave him one – the winner is Robbie Williams.'

Liam Gallagher, another character who frequently pops up in Rob's story, was there to accept the award for Best British Album of the past thirty years for (*What's the Story*) *Morning Glory*. Wearing shades, he came on stage in typical style, swore and chucked his mic and the award into the audience. The host, Peter Kay, watched as he left the stage and said, 'What a knobhead', which got a laugh. Backstage Rob saw Nic Appleton for the first time in ten years. Rob later revealed that it was 'really sweet'. It showed how much he had grown up.

And then, after Cheryl Cole, JLS, Lady Gaga, Jay Z and Alicia Keys, it was Rob's turn to perform. Peter Kay kept the introduction simple: 'This is the accolade that any performer would like to receive and there can be no better recipient this year than the most honoured artist ever in the history of the Brit Awards . . . Please be upstanding for Mr Robbie Williams.'

This was the real return of Robbie Williams. He didn't look like a frightened rabbit in the headlights but a confident artist at the top of his game. He was dressed like a movie star with a dark suit and a black tie loosened around his neck. He clutched his award and started singing verses as if he was about to launch into 'Bodies' but altered them to sing 'Got this award for my lifetime' and 'I guess Jesus really tried for me.' He didn't sing 'Bodies' but, instead, powered into 'Let Me Entertain You'.

The reaction of the audience told the story. Despite the stellar list of performers, Robbie received by far the biggest cheer of the night. Everyone was out of their seat, dancing and cheering, waving their arms about or trying to capture the moment with a picture on their mobile phone. As a live performer, Robbie has the ability to engage the audience immediately. 'One hand in the air,' he commanded. Everyone did as he asked. 'Two hands in the air. Now bounce, bounce, bounce.' Rob managed to pack eight songs into fifteen minutes, blending his greatest hits into one soundtrack of the last dozen years or so of his musical life. He closed with 'Angels' because, he told the audience, 'The song means the world to me.'

In the official programme, the members of Take That sent a message that raised hopes of a public reconciliation: 'Hi Rob, just wanted to say well done mate, we take our hats off to you . . . Lots of love Gary, Howard, Jason and Mark xxxx'. Rob was asked to nominate the things that had given him most satisfaction over the years. He answered, 'Knebworth, Live 8, my charity, the Albert Hall swing gig – and connecting with so many people.

'I know my nan would be proud.'

25

Union and Reunion

Rob celebrated his Brits triumph by eating cake. He couldn't have champagne or cocaine so cake seemed a good alternative. He knew that he would be flying home to Los Angeles with Ayda the next day to embark on some serious gym work to get fit so this was a last naughty calorie binge. For once the rumour mill was going to be proved right: behind the scenes the details were being worked out for Rob to rejoin Take That.

Rob had met the boys again when they were recording in LA in the summer of 2008. They had got in touch with him and invited him to their hotel. He had a raging toothache and didn't fancy it but Ayda told him he should go. He enjoyed seeing them but at that stage had yet to make peace with Gary. He recalled, 'There's a guy in the room I can't even look at.' Eventually the story of their reconciliation would emerge.

The next day Rob rang Gary, which was definitely not something he did every day, and suggested they all come to his house because 'there are things I want to say that'll help us all move forward.' Gary described the following night to *Q* magazine, 'We had the "you-said-I-was-fat-in-1991" conversation.'

The evening was a momentous one for Rob: 'I went from having a real problem with this person to literally rolling on the floor laughing with him ten minutes later. We were genuinely sorry we had upset each other.'

All five immediately made grand plans to get back together, which came to nothing, but the ice had been properly broken. A year later, Gary was back in California for a family holiday when he contacted Rob to suggest they write a song or two – something they had never done during the first incarnation of Take That. They spent two days together and wrote a song called 'Shame'.

This time grand plans did come to something. In September 2009 Rob agreed to fly to New York to work with all four members of Take That on their new album. Gary, as organized as ever, came prepared with ten backing tracks and Rob joined in crafting what would eventually become *Progress*. The reconciliation was not always easy: Rob still suffered doubts about the future and at one point even told the others he was leaving again. Fortunately Mark was able to talk him round – something nobody had tried to do fifteen years before when Rob had felt so abandoned.

Significantly, the seeds of his dramatic reunion with the band were sown in Los Angeles, where Rob was more settled now he had Ayda by his side. As a sign of his commitment to their life in LA, Rob decided to sell his mansion in Wiltshire. The house had never been a proper home. They had spent little time there together, even though Rob had built a go-kart track in the grounds. It was the height of luxury and would have made a nice home for a family of ten. Rob had never seemed the country squire and while he owned the house the only time he was spotted out and about was having a full English breakfast in a nearby cafe.

Rob had finally woken up to the fact that he probably preferred life in Los Angeles. Certainly Ayda did, having lived there all her life. Rob missed his family and friends like Jonathan but it's not as if he needed to save up to hop on a plane and fly over to see them. He could do it every week if he chose.

Rob is less stressed in LA than elsewhere. He likes his routine of watching reality TV in bed with Ayda or sitting through three games on Saturdays when the football's on. They have a cosy existence. He gets up early to go to a morning meeting of his AA/NA group on Sunset. He goes hiking with his dogs. Fortunately Ayda loves dogs too and her brood of smaller pooches have moved in, including a fluffy white Bichon Frise called Poupette that she carries around most of the time. Sid the wolf is still top dog, however. Every Sunday night Rob and Ayda host a quiz night for friends during which he normally adopts the role of jovial quizmaster. He describes it as a 'pyjama night'.

Rob and Ayda are rarely seen at parties, preferring home comforts, although they usually keep an open house and are happy to have friends pop in at any time. Rob now has two properties in Los Angeles; he's living in one while the other is remodelled to be more family friendly, which may signal the life he expects to be leading in the future. Rob told the *Radio Times*, 'I always used to say, "I only go out to find someone to stay in with", and then I found someone.'

To keep fit Ayda runs and plays tennis. Rob prefers to play five-a-side football with his mates on a pitch he had specially built at his Bel Air house on Mulholland Drive. The artificial pitch, complete with floodlights, was perfect for playing a game as the temperature cooled on sunny days. Vinnie Jones and former Sex Pistol Steve Jones are among those who pop over and kick a ball around. Then everybody jumps into the hot tub to chill out and laugh at each other's stories. How different from Burslem on a wet winter's day to be watching the sun go down overlooking the Valley in Los Angeles.

Rob loves football and regards the game as one of the major stress relievers in his life. He disbanded his LA Vale team, though, because he thought the whole thing was getting too serious, with ill feeling and division creeping into the dressing room, which was not the point of starting a team for friends.

For a while Rob had to give up football because of a dodgy knee but he was back playing again in time to captain the England team against the Rest of the World in the celebrity Soccer Aid game at Old Trafford in June 2010. The match was to help raise funds for the earthquake victims of Haiti. In his role as a UNICEF ambassador, Rob had flown in to the devastated island and had been visibly moved by the distress of the people he met, especially the children. He visited a football pitch that was just rubble and dust and a makeshift camp for thousands of displaced families. The charity football match was a disappointment, however, after his England team lost in a penalty shoot-out. The winner was scored by the actor Woody Harrelson, then aged forty-eight, who hadn't played a game until he was forty. Rob missed his own penalty but sportingly described it as a magical evening. The cameras caught sight of Gary Barlow in the crowd.

To prove the conspiracy theorists right, it was announced a few days later that Rob and Gary were going to release 'Shame'. Goodness knows how Rob had managed to keep it a secret. The track would be the single from Rob's new greatest hits compilation, entitled *In and Out of Consciousness*. Rob observed, 'It's not only a celebration of my past but also a bridge to the future. The fact that part of the future includes a name from my past makes it all the more poignant for me.'

2010 would prove to be a year when Rob's personal and private life merged into one gloriously uplifting experience for him. His return to Take That was officially announced on 15 July. Quite simply it was the music story of the year. Rob was going to rejoin them for a new album and a tour that would bring the five Northern New Kids huge riches. Rob was already rich 'beyond his wildest dreams'; Gary, too, was extremely wealthy but the reunion could net Mark, Howard and Jason an estimated £15 million each. They were all equal partners now.

The initial announcement confirmed that Rob would be a part of Take That for a year. He was full of enthusiasm: 'I get embarrassingly excited when the five of us are in a room.' For once the quotes from the others were just as good. Mark commented, 'It's been an absolute delight spending time with Rob again – but I'm still a better footballer.' Jason observed, 'Life is beautifully strange sometimes.'

Commercially it made perfect sense. The record and the subsequent tour in 2011 would raise Take That's profile abroad, while in the UK there was likely to be a renewed surge of affection for Robbie Williams. Having said that, neither of them actually needed one another. Howard Donald explained the motivation to *Q*: 'We spent five years together and never got the chance as individuals to work with Rob in this way because Gary did all the writing then. We're all involved now. It could have turned out that he had as big an ego now as he had then, but he hasn't.' For all of them, but especially for Rob, the reunion offered the opportunity for closure.

The following month Rob got married. It was Saturday, 7 August. Just like the Take That reunion, it was an event that many people thought would never happen. The laid-back wedding at his home in Bel Air said much about his life today: he was a 36-year-old millionaire putting the wilder times behind him and settling down with the woman he loves. There were still touches of the old mischievous Rob, however, as he decided to dispense with bridesmaids in favour of enlisting their eight pet dogs to accompany Ayda down the rose petal-covered walkway to where he was waiting in the garden to greet his bride. Pride of place in their wedding album is a picture of the happy couple with the eight 'bridesmaids' on white leads sitting in front of them. Bang in the middle is Sid the wolf, a garland of flowers around his neck, staring straight at the lens as if he is contemplating having the photographer for his next meal.

Afterwards Rob described to *Hello!* how he felt: 'When I walked down the aisle with our dogs and heard everyone cheering, it made me so emotional that I'm surprised I held it together. I'm the happiest man alive.' *Hello!* had exclusive coverage of the wedding, which they ran over thirty-five pages. Most of the pictures reveal Ayda and Rob looking blissfully happy.

Rob wore a black tuxedo and a white bow tie and looked more Hollywood star than pop star. He kept his cheeky boy persona firmly in the cupboard for the day. Ayda chose to wear a white garland in her hair, a pair of Louboutins on her feet and a traditional Monique Lhuillier white bridal dress that was made and fitted in just six weeks. Monique seems to hit the right note for California weddings: Britney Spears wore one of her creations when she married Kevin Federline in another ceremony in the sunshine of LA. Ayda did admit that Rob would probably have preferred her to wear a string bikini. He could have no complaints, though. For once the old cliché that the bride looked radiant was completely true.

Jan Williams was there, of course, looking fit and well, and Rob's father Pete couldn't resist a spot of entertaining, joining the swing band for a crooning version of 'I've Got You Under My Skin'. Surprisingly, Rob chose not to have a best man on the day but Jonathan Wilkes was there to give a speech that, presumably, he had been preparing for many years. Rob and Ayda also acknowledged the importance in Rob's life of his PA, Josie Cliff, by asking her to be the bride's maid of honour. The four members of Take That weren't there, perhaps because they would have become the story if they had been. This was a day of union, not reunion. Instead the boys sent a video message wishing the couple good luck.

As was normal round at Rob's, there was no alcohol or drugs anywhere to be seen. His new obsession with cake – particularly chocolate cake – was, however, much in evidence, with Rob declaring, 'Your wedding is a night for guilt-free eating.' The whole event was romantic and a little old-fashioned, with everybody just pleased that Rob had found someone he loved. He revealed that they had fallen in love on their very first date.

It was, said Ayda, an electric moment. In keeping with the mood of the day, the new Mr and Mrs Williams took to the floor for their first dance to the strains of Harry Connick, Jr's version of the classic 'It Had To Be You'. At the end of the perfect day, Rob took the microphone and sang 'Angels' to his bride.

A few days later Rob wrote on his blog thanking all his fans for their messages: 'It seems like there's going to be a happy ending after all. I'm the happiest I've ever been – not only have I gained a wife but I've also got four brothers now too.'

The first phase of being a happy family in public was promoting and performing 'Shame', his duet with Gary. For such a landmark song, 'Shame' was very understated, a quiet country tune reflecting on their troubled relationship. Rob's lyric described how it was a shame that they never listened to one another and the emotional upset it caused him. Instead of talking it through, Rob confesses that he had talked in public or, as he says, through the television. It is a simple but true observation that people can spend a lifetime not talking or listening to each other.

Less than three weeks after his wedding, Rob and Gary launched the song on the Chris Moyles Show on Radio 1. Rob described their 'big chat', when they had put their animosity to bed. He recalled that they had said sorry to each other and had both meant it. Rob added, 'It's lifted so much off our shoulders.' Gary observed, 'We just needed to sit opposite each other and talk.' They made it all sound very cosy, as if they were two old boys meeting up in the British Legion for the first time in twenty years.

The duo performed their song for the first time in public when Rob topped the bill at the Heroes Concert in front of 60,000 people at Twickenham in September. The concert supported Help for Heroes, the charity that helps wounded British servicemen.

The line-up was impressive and included Tom Jones, James Blunt and The Saturdays. But, again, it was Robbie who commanded the stage. Neil McCormick of the *Daily Telegraph* observed, 'Williams delivered the kind of intense, emotional, high wattage entertainment that can make a pop song as stirring as a battleground speech, and a concert feel like a victory. It's a different kind of heroism, sure, but Williams deserves some kind of medal for making this rather cheesy event worth its billing.'

The bravado of Robbie's live performances is the invaluable ingredient he brings to the Take That reunion. He will lift their live tour. His new wife Ayda may be biased of course, but she said, 'He's the best entertainer in the entire world', and she meant it. She added, 'Even if he's nervous before, when he gets on stage he just steps into it and wows everybody.'

Gary and Rob continued to do the promotional rounds, performing 'Shame' on *Strictly Come Dancing* a couple of days before its official release date of 4 October. In some ways it was a pity that the song was such a nice little tune and not a big power ballad that did justice to the emotion of them working together for the first time since 1995. It had mixed reviews: the *Daily Mirror* called it 'sappy', while the BBC Online thought it a 'really sweet song' and Hannah Fernando of *heat* magazine said, 'It's pretty catchy.'

The fans liked it, though, because the single went to number two in the charts on release, only kept off the top spot by 'Forget You' by Cee Lo Green. The song was actually less of a talking point than the video. Some people got the fact that it was a light-hearted pastiche of the Oscar-winning film *Brokeback Mountain*, complete with manly bare chests, and others didn't. It's not that easy for two men to sing a duet to each other with a straight face.

A week later *In and Out of Consciousness* became Rob's ninth number one album. The excuse for a second greatest hits collection was that it marked twenty years of Rob in pop. This time it started with 'Shame' and went backwards through thirty-nine tracks, concluding with 'Everything Changes'. The outcome is a far richer, more complete appraisal of Rob's career than the first 2004 compilation. John Bush, writing for *allmusic* online, thought the album gave glimpses of why Robbie Williams was 'occasionally great, sometimes infuriating, and nearly always worth hearing'. He also made a good point about the way the world viewed Robbie Williams, the greatest artist of the nineties and noughties, who 'few people seemed to respect but everyone enjoyed'. At this stage of his career it was hard to know what more Rob could do to claim that respect.

Before you had time to blink, Rob was back on *The X Factor*, this time appearing with Take That. Everything had moved so quickly since his wedding it looked as if Rob had been fulfilling various solo obligations before he could devote all his time to Take That. They performed 'The Flood', the first single from the reunion album *Progress*. Some thought Robbie was a little jittery but it went a thousand times better than the years before. Ayda had walked into the studios with him, clutching his arm and subsequently cheering him on from her place in the audience. Perhaps Rob's little foibles and mannerisms are more significant on television than in the live arena, where the overall vibe is more important than getting a step wrong or missing a note.

Rob took most of the lead vocals on 'The Flood', a strong, anthem-like song from Gary with a strident, almost marching rhythm to it. The *News of the World* called it a 'mammoth anthem' while Elton John, no less, called it 'brilliant'. The boys were dressed all in black, reflecting the harsh tone of the track. Despite some intense promotion over the next few weeks, it just missed being another number one single. This time 'The Flood' was kept off the top by Rihanna's hit 'Only Girl (In The World)'. It may have been a minor disappointment but the boys already knew the new album was going to be a phenomenal success based on the level of pre-orders. The demand for all things Take That was so great that the 25-date world tour sold out in a day – all 1.35 million tickets. Another ten dates were immediately added.

On its first week of release in November 2010 *Progress* had sales of 520,000 – the second fastest of all time in the UK – and it would prove to be the biggest selling album of the year. *Progress* wasn't a rehash of the old Take That with a selection of happy singalong tracks. Instead they had absorbed all the musical influences of their youth and forged a mature new sound for the group. Andy Gill of the *Independent* summed it up: 'Those who imagined Take That's reunion album would be a predictable blending of forces will be shocked to hear *Progress*. Rather than pop balladry, the album leans heavily on electronic beats and textures, and reflects misgivings about science and humanity.'

The band had found the perfect producer for the sound they developed on this album. The Grammy-winning Stuart Price had produced the Madonna album *Confessions on a Dance Floor* and Kylie's album *Aphrodite* and was a master of a modern electronic sound that acknowledged the great days of the eighties and nineties. Like Rob, Stuart was a huge fan of the Pet Shop Boys and that influence was one Rob had been trying to put into his music for years. The track they wrote for Rob, 'She's Madonna', which featured on the much derided *Rudebox*, would not have been out of place on *Progress*. The acknowledgement of the importance of their influence came when the Pet Shop Boys were confirmed as the opening act on Take That's 2011 world tour.

Adam Woods in the *Mail on Sunday* also noticed that *Rudebox* was the precedent for *Progress*'s 'mildly electronic experimentation'. Gary, while still captain of the musical ship, seemed happy to take a step out of the limelight, as if admitting the sheer force of Rob's charisma was something to harness rather than suppress. He did have one of the best moments on the album, however: the song 'Eight Letters' would make a rousing climax to their world tour set.

Progress was a big surprise to many, simply because it wasn't a disappointment. The craftsmanship could not be faulted. Besides the return of Rob, much of the album's interest was centred on Mark Owen's contribution 'What Do You Want From Me', a deeply personal song made even more poignant by the revelations of his extramarital affairs.

For once Rob's personal problems were not the most interesting in the group. After the stories surfaced of some ten affairs, Mark also admitted that he had been battling a booze problem for a decade. Not only was the formerly squeaky clean Mark repairing his marriage but Howard was also hauled through the tabloids over an affair with a soul singer called Adakini Ntuli. He had taken out a 'super-injunction' preventing details of the affair becoming known but this had been overturned by the Court of Appeal.

Take That returned to *The X Factor* for the final when they sang 'The Flood' and 'Never Forget'. They had intended to sing another track, 'Kidz', but the rumour was it was a little edgy for Saturday night viewing. It was easy to see why Simon Cowell feared Take That would eclipse the rest of the show when they finally performed it at the revamped Brits at the O2 in February 2011. They opened the show with a barnstorming version complete with dancers dressed as police in riot gear. It was more military rally than singalong and whetted the appetite for the tour. *Heat* called it 'flawless and visually stunning'. The *Guardian* described it as the 'campest and most spectacular opening to any Brits'.

There was better to come: Take That were crowned Best British Group for the first time. It was twenty-one years since Rob's days as a double-glazing salesman when he had sat on a wall smoking and dreaming of being a star. It was his seventeenth Brit Award – extending his record. When Dermot O'Leary read out the band's name, Ayda jumped up from their table and let out a shriek of triumph. Rob, dressed in sombre black and grey, looked slightly stunned. Nobody seemed to have prepared a thank-you speech. Gary told the cheering audience, 'Brilliant. Thank you all so much.' Rob unhelpfully said, 'Shaba' and nothing else.

It was left to Mark to put into words what everyone was thinking: 'Can I say, Rob – thanks for coming back, mate. Appreciate it.'

Last Story

This is my favourite Rob story and I have saved it until now so that the book can finish with a smile . . .

It was during those troublesome days when the Take That fans would lay siege to the old family house in Greenbank Road, Tunstall. One day Rob was in the Ancient Briton pub across the road enjoying a few beers in the company of friends. He decided to adjourn to the comfort of his home with a young woman who was most definitely 'up for it'. The tipsy pair pushed their way through the throng of fans and into the house, firmly bolting the door behind them. Just as they had dispensed with their clothes and were getting down to things, there was a loud knock at the door.

Rob, thinking it was another lovestruck fan, shouted out, 'Why don't you just fuck off!'

A voice from beyond the door bellowed, 'Robert. It's your mother. Let me in!' . . .

Life and Times

13 Feb 1974 Robert Peter Williams born in the maternity unit of North Staffordshire Hospital, Stoke-on-Trent. He spends his first year in the family home in Victoria Park Road, Tunstall. His father, Pete Conway, a comedian, reaches the final of TV talent show *New Faces*.

1975 His parents take over the Red Lion, Burslem, close to Port Vale football club's ground.

1977 Makes his 'international' debut when he impersonates John Travolta singing 'Summer Nights' from *Grease* for a talent evening at the Pontinental, Torremolinos. His father, Pete, leaves home.

1981 Mother Jan takes him to his first concert, Showaddy-waddy, at the Queen's Theatre in Burslem.

Sept 1985 Appears as Jeremy in *Chitty Chitty Bang Bang* at the Theatre Royal, Hanley. Afterwards he is introduced to the Lord Mayor backstage. Begins senior school at the St Margaret Ward Roman Catholic High School, a short walk from his home in Greenbank Road, Tunstall.

Oct 1988 Takes the key role of the Artful Dodger in *Oliver!* at the Queen's Theatre, Burslem. His father turns up unexpectedly and watches proudly from the stalls.

July 1990 Leaves school and secures a job as a double-glazing salesman with best mate Lee Hancock.

Aug 1990 Sings a Jason Donovan song at an audition for a boy band in Manchester, and is chosen to join Gary, Mark, Jason and Howard to form Take That.

July 1991 Take That release their first single, the undistinguished 'Do What U Like', which reaches number eighty-two in the charts.

Feb 1993 Take That win first Brit Award for 'Could It Be Magic', Best British Single.

Apr 1994 Sings the lead vocal on 'Everything Changes', Take That's fourth number one record.

June 1994 Secretly attends the Glastonbury Festival but spends the whole time hiding in a tent.

Dec 1994 Jan puts the home in Greenbank Road, Tunstall, up for sale. She cites a lack of privacy from Take That fans as the reason for moving to a smart address in Newcastle under Lyme.

June 1995 Attends Glastonbury Festival with bleached blond hairdo, a blacked-out tooth and a case of champagne. Is pictured dancing madly on stage with Oasis.

July 1995 Robbie leaves Take That after a final meeting at the Cheshire Territorial Army barracks in Stockport. Begins period of partying that leads to him being voted *NME* Ligger of the Year.

Aug 1995 Proves a big hit presenting *The Big Breakfast* on Channel 4.

Sept 1995 Dons black wig, high heels and white Y-fronts for a soft drink advert, which reportedly makes him £100,000. Appears as an extra in *EastEnders*, talking on the telephone in the Queen Vic.

Dec 1995 Begins dating his first serious girlfriend, make-up artist Jacqui Hamilton-Smith, the daughter of Lord Colwyn. They see each other for nine months.

Feb 1996 Reaches out-of-court settlement with BMG to enable him to pursue a solo career. The four remaining members of Take That split.

June 1996 Signs a three-album record deal with Chrysalis/EMI rumoured to be worth £1 million. Shortly afterwards parts company with manager Tim Abbott and hires IE Music to represent him.

July 1996 His first solo release, 'Freedom', a cover of a George Michael song, just misses the top chart slot. It sells a respectable 270,000 copies.

Oct 1996 Reveals he is being treated by celebrity therapist Beechy Colclough for drink and drugs problems.

May 1997 Robbie is pictured embracing actress Anna Friel on a hotel balcony in Rome but the romance is short-lived.

June 1997 Checks into the Clouds House clinic near Salisbury in Wiltshire for his first serious stab at rehab. He stays six weeks.

July 1997 Attends High Court in London to face legal action from former Take That manager Nigel Martin-Smith, who is claiming £200,000 in unpaid commission.

Sept 1997 His first solo album, *Life Thru a Lens,* is finally released, more than two years after he left Take That.

Nov 1997 Meets Nicole Appleton of girl band All Saints on a TV show. The romance begins in earnest over the New Year.

Dec 1997 'Angels' reaches number four in the UK chart. It spends thirteen weeks in the top ten and becomes his biggest selling single to date, selling more than a million copies including downloads. *Life Thru a Lens* re-enters the album charts and goes to number one.

Feb 1998 Fails to win a Brit Award but performs a show-stopping duet with hero Tom Jones. He describes it as the happiest five minutes eleven seconds of his life.

May 1998 Achieves ambition of scoring a goal in Port Vale colours when he plays in testimonial game for Dean Glover. He nets a penalty a few minutes into the second half. Minutes later he is sent off for arguing with the referee.

Sept 1998 Secures first UK number one single with 'Millennium', which samples the theme from the James Bond film *You Only Live Twice.*

Dec 1998 Finally splits from Nicole Appleton after a rollercoaster year during which they had been engaged twice.

Feb 1999 Wins three solo Brits, having been nominated for a record six awards. Also wins two Ivor Novello Awards for 'Angels' (Most Performed Song) and Songwriter of the Year (with Guy Chambers).

April 1999 Buys his mother a £1 million luxury home in the village of Batley, near Newcastle under Lyme. The house has twenty-four acres of land around which Robbie, who does not have a licence, can drive his Ferrari.

May 1999 Flies back from the US to play in a testimonial football match for Port Vale hero Neil Aspin. He scores a goal in his side's 5–3 win over Leicester City. Efforts to kick-start a romance with Andrea Corr fail despite sending her two bouquets of 101 roses with the message 'What can I do to make you love me?', the title of her biggest hit.

Aug 2000 *Sing When You're Winning* is released and becomes his third number one album. He dedicates it to collaborator Guy Chambers.

Nov 2000 Flies off for a holiday in Barbados after a bad night at the MTV Europe Music Awards in Stockholm, where he had a scuffle with a record producer and ended the evening passed out.

Feb 2001 A disturbed fan throws him off the stage during a concert in Stuttgart. To great acclaim, he refuses to abandon the concert. Dedicates Brit Award for Best Video to his sister's son, Freddie.

Oct 2001 Showcases his *Swing When You're Winning* album at a triumphant concert at the Royal Albert Hall, London. Lifelong friend Jonathan Wilkes joins him on stage to sing 'Me and My Shadow'.

Dec 2001 Achieves his first Christmas number one when his duet, 'Somethin' Stupid', with Nicole Kidman tops the charts. Moves to Los Angeles, initially as a temporary measure.

June 2002 Steamy pictures of Robbie and a topless Rachel Hunter appear in the Sunday newspapers.

Oct 2002 Tells a press conference in London that he is 'rich beyond his wildest dreams', after announcing a new contract with EMI, reputedly worth £80 million, the biggest deal in British music history. Splits from his songwriting partner Guy Chambers.

Nov 2002 His fifth album, *Escapology*, is released and goes straight in at number one. It becomes the biggest selling album of the year despite not being released until 18 November.

Feb 2003 Rachel Hunter confirms she has split from Robbie but that she will always 'absolutely adore' him'. He wins a record fourteenth Brit Award (Best British Male) and recites a joke Lonely Hearts advertisement as his acceptance speech: '29-year-old Aquarian, slightly chubby, seeks boy or girl for nights of poker and AA meetings . . . See you next year.'

Aug 2003 Performs for three nights at Knebworth before 375,000 people, confirming his position as the UK's number one pop star. His mother takes a bow and the crowd sings 'Happy Birthday' to his best friend.

Nov 2003 Tours Moscow in his role as a special representative for UNICEF as part of the organization's End Child Exploitation campaign. Plays a concert at the city's Olympic stadium.

Jan 2004 Is best man at the wedding of Jonathan Wilkes to dancer Nikki Wheeler. The wedding takes place in the meditation garden of Robbie's home in Los Angeles. The newlyweds describe it as a fairy-tale setting.

Feb 2004 Celebrates his thirtieth birthday with a party at his mansion on Mulholland Drive. His sister Sally and long-time partner Paul Symonds decide to get married and Robbie pays for the wedding in Las Vegas.

March 2004 Fifty guests, including Ant and Dec, attend another birthday party at Skibo Castle, a luxury hotel in Inverness. Rob checks in as Jack Farrell Jnr in memory of his grandfather.

June 2004 The Robbie Williams Performing Arts Suite opens at his old high school in Tunstall, after he donates £50,000 to the project. Both his mother, Jan, and Sally, his sister, attend.

Oct 2004 Achieves sixth UK number one single with 'Radio', his first collaboration with Stephen Duffy, an original member of Duran Duran. His *Greatest Hits* album sells 350,000 copies in the first week and is the biggest selling of the year.

Feb 2005 'Angels', which never made number one, is voted best single of the last twenty-five years at the Brit Awards.

July 2005 Begins a triumphant set at the Live 8 concert in Hyde Park with a version of Queen's 'We Will Rock You' in honour of the late Freddie Mercury. The performance is one of Rob's proudest moments.

Nov 2005 Shifts 1.6 million tickets for his world tour in a day, beating the previous best of 1 million by 'N Sync. The album *Intensive Care* is released and becomes his biggest seller around the world.

Dec 2005 Wins a libel action against MGN and Northern & Shell after publications suggested he lied about his sexuality in the autobiographical book, *Feel*. Settles out of court for a reported £200,000.

Feb 2006 Becomes the majority shareholder in Port Vale football club after investing £260,000. His father, Pete Conway, says, even though his son is in LA, the first thing he wants to know is how Vale got on in their last match.

April 2006 Begins his Close Encounters World Tour in Santiago, Chile. He will have played in front of three million people by the time it ends in Melbourne in December.

July 2006 New single 'Rudebox' receives mixed reviews. The *Sun* describes it as 'the worst song in history' and it stalls at number four in the charts.

Oct 2006 Despite reaching number one, *Rudebox* is by far his lowest selling album in the UK, with sales of just over 500,000 copies.

Feb 2007 The day before his thirty-third birthday admits himself into the Meadows Clinic in Arizona to receive treatment for his addiction to prescription drugs. Says he would have died if he had not gone to rehab. Decides to take a break from the limelight, a sabbatical that would last two years.

Nov 2007 Is pictured on holiday in Amsterdam with his girl-friend, actress Ayda Field. Robbie is barely recognizable in an orange puffa jacket, beanie hat and bushy beard.

April 2008 Takes part in a Radio 4 documentary on UFOs. Says he once saw an object the size of a football field whizzing over his house in LA.

Dec 2008 Jets back to Britain to be at his mother's bedside after she undergoes heart bypass surgery at a hospital in Cheshire.

Jan 2009 Announces that he is going back into the recording studio to fulfil his contractual obligations with EMI.

Feb 2009 Takes Ayda on a Valentine's Day treat to watch Port Vale lose two–nil at Brentford.

Oct 2009 Performs his new single 'Bodies' on *The X Factor* but is put off stride when the entrance doors to the stage fail to open. Reunited with Gary Barlow at the BBC *Children In Need* concert at the Royal Albert Hall. New album *Reality Killed the Video Star* is pipped to number one by boy band JLS.

Nov 2009 Proposes to Ayda Field during a radio broadcast in Australia. It turns out to be a joke but forgets to tell his mother, Jan, who says she is 'really pleased' for them.

Feb 2010 Collects the Outstanding Contribution to Music Award at the Brits, his sixteenth win. Performs a medley of his greatest hits, ending with 'Angels'.

June 2010 Captains England against the Rest of the World at the UNICEF UK Soccer Aid charity match to raise funds for the victims of the Haiti earthquake. Misses a penalty in the shoot-out at Old Trafford and fails to lift the trophy.

July 2010 It's official. The biggest pop news of the year is confirmed when Take That announce Robbie is rejoining them. A new album has already been recorded.

Aug 2010 Marries his long time girlfriend Ayda Field in the garden of his home in Los Angeles. The couple's eight dogs are bridesmaids. Robbie sings 'Angels' to his bride and says he's the 'happiest man alive'.

Sept 2010 Performs his new duet 'Shame' with Gary Barlow at the Heroes Concert at Twickenham. He calls it 'one of the most memorable moments in my professional career so far'.

Oct 2010 His second greatest hits compilation, *In and Out of Consciousness*, becomes his ninth solo number one album. Marks ten years of his charity Give It Sum by visiting some of the 300 projects it has helped in Stoke-on-Trent. More than one million tickets are sold for the 2011 Take That live tour in one day.

Nov 2010 Take That, including Robbie, perform 'The Flood' on *The X Factor*. The new album, *Progress*, sells 520,000 copies in the first week and will top the charts at Christmas.

Feb 2011 Take That finally win Best British Group at the Brit Awards.

May 2011 The tour begins.

Acknowledgements

I loved speaking to people about Robbie. They shared their memories of him with such enthusiasm. I have respected the wishes of those who did not want to be named and I hope they enjoy the book. My sincere thanks go to George Andrews, Bill Bache, Carole Banks, Paul Colclough, Suzanne Coppin, Sam Evans, Zoë Hammond, Lee Hancock, Keith Harrison, Margaret Heath, Dave Johnson, Philip Lindsay, Mindy McCready, Kelly Oakes, Jane Oddy, David and Val Ogden, Jim Peers, Paul Phillips, Brian and Joy Rawlins, Giuseppe Romano, Phil Rossiter, Rick Sky, Hamid Soleimani, Eric Tams, Brian Toplass, Eileen Wilkes and the late Graham Wilkes.

My old friends Cliff Renfrew and Gill Pringle were an enormous help in Los Angeles. I must give a special mention to Dan 'Danno' Hicks, a great storyteller and a mine of information.

At Simon & Schuster, my thanks to Mike Jones, who commissioned this book; editors Colin Midson and Rory Scarfe for their expert advice; editorial assistant Emily Husain for helping to coordinate everything; Paul Gooney for his striking cover design; Jo Edgecombe for overseeing production; Emma Harrow for publicity; and Grainne Reidy and Richard Clarke for looking after the all-important sales.

My agent, Gordon Wise, has made a huge difference to my career. His assistant at Curtis Brown, John Parton, is also a great asset to the team. I am grateful to Jen Westaway for her research and for transcribing my tapes, and to Arianne Burnette for her stellar work copy-editing my original manuscript. Finally, I am grateful to Jo Westaway for her patience and support and for coming down the pub to discuss it.

Select Bibliography

Gary Barlow, *My Take* (Bloomsbury, 2006)
Chris Heath, *Feel: Robbie Williams* (Ebury Press, 2004)
Mark McCrum, *Robbie Williams: Somebody Someday* (Ebury Press, 2001)
Martin Roach, *Take That: Now and Then* (HarperCollins, 2009)
Robbie Williams, Chris Heath, *You Know Me* (Ebury Press, 2010)

Picture Credits

The Staffordshire Sentinel: 1, 4
Brain Rawlings/North Staffs Amateur Dramatics and Operatics Society: 2, 3
Lee Hancock: 5
Provided courtesy of the author: 6
Rex Features: 7, 8, 12, 16, 18, 22, 24, 26, 29, 30, 31, 33, 39
Getty Images: 9, 11, 17, 20, 21, 27, 32
Reuters: 13, 14, 23, 34, 35, 36
NI Syndication: 15
Mirrorpix: 10, 19, 25, 37
PA Photos: 38

Index

(the initials RW in subentries refer to Robbie Williams)

Abacus Windows, 38

Abba, 215

Abbott, Tim, 111–12, 113, 118, 127

Ackroyd, Dan, 184

Adams, Bryan, 175

Aerosmith, 118, 186

Aguilera, Christina, 190

Aizlewood, John, 157

albums and songs by RW and Take
    That:
  'Actor, The', 221
  'Angels', 125–7, 128, 130, 135,
      144, 149, 157, 158, 200, 208,
      209, 225, 255, 262
  'Are You Gonna Go My Way',
      129–30
  'Baby Girl Window', 106
  'Back for Good', 93, 128, 202,
      212
  Beautiful World, 223–4
  'Better Man', 157, 175
  'Bodies', 246, 247–8, 254
  'Bongo Bong', 220, 223
  'Cheap Love Song', 118
  'Come Undone', 185, 198, 199
  'Could It Be Magic', 74–5, 76, 99
  'Do What U Like', 66, 72
  Ego Has Landed, The, 147, 148–9,
      209
  '80s, The', 221–2
  Escapology, x, 191, 196–9, 201,
      209–10
  'Everything Changes', 88, 99, 148
  Everything Changes, 88, 89, 148
  'Feel', 197, 210

'Flood, The', 264, 266

'Freedom', 116, 117

'Good Doctor', 220

'Grace', 142

Greatest Hits (RW) 206–7

Greatest Hits (Take That), 218

'How Peculiar', 197

'I Found Heaven', 74, 89, 147

'I Will Talk and Hollywood Will
    Listen', 166

'If I Ever Had a Son', 132

In and Out of Consciousness, 259,
    263

Intensive Care, 207–9, 223

'It Only Takes a Minute', 73, 74,
    88

'It Was a Very Good Year', 166

'It's Only Us', 148

I've Been Expecting You, 139, 142,
    146–8, 157

'Jesus in a Camper Van', 147–8

'Keep On', 220

'Kids', 156, 158

'Kidz', 266

'Kiss Me', 204, 220

'Knutsford City Limits', 157

'Lazy Days', 120, 124

'Let Love Be Your Energy', 201

'Let Me Entertain You', 126, 146,
    201, 225, 254

Life Thru a Lens, 32, 106, 119,
    121, 125, 126–8, 135, 147,
    157, 266

Live at Knebworth, 202

'Louise', 220

albums and songs by RW and Take
That: – *continued*
'Lovelight', 220, 223, 224, 225
'Mack the Knife', 166
'Me and My Shadow', 176,
213–14
'Millennium', 139, 146, 149, 158,
208, 249, 259, 266
'Million Love Songs' 49, 50, 74–5
'Mr Bojangles', 166
'Misunderstood', 207
'Monsoon', 197
'Morning Sun', 248, 259
'My Culture', 16
'Nan's Song', x, 198
'Never Forget', 266
*Never Forget: The Ultimate
Collection*, 218
'90s, The', 221–2
'No Regrets, 142, 146
Nobody Else, 92–3, 97, 99
'Old Before I Die', 119, 121, 212
'Once You've Tasted Love', 73
'One of God's Better People', 127
'Patience', 224
'Phoenix from the Flames', 142
'Pray', 85, 88, 89
'Promises', 72
'Radio', 206, 207, 224
Reality Killed the Video Star, 243
'Relight My Fire', 89
'Revolution', 198
'Rock DJ', 156–7, 158, 159, 208,
228
'Rudebox', 222, 224, 225
Rudebox, 118, 219–23, 224–5
'Sexed Up', 176
'Shame', 255
'She's Madonna', 220
'She's the One', 119, 146, 162,
176
'Shine', 224
'Sin Sin Sin', 205
Sing When You're Winning, 156–8,
159, 197, 199
'Somethin' Stupid', 167
'South of the Border', 118, 124
'Strong', 16, 146–7

'Summertime', 220, 224
'Supreme', 157, 161, 182
'Sure', 95
Swing When You're Winning,
164–7, 176, 182, 196, 213
Take That & Party, 60, 74
'Tripping', 207–8
'We're the Pet Shop Boys', 220
'Why Can't I Wake Up With You',
49, 84
'Win Some Lose Some', 142
Ali, Muhammad, 40, 44
All Saints, x, 132, 133–4, 135,
136–7, 138, 139, 140, 141–2,
220
split, 141–2
Allen, Lily, 220
Allmusic, 127, 264
Ancient Briton pub, 9, 77, 81, 85
Andrew, Prince, 106
Andrews, Ann, 240
Andrews, Dawn, *see* Barlow
Andrews, George, 43
Andrews, Kelvin, 222, 242
Aniston, Jennifer, 238
Anne-Marie (teenage friend), 31
Annie, 22, 26
'Another Brick in the Wall', 99
Ant and Dec, 104, 176
Appleton, Lee, 132–3
Appleton, Lori, 132–3
Appleton, Natalie, 132–3, 134,
139–40
autobiography of, 134, 136,
141–2, 145–6
Appleton, Nicole, x, 132–43, 145–6,
155, 169, 254
autobiography of, 134, 136,
141–2, 145–6
pregnancies of, 136, 141, 142
RW's proposals to, 137, 139
RW's splits from, 138–9, 140
'Are You Always Going to Be
Alone', 173
Aspin, Neil, 131
Astley, Rick, 50
Aston Villa FC, 130
Attitude, 116, 214

B, Mel, 185, 214, 253
Babybird, 120
Babylon Zoo, 120
Back to You, 239
Baldwin, Stephen, 105
Banks, Carole, 12, 19, 21
Bannon, Conrad, 34–5, 151, 152
Barbarella, 203
Barlow (née Andrews), Dawn, 153
Barlow, Colin, 48
Barlow, Daniel, 153
Barlow, Gary, 47–51, 52–3, 59,
    60–1, 66–7, 71, 88, 96, 112,
    113, 115–16, 124–5, 133, 134,
    149, 199, 213, 217, 256–7, 259,
    262, 265, 267
  at Take That's first meeting, 55
  BMG drops, 153
  club residencies undertaken by,
    48–9
  debut record of, 116
  feud between RW and, 61
  first solo album of, 116
  Ivor Novello Awards for, 95, 153
  Martin-Smith meets, 47, 50–1
  memoir of, 50, 60, 71, 89, 96,
    117, 219
  new RW impresses, 126
  Pebble Mill contest entered by,
    49
  royalties enjoyed by, 118
  RW's continued animosity
    towards, 144
  RW's harsh words about, 116
  second single of, 121
  songs written by, 72, 73, 75, 85,
    95, 223
  Take That's demise and, 100
  teenage earnings of, 49
  Virgin Music Publishing contract
    and, 71
  wealth of, 71, 95
  see also Take That
Bartram, Dave, 11
Basinger, Kim, 105
Battery Studios, 120
Bazilian, Eric, 118
BBC Choice, 174

BBC Music, 207
BBC Online, 263
BBC Stoke, 58
'Be Back Soon', 23
Beatles, 88–9, 148, 222, 224
'Because of You', 120
Beckham, David, 44–5, 54
Beckham, Victoria, 214
Beckinsale, Richard, 106
Beckinsale, Samantha, 106
Beesley, Max, 185, 221–2
Beverly Hills 90210, 184
Bez, 94
Big Breakfast, 104–5
Billboard, 149, 157, 210
Blatt, Lilyella, 140
Blatt, Melanie, 133, 136, 140
Blue, Callum, 236
Blue Collar TV, 238
Blunt, James, 262–3
BMG, 111, 113, 116, 153
Bon Jovi, 118
'Bootie Call', 139
Borrowed Wings, 175
Boss Agency, 47
Boyzone, 218
Brand New Heavies, 185
Brand, Russell, 226
Bresnark, Robin, 127–8
Bridget Jones's Diary, 164
Bridget Jones: The Edge of Reason, 207
Briggs, Chris, 112, 117, 120, 124
Brit awards, 42, 88, 128–9, 135–6,
    140, 141, 144, 149, 155, 192,
    217, 224, 243, 266
Brit Pop, 119, 121, 124, 205
Britain's Got Talent, 6, 52
Brogan, Pat, 14
Buggles, 243
Bugsy Malone, 22
Bunton, Emma, 214
Burslem Golf Club, 41, 77
Bush, John, 127, 264
Butler, Bernard, 200

C, Mel, 158
Cameron Mackintosh Young
    Entertainer of the Year, 173

Campbell, Alastair, 194
'Can't Stop the Music', 65
'Candle in the Wind', 125
Candy Flip, 222
Cannes Film Festival, 141
Capital Radio, 127Capital Radio
    Road Show, 120
Capitol Records, 209
'Careless Whisper', 75
Carey, Mariah, 185
Carson, Frank, 173
Carter, Lynda, 229
Catalogue (Hoare, Heath), 244
Catatonia, 129
Cécillon, Jean-François, 112
Celebrity Big Brother, 217
Chambers, Dylan, 199
Chambers, Guy, 119–21, 125, 140,
    146, 147–8, 149, 156, 164, 166,
    201, 205, 207, 222
  RW splits from, 198–200
Chapman, Nicki, 71
Cheshire Territorial Army
    Barracks, 97
Chester FC, 172
Child, Desmond, 118–19
Children's Royal Variety
    Performance, 74
Chitty Chitty Bang Bang, 12–13,
    19–22, 29, 263
Christy, Brandon, 221, 239, 240–1
Christy, Lauren, 221
Chuckle Brothers, 32
Clark, Tim, 114, 115, 226, 242
Cliff, Josie, 186–7, 261
Clifford, Max, 190
Clothes Show, The, 67
Clouds House clinic, 122, 127
Clough, Brian, 8
Cockney Rebel, 129
Cokes, Ray, 92
Colclough, Beechy, 108–9, 122, 265
Colclough, Coco, 42–3, 44, 58, 59,
    60, 68, 77, 85–6, 130–1, 213
Cole, Cheryl, 70, 254
Colwyn, Lord, 106
'Come Up and See Me', 129
Comic Relief, 150

Compton Bassett House, 244
Concert of Hope, 134
Connery, Sean, 146
'Consider Yourself', 23
Conway, Pete, (father), x, 4–9,
    14–16, 32, 77, 122, 125, 192–3,
    232, 240
  amateur boxer, 40
  Conway stage name chosen by, 6
  documentary on, 192
  family abandoned by, 4, 7–8
  news of RW's engagement
      reaches, 137
  ping-pong played by, 41
  pub licensee, 7
  real name of, 4
  RW's fame and, 89
  RW's wit inherited from, 84
  similarities between RW and, 15
  stage name chosen by, 6
Cool Cube, 65
Cooper, Alice, 146
Cope, Julian, 119, 120
Coppin, Suzanne, 228–35
Corr, Andrea, 154
Corrs, 154
Cousins, Robin, 162
Cowell, Simon, 6, 266
Cox, Leanne, 30
'Cross, The', 72
Cutest Rush, 52

Daily Mirror, 75, 223, 226, 243,
    263
Daily Telegraph, 148, 263
D'Amato, Lisa, 226
Dance UK, 66
Dancing on Ice, 162
'Dave's House', 175
Davidson, Jim, 49
Davies, Lucy, 207
Davis, Sammy Jr, 164, 166
Davro, Bobby, 49
Davy, Damian, 47
Day, Darren, 109
Day, Doris, 12
Days of Our Lives, 238
Dead Like Me, 236

Deevoy, Adrian, 163, 209
Déjà Vu, 231
'Delilah', 129
Dennis, Les, 6
Depeche Mode, 48
Dexys Midnight Runners, 120
Diana, Princess of Wales, Memorial
    Fund, 134
Dimmock, Jack, 21
Doctor Who, 109
Dodd, Ken, 49
Doherty, Shannon, 184
'Don't Walk Away, Renée', 189
Donald, Howard, 51–2, 59, 71, 96,
    214, 217, 260, 266
  Martin-Smith meets, 51, 52
  nipple-ring incident concerning,
    75
Donna Louise Trust, 151
Donovan, Jason, 55, 215
Dow, Nancy, 238
Downey, Robert Jr, 186
Duffy (née Worrall), Claire, 205,
    208
Duffy, Nick, 205
Duffy, Stephen, 203–6, 207, 208,
    220
Duran Duran, 203–5

EastEnders, 105
Eastwood, Clint, 243
Elan, Priya, 223
Elastica, 118
Elizabeth II, Queen, 106
Emerson, Lake and Palmer, 114
EMI, 112–13, 125, 156, 159, 161,
    194, 201, 204, 209, 242
Eminem, 34
Emperor's Wife, The, 222
Entertainment Weekly, 157
Enthoven, David, 114, 117, 120,
    155, 184, 194, 226
Evans, Chris, 155, 160
Evans, Sam, 7
Evecan, Hal, 237
Evening Standard, 243
Everton FC, 172
'Every Time We Say Goodbye', 37

Face, 94, 215
Farrell, Jack (maternal
    grandfather), 10
Farrell, Janetta (maternal
    grandmother), 10
Federline, Kevin, 261
Feel (Heath), 60, 82, 187, 211, 212,
    244
Fernley, Sharon, 30
Fernando, Hannah, 263
Ferry, Bryan, 228
Fiddler on the Roof, 22
Field, Ayda, 236–42, 253, 256, 257,
    258, 260, 261, 263, 266
Field, Gwen, 237
Field, Marjorie, 237
Filth and the Fury, The, 160
Financial Times, 195
Fitzgerald, Ella, 37
Fleming, Ian, 19
Florey, Nicholas D., 20
Flynn, Paul, 223
'Forever Love', 116
Foster, Sara, 188
Four Tops, 189
Frankie Goes to Hollywood, 243
Free, 115
Friel, Anna, 109–10, 127
Fry, Stephen, 194, 225
Full Monty, The, 129
Fun Lovin' Criminals, 140
Fundamental, 243–4

Gallagher, Gene, 145
Gallagher, Liam, 91–2, 93–4, 112,
    124, 127, 141, 143–5, 148, 200,
    212, 254
Gallagher, Noel, 93, 109, 112, 127,
    143–4, 148, 200
Gascoigne, Paul, 108
Genn, Ant, 118, 220
Gill, Andy, 265
Gilson, Rachael, 61–5, 67–9, 70,
    81–3, 87, 170, 229, 243
  modelling work of, 67–8, 82
  musical skills of, 72
  RW's long-lasting affection for,
    86

Girls Aloud, 54, 198
Gittings, Mrs (teacher), 35
Give It Sum, 150–2
Glastonbury Festival:
    1994, 90–1
    1995, 93–4, 118
Glitter, 185
Glover, Dean, 130
G-MEX, 85, 88
Golden Shot, The, 15
Golding, James, 158
Grammer, Kelsey, 239
Grease, 8
Greek Star, 26
Green, Cee Lo, 263
Grumbleweeds, 173
Guardian, 207, 208, 223, 266
Guildhall School of Music, 119,
    185, 222
Gyllenhaal, Jake, 238

Halliwell, Geri, 158–60, 162–3, 190,
    253–4
Hamilton, Alana, 184
Hamilton, Ashley, 184, 188
Hamilton-Smith, Jacqui, x, 106–8,
    109, 155, 161
Hamilton-Smith, Lady, 107
Hammond, Tony, 78
Hammond, Zoë, 3–4, 10–11, 12,
    13–14, 18–20, 21, 22, 23 24–7,
    34, 39, 51–2, 59, 77, 86, 170,
    171
    RW meets, 18
Hancock, Lee, 10, 12, 28, 29, 30,
    31–3, 34, 35–6, 37–8, 39, 40,
    43–4, 56, 57–8, 68, 90, 146,
    213, 221
    aspirations of, 35
    soccer played by, 42
Hands, Guy, 242
Hans Christian Andersen, 18, 169
Happy Mondays, 94, 219
Harrelson, Woody, 259
Harrison, Fraser, 186
Harrison, Keith, 151
Hatch, Tony, 6
'Have You Met Miss Jones?', 164

Hear'Say, 54
Heat, 144, 225, 263, 266
Heath, Chris, 60, 187, 199, 227, 244
Heath, Margaret, 62, 63, 64–5,
    67–8, 81–2, 170
Heaven nightclub, 138
Heffernan, Ray, 126
Hello!, 191, 260–1
Hendrix, Jimi, 44, 63
Heroes Concert, 262
Hill, Norman, 48
Hitman and Her, The, 52, 66, 67, 77
Honeyghan, Lloyd, 144
Hooper, Nellee, 107, 109, 161–2,
    200
Horn, Trevor, 243–4
Hot Stars, 211
Houdini, Harry, 197
Houston, Whitney, 227
Howes, Bob, 49
Human League, 205, 219, 220
Hunter, Janeen, 190–1
Hunter, Rachel, 188–92, 193
    RW splits from, 191
Hutchence, Michael, 138
Hype, The, 174

'I Am the Way', 147
'I Believe I Can Fly', 121
IE Music, 113, 114
If Only (Halliwell), 159
In Rainbows, 242
Independent, 265
Innocent Records, 175, 175–6
International Music Managers
    Forum, 121
Ivor Novello Awards, 95, 149, 153,
    224

Jackie, 72
Jackson, Michael, 75, 108
James Taylor's Greatest Hits, 177
James, David, 104
Jay-Z, 254
Jean, Wyclef, 129
Jeffery, Ray, 23–4
'jelly video', 66
Jim'll Fix It, 76

JLS, 249, 254
Jo (aunt), 125, 221
John, Elton, 36, 88, 108, 125, 146,
    148, 200, 264
Jonathan Wilkes and the Space Girls,
    173
Jones, Brian, 94
Jones, Linda, *see* Woodward
Jones, Steve, 258
Jones, Tom, 129–30, 136, 188
'Just Another Day', 175
Just for the Record (Halliwell), 160
Just Seventeen, 72

Kajagoogoo, 18
Kay, Peter, 254
Kelly, R., 121
Kensit, Patsy, 107, 138
Keys, Alicia, 254
Kidman, Nicole, 167–8
King Crimson, 114
King and I, The, 22
Kinsella, Kevin, 111–12, 214
Kirkham, Richard, 36
'Kiss', 173
'Kiss From a Rose', 243
Knebworth, x, 201–2
Kravitz, Lenny, 129

LA Lakers, 191
LA Vale FC, 229
Lady Gaga, 254
Larkin, Philip, 16
Laughton, Fred, 53
Le Bon, Simon, 203
Leicester City FC, 131
Lemon Trees, 119, 120
Lennon, John, 183
'Let's Pray for Christmas', 49
Lewis, Leona, 182
Lewis, Shaznay, 133–4, 140
Lhuillier, Monique, 261
Licks, 199–200
'Lift Me Up', 160
Light Years, 156
Lilac Time, 205
Lindsay, Phil, 28, 29–30, 31, 36,
    37–8, 42

Lineker, Gary, 105
Live at the Albert Hall, 202
Live 8, 207
Liverpool FC, 172
Lloyd Webber, Andrew, 147, 200
Lodge, Lee, 186–7
London's Burning, 106
Lonestar, 118
Longthorne, Joe, 173
Looking for a Day in the Night, 205
Lorraine, Peter, 124
'Love Is Where I'm From', 140
'Love Won't Wait', 121
'Loveboat', 156

Macc Lads, 31, 32
McCartney, Paul, 125, 196
McCready, Mindy, 118
McCrum, Mark, 155, 164, 184, 186
McCutcheon, Martine, 175
McDonald, Richie, 118
McKenna, Paul, 159
McNab, Neil, 44
Madonna, 60, 155, 215, 220
Making It Legal, 238
Manchester City FC, 44
Manchester United FC, 44, 53
Manilow, Barry, 67
Margaret, Princess, 74
Marley, Bob, 115
Marshall, Ben, 214
Martin, Dean, 164
Martin, Gavin, 250
Martin-Smith, Nigel, 46–8, 50–1,
    52, 54, 55, 59, 60, 65–7, 79, 87,
    100, 113, 116, 127, 200, 226
  court case against, 103
  fictional history created by, 53
  'no girlfriends' edict of, 70, 86
  objects to RW lyric, 221
  record deal negotiated by, 71
  RW's 'Satan's son' description of,
    60
  RW's continued animosity
    towards, 144
  RW's harsh words about, 116,
    127
  RW's legal battle with, 114

Martin-Smith, Nigel – *continued*
　safe-sex tour strategy of, 73
　sexuality of, 65
　Take That part company with,
　　218–19
　see also Take That
Matrix, 221
'Maybe He'll Notice Her Now', 118
McCormick, Neil, 263
Meadows Clinic, 225–7
Meehan, Jerry, 221–2
Melody Maker, 127–8
Melvin, Joanna, 29, 146
Mercury, Freddie, 207
Met Bar, 104
Michael, George, 51, 75, 116, 117,
　149
Mill Hill Primary School, 17
Minogue, Kylie, 55, 87, 138, 155–6,
　158, 161, 215
Mr Blobby, 89
Mohan, Dominic, 197
Mojo, 157, 203
Monkhouse, Bob, 200
Moran, Nick, 161
Morgan, Huey, 140
Morgan, Piers, 96
Morris, Owen, 118
Morrison, Jim, 44
Morrissey, 196
Moss, Kate, 61, 108, 227
Most Wanted, 92
Moulin Rouge, 167
MTV Awards, 157, 161
Music Week, 120
'My Girl', 72
'My Way', 158
My Take (Barlow), 50, 60, 71, 89,
　96, 117, 219

Naked Elvis, 155
Neighbours, 6, 55
'Never Ever', 134, 135
New Faces, 6
New Kids on the Block, 47, 51, 54,
　218
New Musical Express (*NME*), 148,
　207, 223

News at Ten, 98
News of the World, 155, 168, 189,
　226
Newton, Ro, 65–6
Nirvana, 99
Nobody Someday, 163
Norma Jean's, 36
Norman, Carolyn, 72
North Staffordshire Amateur
　Operatic and Dramatic Society
　('North Staffs'), 18, 22–3
'Nothing Can Divide Us', 55

Oakes, Kelly, 11, 16, 30–1, 32
Oasis, 93, 104, 116, 118, 124, 143,
　144, 148, 197, 200, 201, 209
Observer, 223
Ogden, David, 12–13, 21
Ogden, Val, 12
OK!, 159
'Old Before I Die', 119, 121, 212
Oliver!, 3–4, 13, 17, 23–5, 25–6, 34,
　39, 69, 171
Open Road, 124
Openshaw, Mr (teacher), 35
Orange, Jason, 51–2, 59, 71, 84, 96,
　97, 217
　antipathy to RW shown by, 94
　Martin-Smith's antipathy
　　towards, 60
　Martin-Smith meets, 51, 52
　RW's harsh words about, 116
　see also Take That
Orange, Justin, 52
Orbit, William, 220
O'Reilly, Peter, 28, 29–30, 36
Orgasmatron, 199
Orton, Beth, 222
Osbourne, Jack, 187–8
Osbourne, Kelly, 187
Osbourne, Ozzy, 187
Osbourne, Sharon, 187–8
OutRage!, 215
Outsiders, The, 84
Owen, Mark, 52–4, 60, 71, 77, 79,
　84, 87, 92, 95, 202, 212–13,
　217
　Buddhism practised by, 96–7

favourite, 99
sexuality of, 212
see also Take That
Owen, Michael, 172

Palmer-Tomkinson, Tara, 106,
227
Parkinson, 167
Parkinson, Michael, 167
Peers, Jim, 41
Peers, Joan, 54
Peers, Tim, 11, 41, 76–7, 81, 209
People, 211
Perry, Matthew, 186, 238
PerthNow, 225
Pertwee, Jon, 109
Pertwee, Sean, 109
Pet Shop Boys, 146, 205, 219, 220,
243–4
Peter Kay's Phoenix Nights, 49
Petridis, Alex, 207, 208, 223
Phillips, Paul, 34
Pickwick, 22–3
Piers Morgan's Life Stories, 160
'Pinball Wizard', 146
Pink Floyd, 99
Piper, Billie, 155, 175
Play Dead, 241
Pointer Sisters, 230
Pop Idol, 71
Popstars: The Rivals, 198
Port Vale FC, 7, 42, 43–4, 129,
130–1, 171, 172, 241–2
Porter, Cole, 148
Power, Steve, 120–1, 129, 207
Prince, 72, 173
Progress, 257, 264, 265
Proper Management, 111, 114
Public Enemy, 219
Pulp, 118
purerobbie.com, 222, 223
PWL, 115

Q, 157, 212, 214
Q Awards, 145
Queen Nation, 213
Queen's Theatre, Burslem, 3, 11,
13, 22, 147

Radiohead, 242
Rawlins, Brian, 23–4, 56–7, 76
Ray of Light, 220
Raymonde, Nick, 71
RCA, 71, 72, 73, 111, 115
Red Lion, Burslem, 6–7, 90
Redknapp, Jamie, 104
Reed, Oliver, 7
Reeves, Vic, 31–2, 84, 104
Regime's club, 61
'Relax', 243
Reload, 129
Renfrew, Cliff, 187, 190
Respect agency, 67
Rhodes, Nick, 203
Rice, Tim, 200
Richards, Keith, 92, 153–4, 183
Richie, Lionel, 67
Ridgley, Andrew, 51
Right Said Fred, 71
Ritchie, Guy, 155, 220
Ritzy nightclub (formerly
Zanzibar), 36, 51, 59, 68–9
Roach, Martin, 218
Robbie Williams Is My Son, 192
Robinson, Bill, 166
Robson, Bryan, 11, 44
Rocky Horror Show, The, 47, 190
Rolling Stone, 157
Rolling Stones, 94, 153
Romano, Giuseppe, 26, 28, 29–30,
31, 33, 35–6, 39, 40, 78, 150
aspirations of, 35
soccer played by, 42
Ronson, Jon, 240–1
Ronson, Mark, 2120, 223
Rossiter, Phil, 17
Roxy Music, 114, 228
Rudge, John, 131
Russo, Craig, 221
Rutherford, Tilly, 115

St Margaret Ward School, 17, 22,
29, 60, 150–1, 152
religion at, 37
RW's donation to, 150
'Saturday Night's Alright (For
Fighting)', 36, 146

Saturday Night Fever, 8, 73
Scantlin, Wes, 191
Schnorbitz, 173
'School's Out', 146
Seal, 243
'Sentimental Journey', 12
Sentinel, 19, 33, 46, 88, 151
Sex Pistols, 128, 160
'Shame', 257, 259, 262, 263
Shamrock Tattoo Parlor, 185
Shark Week, 234
Sharkey, Feargal, 91
Sharrock, Chris, 119
Shields, Tom QC , 211
Shooting Stars, 31
Showaddywaddy, 11
Signal Radio, 43
Simply Red, 37
Simpson, Jeff, 74
Sinatra, Frank, 148, 158, 164, 167
Sinatra, Nancy, 167
'69', 199
Sky, Rick, 47, 67, 84, 91–2, 209, 213
Sleeper, 122
Smash Hits, 65, 88, 218
'Smells Like Teen Spirit', 99
Smith, Angie, 66–7
Soli House, 37
Some Mothers Do 'Ave 'Em, 136
Somebody Someday (McCrum), 155
Somerville, Jimmy, 213
'Sorry Seems to Be . . .', 125
Soul Mekanick, 222
'Sound of the Underground', 198
Sounds, 204
'Spaceman', 120
Spearmint Rhino, 168
Spears, Britney, 70, 190, 230
Spector, Phil, 243
Spencer, Danny, 222, 242
Spice Girls, 54, 116, 117, 135, 158, 214
Sports Illustrated, 188
Standing on the Shoulders of Giants, 200
Staples, Clare, 159
Star, 211
Star Trek, 105

Star Wars, 84
Stereophonics, 129
Stewart, Kimberly, 188
Stewart, Liam, 189
Stewart, Renee, 189
Stewart, Rod, 184, 188, 189, 191
Stock, Aitken and Waterman, 55, 156
Stoke City FC, 42, 43, 44, 78, 129, 130–1
Stoke-on-Trent Alcohol Advisory Service, 90
Stoke-on-Trent Charity Pantomime and Drama Company, 19
Stone, Rosa, 198
Stoppard, Dr Miriam, 226
Strachan, Michaela, 52
'Strawberry Fields', 222
Strecker, Tanya, 155, 181, 220
Street Beat, 52
Studio 60 on the Sunset Strip, 238
Subterranean Hawks, 204
Sun, 98, 100, 107, 136, 144, 159, 197
Sunday Times, 195
'Sweet Transvestite', 190
Sylvia Young Theatre School, 133
Symonds (née Williams), Sally (half-sister), 4, 6, 10–11, 12, 56, 67, 86, 90, 209, 244–5
  marriage of, 206
Symonds, Paul, 90, 206

T.Rex, 114
Take That:
  albums and songs of, *see* albums and songs
  Beesley drums with, 185
  bestboyband vote for, 218
  Brit Awards for, 224, 225–6
  camp first incarnation of, 65
  change in appearance of, 72
  consecutive numberone singles for, 89
  dance routines of, 52
  demise of, 100, 115–16
  documentaries on, 214, 217–18
  fan club of, 90

first album of, 73
first sell-out arena tour by, 85
first gig by, 65
first meeting of, 55
first number-one single of, 84–5
first post-reunion album of,
    223–4
first record deal signed by, 71
first single of, 66
first *Top of the Pops* appearance of,
    74
foundations laid for, 50
gay fan base of, 65
HMV cancel tour of, 74
'jelly video' of, 66
music-publishing contract signed
    by, 71
naming of, 59–60
'no girlfriends' rule concerning,
    70
re-formation of, 218
reunion tour of, 218–19
Robson meets, 44
RW accepted into, 56
RW's audition with, 54–5
RW becomes marginalized
    within, 92–3
RW becomes too dangerous for,
    94
RW joins, ix, 38, 151
RW is Minogue's favourite
    among, 156
RW's 'movie' jibe concerning,
    160–1
RW's progressive isolation within,
    96
RW's release from contract with,
    111
RW's split from, 95, 97–9
safesex tour by, 73
silver disc for, 76
small clubs played by, 47
Smash Hits awards for, 88
under-18s marketing of, 72
whispers about sexuality of, 212
Take That – For the Record, 217
Talisman pub, 77–8
Tams, Eric, 4, 6, 19–20, 20–1

Tatchell, Peter, 215
Taupin, Bernie, 200
Tavares, 73
Taylor, John, 203
Temptations, 72
Tennant, Neil, 146
Terra Firma, 242
Theatre Royal, Hanley, 22, 29, 169
Thompson, John, 37
Timberlake, Justin, 70
'Time Warp, The', 47
Tin Tin, 204
Today Show, The, 215
Together (Appleton, Appleton), 134,
    136, 141–2, 145–6
Tonight Show with Jay Leno, The, 164
Top of the Pops (magazine), 124
Top of the Pops (TV show), 47, 48,
    67, 74
Travolta, John, 8
'Truly Scrumptious', 19, 21
Truth About Take That, The, 214
Turner, Anthea, 190

Underwood, John, 107

Van Dyke, Dick, 19
van Outen, Denise, 133, 135
Vanilla Ice, 34
Vaughan, Norman, 15
Vic Reeves Big Night Out, 31
Vicious, Sid, 128
'Video Killed the Radio Star', 243
Village People, 65, 72
Virgin Music Publishing, 71
Vox, 127

Wadsworth, Tony, 196
Wainwright, Loudon III, 147
Wallinger, Kurt, 119
'Wannabe', 116
Washington, Denzel, 231
Waterboys, 119
Waterman, Pete, 52
Wayne, Bill, 15
'We Will Rock You', 201, 207
Westlife, 218
Wham!, 51

'What Do You Want From Me', 266
What We Did Last Summer, 202
Wheeler, Nikki, 181, 193
White Album, The, 224
'Wig Wam Bam', 47
Wilkes, Eileen, x, 5, 9, 16, 169,
    170–1, 172, 173, 174, 177,
    183–4, 192, 201
Wilkes, Graham, 169, 172, 173, 174
Wilkes, Jonathan, x, 5, 39, 127, 155,
    158, 168–77, 181, 183, 190,
    192–3, 201–2, 242, 244
    RW's duet with, 176
    wedding of, 193
Wilkes, Kay, 61, 62, 68–9, 169
Wilkes, Mickey, 242
Will and Grace, 238
Williams, Betty (paternal
    grandmother), ix–x, 5, 9, 12,
    57, 79, 86, 136
    death of x
    RW's tribute to, 198
Williams, Jan (mother), ix, 6, 7,
    8–14, 16, 17–18, 21–2, 28, 38,
    56, 57, 68, 98, 117, 135, 151–2,
    169, 198, 209
    boutique run by, 9
    boyband ad spotted by, 46
    charity work of, 150, 151
    coffee shop run by, 9, 25
    drinkanddrugs counsellor, 90,
        150, 188
    drugandalcoholabuse expertise
        gained by, 115
    florist's run by, ix, 9, 32, 78
    golf played by, 11, 41
    heart bypass on, 244–5
    'Killing Me', 127
    at Knebworth, 202
    news of RW's engagement
        reaches, 137
    news of RW's split from Appleton
        reaches, 139
    Port Vale shareholder, 241–2
    RW buys houses for, 89–90,
        149–50
    RW's birthday surprise for, 78–9
    RW's fame affects, 80

    on RW's rehab, 226–7
    RW's song about, 127
    RW's split from Take That and,
        98, 99
    RW's strained relationship with,
        103
    sits in on RW's interviews, 113
    socialstudies course taken by, 90
    at Take That audition, 55
    video shocks, 67
Williams, Pete (a.k.a. Pete Conway)
Williams, Phil (paternal
    grandfather), 5, 9, 125
Williams, Robbie:
    Abbott's claim against, 113
    accepted for Take That, 56
    acid taken by, 85
    albums and songs of, *see* albums
        and songs
    Alcoholics Anonymous (AA)
        attended by, 139, 162, 184,
        186
    best man at Wilkes's wedding,
        193
    Big Breakfast presenter, 104–5
    birth of, 6–7
    Brit Awards for, 149, 192, 217
    casual sex and, 85–7, 105–6, 110,
        154, 182
    charity of, 150–2
    clown reputation of, 30, 64, 67,
        95, 148
    cocaine used by, 85, 91, 103, 104,
        108, 121, 154
    Compton Bassett House bought
        by, 244
    courtesy shown by, 42
    dance training for, 59
    depression suffered by, 194, 225,
        233, 235
    drinking culture of, 38, 42, 85,
        90, 97, 103, 108, 121–2, 153,
        174, 187
    drugs taken by, 38, 42, 85, 88, 91,
        103, 104, 108–9, 121, 139,
        153–4, 174, 187, 220, 226–7
    early impressions performed by,
        8

EastEnders appearance of, 105
EMI deals with, 112–13, 195–6, 209, 242
engagements of, 137, 139
fame catches up with, 79–80
Farrell alias of, 10
feud between Barlow and, 61
first juvenile lead played by, 19–22
first lead vocal sung by, 74
first sole writing credit of, x
first tattoo of, 57
frozen career of, 111
Gallagher's sexuality taunt against, 145, 212, 214
Gilson meets, 61
golf club junior captain, 41
golf played by, 11, 41
heroin used by, 122
Ivor Novello Awards for, 149
largest world tour of, 208
Los Angeles move by, reasons for, 183
'lost year' of, 108, 112, 121, 220
marijuana smoked by, 38, 85
Martin-Smith's legal battle with, 114
'Maximilian' invented name of, 59
most entertaining member of Take That, 84
Narcotics Anonymous (NA) meetings attended by, 186
O-level results of, 56
personal fortune of, 195–6
pet parakeets kept by, 9
pub birth myth surrounding, 6–7
in rehab, 122–3, 225–7
'Robbie' name first applied to, 58
school life of, 17, 22, 28–32, 34–5, 37–8
security concerns of, 182–3, 184

security guard assigned to, 91
sexuality of, 211–16
similarities between father and, 15
smoking taken up by, 34
soccer played by, 42–3
soccer team of, 229
in softdrink advert, 265
songwriting partners sought by, 117–19
sport and, 40–5
Stuttgart attack on, 182–3, 267
Take That audition of, 54–5
Take That split with, 95, 97–9
UFOs seen by, 240, 270
UNICEF ambassador, 254–5, 268
voice abused by, 93
weight gain by, 103
Willwogs nickname of, 28, 34, 43
windowsales job of, 38, 263, 264
see also Take That
Williams, Sally (half-sister), *see* Symonds
Willis, Bruce, 189
'Wimmin', 185
Winwood, Stevie, 115
Wonder, Stevie, 222
Woodward, Linda, 188
World Party, 119, 146
'World Shut your Mouth', 120
Worrall, Claire, *see* Duffy

X Factor, The, 246–8, 249, 251, 258, 271

Yates, Paula, 104
'Yesterday', 125
'You Can Leave Your Hat On', 129
You Only Live Twice, 146, 266
'You're Gorgeous', 120
'Your Disco Needs You', 156
YouTube, 234

Zuttis of Oldham, 53

Also available from Simon & Schuster UK:

Sean Smith

CHERYL

THE NUMBER ONE BESTSELLER

Cheryl is the definitive biography of the nation's favourite star. From her Newcastle childhood to her stellar success with Girls Aloud, as a number one solo artist and on TV with *The X Factor*, Sean Smith tells the true, roller-coaster story of how a cheeky and feisty girl from a grim, working-class area became the iconic figure for modern women in Britain today.

Cheryl's path to fame and fortune has often been difficult, facing the problems drugs and unemployment have brought to those she loves. Now, her turbulent marriage to footballer Ashley Cole is sadly under the spotlight, but with insight and understanding, Sean Smith reveals the real woman behind the beautiful public face.

ISBN 978-1-84739-317-3
PRICE £7.99

Also available from Simon & Schuster UK:

Sean Smith

KATE

The sun shone, the crowds waved and cheered wildly and billions watched on TV all around the world as Kate lovingly kissed William on the balcony of Buckingham Palace – not once but twice! The world, it seemed, still believed in their favourite fairytale – any girl could dream of becoming a princess.

Kate is the definitive biography of the nation's newest princess. Sean Smith has retraced the steps of Kate's journey, from her childhood in rural Berkshire and her unhappy time as a victim of school bullies, to her transformation from a plain, gangly girl into the beauty she is today.

Fully illustrated this is the one book you will want to read about the event of the decade.

ISBN 978-1-84737-868-2
PRICE £14.99